Engage & Activate

Navigating College and Beyond

C. KYLE RUDICK

University of Northern Iowa

NICHOLAS A. ZOFFEL

Global Forum for Civic Affairs

KATHERINE GRACE HENDRIX

University of Memphis

SAN DIEGO

Bassim Hamadeh, CEO and Publisher
Todd R. Armstrong, Publisher
Tony Paese, Project Editor
Abbey Hastings, Production Editor
Abbie Goveia, Graphic Design Assistant
Stephanie Kohl, Licensing Coordinator
Kim Scott/Bumpy Design, Interior Designer
Natalie Piccotti, Director of Marketing
Kassie Graves, Vice President of Editorial
Jamie Giganti, Director of Academic Publishing

cognella® | ACADEMIC PUBLISHING
3970 Sorrento Valley Blvd., Ste. 500, San Diego, CA 92121

Brief Contents

Contents

Preface

Over the years, we have conducted an experiment in our classes. We ask students to name the problems that they will face regionally, nationally, or globally over the next 50 years. As they volunteer their ideas, the chalkboard space where we write them becomes increasingly full: global climate change, racism, sexual assault, pollution, student debt, political divides, ongoing wars, cybersecurity, privacy, wealth inequality, immigration, and they continue with topic after topic. Finally, we ask, "Okay, so how much of your time in education has prepared you to address these issues?" Some students smile uncomfortably, others fidget, but none want to say what we all know is the answer—that they have received very little education that will help them navigate these problems in the years and decades to come.

One year, a student raised their hand, said, "Look, I think we all know these are problems. But I'm just trying to get through college and get a job." And, even though only one student expressed it, other students in the room nodded their heads in agreement. That moment still stands out to us because it exemplifies a pervasive, and tragic, myth among many people—that addressing the economic, cultural, environmental, and political problems of the world are somehow separate from their everyday lives. That is, many people believe that if they just keep their head down and follow the path of least resistance that society has laid before them, things will eventually resolve themselves. Activism, as a result, is increasingly viewed as an arena reserved for troublemakers and malcontents.

We wrote this book for that student and for the many others who we have taught and will teach in our careers. Students cannot afford to view their college experiences through the narrow lens of job training, nor can they separate themselves from the problems that face us as community members, a nation, or a species. However, our hope is that students don't see activism as something added to or separate from their experiences. Rather, our book is premised on the belief that students' everyday lives are sites for intervention, renewal, and growth. In other words, this is not a book about activism, it is a book that helps students connect the important issues that face them each day such as time management, negotiating authority, financial stability, romance, and (yes) job preparation, to the larger context of issues that they will need to address in their lives.

Our purpose in this book is to help students address both the individual and social aspects of higher education. We believe that higher education should help students meet their personal goals in life, find a community of justice-minded people, and seek out strategies when differences arise. As such, this book explores problems that new continuing students will encounter (e.g., time management, financing college, and sexual health) and offers advice for overcoming those obstacles. In this way, our book addresses many of the concerns that other student orientation texts might by offering practical advice about common student issues. However, what makes our book unique is how we make explicit that the problems students face are never just individual problems, they are opportunities to see the cultural, economic, and historical dimensions of issues that face our increasingly global society. We hope students recognize their problems as opportunities to organize with others around them, and to become activists, thereby ensuring that no one else must suffer from the same issues they have navigated. We think that this approach to activism—of taking the saying "the personal is political" seriously—is key for creating communities and a society that is more just, humane, and sustainable while increasing student success, retention, and engagement. As instructors, we cannot think of any higher achievement than to help students see themselves as empowered, educated, and empathetic change-makers and hope you will join us in the work by using this book.

Outline of the Book

The purpose of the book is embedded both in the content and structure of the text. The text begins with two chapters that serve as an introduction to the book and the framework from which the book will proceed. In Chapter 1, "Hired or Higher Education? Making the Most of Your Education," we introduce ourselves as authors to readers, and provide a justification for why the book should be important to students. We find many authors simply start from the premise that students should read their books because they are assigned course materials. However, we offer stories about ourselves, and our reasoning for creating this book, because we feel that it is important to treat students as discerning, competent adults who will make a choice as to whether to purchase, read, or agree with our book. As such, the first chapter sets the tone for the rest of the book: dialogic, nuanced, and vulnerable. Chapter 2, "Reflective Practice: Building a Vocabulary for Justice," offers an overview of social justice—what the term means and why we think it's important to strive for in society. We'll also discuss some of the common misperceptions about social justice, and offer a vocabulary for understanding individual problems as shared, social issues. Our intention is to set the foundation for students to understand that a world in which all human capabilities are met is one that is necessary but above all, achievable, with their activism and energy.

Each successive chapter addresses a specific problem that faces students. After identifying the issue, we provide practical advice for how students can navigate their way to success. The end of each chapter returns to the social justice approach to the problem, asking the question, "How can you be an activist in this area? What commitments will you make to ensure that no one has to navigate this problem as you had to in the future?" In Chapter 3, "Authority and Cultural Capital: Demystifying Institutional Culture," we make explicit the institutional structure of higher education in order to make it easier for students (particularly first-generation students) to navigate as well as provide an impetus for greater shared governance. We provide advice for students on how to interact with various authority figures on campus (e.g., email etiquette). We conclude by articulating avenues for activism for greater shared governance among students, faculty/staff, administrators, community members, stakeholders, and politicians. Chapter 4, "Study Habits and Self-Care: Cultivating Skills, Challenging Busywork," is where we discuss the rise of "busyness" as a destructive habit and its influence on college life. We then map out the study habits that students can engage in that will increase their control over their life and schedule. Finally, we argue that self-care is an important component of realizing a social justice framework both within higher education and as a balanced citizen.

Next, in Chapter 5, "The Environment and You: Healthy Living, Healthy World," we argue that campus living provides new challenges for students in their eating, sleeping, and exercise behaviors as opportunities for connecting everyday life to environmentalism. We first outline the newfound freedom many students face in making decisions about a host of important, but quotidian, choices (e.g., what to eat). We then outline common ways that student can engage in healthy living practices. We close by articulating how students, healthy living can be a part of an ethic of sustainable consumption patterns and the foundation for advocacy regarding environmental causes (e.g., campus divestment of fossil fuels). In Chapter 6, "Romance, Fluidity, and Consent," we recognize the sexual norms that characterize higher education while connecting those to activism about sexual violence. We discuss consent as an affirmative act ("yes means yes"), how to navigate giving/receiving consent for sexual activity, and sexual health practices. We finish by providing ways for activism concerning bystander intervention.

In Chapter 7, "Building Cross-Cultural Relationships," we address the institutional shock that many (White) students experience when enrolling in higher education and articulate that discomfort as a place for both reflection and activism. We first recognize that many White and domestic students have lived in de facto segregated communities and schools until college and address how this lack of meaningful experience can make intercultural friendships daunting. We then provide common pitfalls to avoid when hoping to establish open, authentic relationships with a person whose race or ethnicity is different from the student. We conclude with avenues for students to use their experiences as catalysts for creating inclusive communities and colleges. In Chapter 8, "Mental and Physical Health: Navigating the Chronic and Situational," we show how mental and physical health issues are not "added burdens" but are parts of human variability. As such, they should be viewed as valued and differing types of human experiences. We first provide a brief history of languaging disability (i.e., moral, legal, and social justice). We then identify the legal structures in place that secure equal access and treatment for students with disability and the various institutional services that students can use. We conclude by identifying avenues for student activism about universal design on campuses and the destigmatization of health issues. In Chapter 9, "Financing College: Student Debt in an Age of Rising Tuition Costs," we provide tips for students on how to finance college while connecting their financial struggles to neoliberal capitalism. We outline a brief history of state retreat from higher education funding, the rise of student debt, and the explosion of the student debt industry. We then provide ways for students to ease their financial hardship through financial literacy, scholarships/grants, and everyday life hacks. We argue that student debt is a part of a larger ethic of precarity and urge students to become activists about wealth inequality and corporatism.

We end the book with Chapter 10, "Succeed While Changing Your Community! Student Activism for a Better World," to summarize the book's message and reemphasize the importance of a social justice ethic to solving personal and social problems. We first remind students of connecting their personal problems and issues with systems of power and privilege. We argue that their time in higher education is sacred, and that they should work to protect it for themselves and those who come after them. We close with a utopic vision of society that has committed itself to foregrounding social justice in its decision-making processes.

Major Features of the Book

Student Resources

As authors, we recognize textbooks must provide content in multiple ways in order to attract student interest. As such, we have incorporated a number of features throughout the text to help guide students' reading practices and provide ways for student engagement. They include:

Accessible writing: Nothing is worse than writing that no one wants to read. Throughout the text we have striven to maintain an open, dialogic tone with readers, so students don't feel like they are being talked down to or excluded. We situate ourselves as people through sharing personal stories and voice and minimize jargon or abstract language.

Student Voices: Throughout the text, there are quotations from students we interviewed who were kind enough to offer advice, examples, or recommendations based on their experiences. These quotes help connect readers to important material by letting them see themselves in the writing.

Content-specific breakout boxes: These boxes provide in-depth information in a concise way to increase reader interest. They feature lists, common myths, and resources for further information.

Bold key terms and glossary: Students need a vocabulary to identify and address the issues they face, and these concepts provide an easy-to-access way to help them in this process.

Beginning/ending materials for each chapter: Sometimes students need help guiding their reading, so we have provided chapter objectives and orienting questions at the beginning of every chapter. We have provided discussion questions and a student challenge activity at the end of each chapter for further student discussion and engagement.

Distance Learning Materials: Students in online learning have different needs than their face-to-face counterparts. That's why we created engage-activate.org for a host of online learning resources to make sure students are successful whatever the medium of instruction.

Instructor Resources

In addition to student resources, our textbook comes with a number of instructor resources to help you plan and teach your course. Upon adoption of the text, you can request instructor resources, which include:

NCA *Communication Teacher* activities: The National Communication Association's journal, *Communication Teacher*, provides single-class, unit, and semester-long activities that can be used by instructors. We have identified a least one activity per chapter that can be used, and have provided the relevant citation so you can find it quickly and easily.

Resources: New and continuing instructors who wish to develop their understanding of social justice will find our resources guide a helpful place to start. Each chapter is accompanied by a sample quiz that can be used or amended for your instructional needs. Additionally, PowerPoint slides, chapter outlines, and a sample syllabus are available through a password-protected instructor's site.

Ongoing Pedagogical Support: The authors are available to give continuing support to instructors who adopt the text. Listen to their podcast, read their blog, contact them through email, or schedule an instructor workshop presented by the authors. Visit engageactivate.org for more information.

Acknowledgments

As with any intellectual project, the names that appear on the cover are not the only people who contributed to the project. The influence of colleagues, friends, family, and students are present throughout the text. Without their advice, help, and support, we would not have been able to put this book in your hands. We are deeply indebted to them.

We would like to thank those who reviewed the textbook and provided feedback on earlier drafts of the chapters. Reviewing is often undervalued intellectual labor, but we know that our book is stronger for the comments and edits offered by the long list of superb scholars who gave their time and energy. They are Nancy Bressler (West Virginia Wesleyan College); Sonja M. Brown (Ashland University); Sheila Bustillos (Texas Woman's University); Christopher J. Claus (California State University, Stanislaus); Kristopher Copeland (Tulsa Community College); Matt Crick (William Patterson University); Deanna L. Fassett (San José State University); Matt Foy (Upper Iowa University); Bina Lefkovitz (Sacramento State University); Armeda C. Reitzel (Humboldt State University); Sarah Riforgiate (University of Wisconsin–Milwaukee); and Vicky Szerko (Dominican College). Thank you for all of your contributions.

We would also like to thank our students. Many of them have influenced our thinking throughout the process, and helped us understand what problems students feel need to be addressed. We also would like to acknowledge the students who shared their experiences with us to be used in the textbook. Their stories and advice were invaluable to our process, and (we hope) helpful for student readers.

Finally, we would like to thank our families. Since we began this book they have looked the other way at our mounting coffee shop purchases, forgiven the amount of time we have spent writing, and listened to us express our excitement, joys, and frustrations throughout the process. Without their support, it's easy to say that this book would have never come to fruition. We promise that our coffee bills will go down now that the book is finished. At least, until the next edition is due.

CHAPTER 1

Hired or Higher Education?

Making the Most of Your Education

CHAPTER OBJECTIVES

By the end of the chapter, you should be able to:

Describe the reasons that society has traditionally promoted higher education.

Identify the importance of education for social transformation

Explain the connection between activism and college life

Orienting Questions

As you read the chapter, try to answer the following questions:

Why did you decide to attend college? Why this particular college?

What role do you think higher education plays in society?

What did you think college would be like? Does it measure up?

CHAPTER 1

Hired or Higher Education?

Making the Most of Your Education

CHAPTER OBJECTIVES

By the end of the chapter, you should be able to:

- Describe the reasons that society has traditionally promoted higher education

- Identify the importance of education for social transformation

- Explain the connection between activism and college life

ORIENTING QUESTIONS

As you read the chapter, try to answer the following questions:

- Why did you decide to attend college? Why this particular college?

- What role do you think higher education plays in society?

- What did you think college would be like? Does it measure up?

When I (Kyle) enrolled in college, I did it because I wanted a good-paying job. Growing up in a White, middle-class home, I felt the need to build on the professional ambitions of my family, and the masculine pressure to be the one to "take home the bacon" by having a high-paying job. In fact, I wanted to start in human resources and work my way up the corporate ladder until I made at least a healthy six-figure salary. My mother (who was a public school teacher) and my father (who was a police officer), provided the impetus for this decision. I remember, when I was very young, my mom would stay up late into the night grading papers, making notes for parents, and preparing reports for her administrators while dad would work the graveyard shift, working all night only to come home and sleep all day. Both worked hard for other people, to help their children learn or keep their families safe. Both, in my mind, worked entirely too hard for the money they made. I would never, I vowed, work in public service. And, college was the way I would ensure I never had to scrimp or save.

Well, life had another plan in store for me. I volunteered at my college's communication lab, where students go to get help on their public speeches. I was in competitive speech and debate and thought working at the lab would be a good line on my resume when I completed college. I found that I loved teaching, that I craved those moments when students learned something new and recognized they could do something that they didn't think possible. And so, in my second year of college, I switched my major to communication education so I could teach high school speech and debate.

My journey wasn't over. I attended a communication studies conference, the Central States Communication Association, in the spring of my second year

Figure 1.1

and fell in love with the people I found there. Each of the professors I met was a dedicated teacher, but they also conducted research and debated important ideas about communication, which sparked my passion for creating new knowledge. So, I completed my degree, but instead of working in a high school, I went on to get my MA and PhD, and now I work as a professor in a university. I most certainly don't make anywhere near six figures, and sometimes I feel like I work too hard (the average professor works over 60 hours a week!), but I understand now why my mom and dad made the choices they did. Dedicating one's life to the service of others isn't the weakness I thought it was—it was the foundation for a happy, sustainable life.

****

Figure 1.2

Why are you in college? Maybe you are in college to earn a degree, get hired, and have a professional-class livelihood. There's certainly nothing wrong with that! We live in a society where it is increasingly necessary to have a college education to perform the wide range of tasks organizations need (Hart Research Associates, 2018). Furthermore, there is a lot of evidence that indicates that the United States is moving toward a "gig" economy, where a person has many part-time jobs or a main job with a side hustle to make a livelihood (Hathaway & Muro, 2016). These changes mean it will be increasingly rare that a person has one job with one organization over the course of their lifespan—something that was quite common for the baby boomer generation (Associated Press, 2016). Add the fact that college degree-holders earn substantially more than their non-degreed counterparts over their lifespan (Bureau of Labor Statistics [BLS], 2018), and it's no wonder why you would be in college to invest in your career.

We hope you, like Kyle, don't stop there. Whether you dedicate your career to serving others in direct ways or in ways that aren't as obvious, there is a place for everyone in making our communities and our world a better place to live. Everyone can do their part to change the world. But to do that you're going to need two things. First, you're going to have to complete your college degree. The knowledge, skills, and dispositions you accrue over your time in college will be invaluable for your personal growth and the health of your community. Of course, people who don't have a college education also have a wide range of resources with which to transform themselves and society—a college degree isn't the only way to these goals. But, as a college-educated citizen in the United States, you will have unique opportunities for activism and a different way of seeing the world. Completing your degree will give you the tools to navigate and access avenues for change, many of which will be uncharted until *you* get involved.

Second, you're going to need a language for talking about the problems that face society. We bet that much of the talk you hear in your life doesn't do justice to the full complexity of the issues that face our society. Because the United States is a highly individualistic nation, we tend to see social problems as individual concerns. For example, many people with physical disabilities were barred from accessing jobs, goods, and services because many buildings were not built in an accessible way (e.g., lack of elevators or ramps). It wasn't until the passage of the Americans with Disability Act in 1990 that federal regulations were passed mandating accessible buildings. That's right—for nearly 200 years of U.S. history we structured our communities against people with mobility issues and made them, as individuals, figure out how to navigate society. Individualistic approaches to social problems, whether it regards disability, racism, poverty, or pollution are, in our mind, inadequate responses the challenges that face society. Only by acting on problems with a social and individual approach can we hope to work together to change the world. Higher education can become that place where you navigate your learning to build a sustainable future.

That is the purpose of this book, to help you address both the individual and social aspects of higher education. Like many of the teachers you'll have in your higher education, we want you to succeed in college. We want you to meet your personal goals in life, find a community of justice-minded people, and seek out strategies for dialogue when differences arise. As such, this book will explore emerging issues, identify problems that new and continuing college students encounter, offer advice for how you can best overcome those obstacles, and share some stories of people who at one time were in the very spaces you're in right now. But, and this is crucial, we hope that you don't stop with just succeeding in college. We want you to see the problems you face not as a series of overwhelming obstacles, but rather as opportunities to organize with others around you—ensuring that no one else must suffer from the same problems you've surmounted. We think that this approach to activism, of taking the saying "the personal is political" seriously, is key for creating communities and a society that is more just, humane, and sustainable. When we see our personal struggles as shared problems, we can build coalitions for change, and realize a better future.

Why Does Higher Education Exist?

When I (Nic) enrolled in college, I did it because it was expected. I couldn't decide between wanting to be a lawyer or philosopher, but I knew I wanted to work my way up a corporate or intellectual ladder until I was wealthy or had an idea to call my own. My parents were public school teachers. Students called them by "Mr." and "Mrs." They met in a lab while working with special education students. We, along with my sister, over dinner, in our living room, and during family vacations routinely discussed our dreams, faith, social justice, politics, teaching, and intense feelings of being lost in the world, in public education, in systems, all as teachers, students, and members of various communities.

Figure 1.3

I volunteered at our college's communication lab; however, for me this was a place to get access to what professors wanted. Students here seemed to have a personal relationship with their teachers, and I wanted that, too. I was on the competitive speech and debate team, but I saw the activity as a means to an end. Engaging in this activity seemed to provide access to people, information, mentorship, and what seemed like an important leg up on my peers to accomplish what was expected. I also noticed something in the classroom, in the lab, and around their department offices—professors always seemed to help those who engaged them through academic curiosity just a bit more. Professors seemed to be dedicated to these students' success as though they would be future carriers of their knowledge. These moments seemed as valuable as money, and I wanted to experience them as a career.

In my second year of college, I switched my major to communication. Please don't read this as though I had things figured out by my second year; the only thing clear for me was that I had an insatiable curiosity for learning (and privilege afforded me opportunities to indulge). My journey to communication came after counseling appointments, talking to friends and professors, and switching my major for the sixth time. I eventually finished my bachelor's degree, completed my MA and PhD, found a position at a community college, earned tenure, and left academia 9 years later to become the executive director of a nonprofit. By my original standard, I was successful. But, more than that, I had found a community of people who were dedicated to the same things I was: learning, teaching, and mentorship. I made some of my best friends in the classroom, which translated into personal growth. And, the chance to work with others on transformative projects, and to make a difference, are still things that motivate me to be my best as a leader of a non-profit dedicated to education around the world.

****

As you think about your personal goals for attending college, we want you to put them in the context of the larger scope, history, and purpose of higher education. Every year millions of students of all ages and from all over the world enroll in college, and billions of dollars in taxes, tuition, loans, scholarships, and grants are spent to educate them. Although you may have personal goals for going to college, the truth is that your goals are likely structured by a combination of the three primary social functions that education has for society: national economic development, personal advancement, and societal transformation (Labaree, 1997; Sprague, 1999). Understanding the role of higher education in society is an important step in developing ways to transform it and our communities.

Figure 1.4

The first reason that a society offers higher education is to create a globally competitive workforce. If you've ever listened to a politician talk about higher education, you'll have heard this is a common talking point. In this view, America is in competition with other nations for creating and profiting from new industries, technologies, and natural resources. Historically, the role of chief competitor has varied from the United Kingdom, to France, to Germany. However, this reason was probably most explicitly invoked when the United States was competing with the Soviet Union, and a lot of political talk revolved around how everyday Americans could "fight the communist threat" through excellence in the workplace. With the collapse of the USSR, the role of chief competitor has been filled by China. So, when you hear politicians talk about education as a national investment today, they might make veiled or overt remarks that America is "losing its edge" or "losing ground" or "being beaten by" other countries, primarily China.

This approach to higher education is based on the premise that the national economy is like a machine, and that every person has a proper place that keeps that machine running. This approach manifests most explicitly in a variety of educational tracking programs and processes that begin at a young age and can follow a person well beyond their compulsory education, and even throughout their lifetime. For example, most high schools offer a variety of special education, vocational technical, so-called normal or regular, gifted and talented, and college preparation courses—and each type of course (and how well funded it is) corresponds, largely, with students' post high school–graduation ambitions.

Because PK–12 schools are paid for primarily through property taxes and bond measures, schools in poorer neighborhoods often struggle to find needed funding, while wealthier neighborhoods are better funded because of their greater access to funding. This system is why we have schools that may only be a few miles apart or even within the same district but have vastly different access to educational opportunities (Kozol, 2005).

Although we may look at these disparities as problems, those who see education primarily to create a globally competitive workforce welcome these inequalities. To these people, we need unskilled labor as much as we need skilled labor, blue collar and white collar, laborer and manager, to make sure that everyone has a place in the machine that makes up the national economy, which also has a place in the greater global economy. Higher education, in this thinking then, ensures that those who have demonstrated their worth to the national economy (i.e., the middle class and wealthy) continue down their socioeconomic track through their children and children's children. This is not to say that these people do not recognize exception—they realize some people achieve things that propel them into a higher socioeconomic class. However, many of those living in poverty or part of the working or middle class are largely ignored or barred from participation in the highest echelons of the professional economy regardless of their talent due to social problems such as poor school funding, corporate greed, various sociopolitical agendas, standardized practices, access to addictive substances, and restrictions from early educational opportunities (e.g., preschool). Because people who rise above their status are viewed as disrupting the balance of that machine, much is done to maintain a status quo.

The second reason a society offers higher education is because it is a means to personal economic advancement. As we noted earlier in the chapter, this is

Figure 1.5

probably the most common reason that everyday Americans think of when deciding whether to attend college. A college degree is viewed as a means to enter the professional-class workforce and secure a perceived middle-class lifestyle. Political commentary that draws on this idea is usually characterized by statements such as "students need to be prepared to be successful for the 21st-century economy" or "the path to a good job is a good education." This view of education gained prominence in the 1980s when the national economy shifted from an industrial-labor to a customer-service economy (Hernandez, 2018). Now, for example, it is less likely that you will get a job building a computer and more likely that you will get a job providing technical assistance, creating software, or developing marketing outreach using a computer. Within this framework, it is important that you get an education that helps you realize your economic and professional aspirations.

In this view, education is understood as a personal investment, one whose return-on-investment is proportional to the amount of money, time, and effort you put into it. If the previous reason's metaphor was a "machine," then this reason's metaphor would be the casino. Your job is to find the best university, at the best price, and pick the major/classes (regardless of your talent, ambitions, or feelings) that will provide you with the best chances for a job that will provide some type of economic success. But, unlike a customer who is paying for goods or services that they immediately enjoy (e.g., I buy a hamburger and eat it), the process of getting an education doesn't guarantee that you will obtain your dream job or understand happiness. Instead, much of your educational experiences are largely shaped by a calculating logic of how to increase your chances to "hit it big" (i.e., get a dream job). So, you may love music and want to learn how to play the piano, but that isn't in your major, so you shouldn't spend the time and money to take the class. Or, you may have a real talent for writing novels, but that's a hard industry to be successful in—much better to choose a major that has higher employment and earning potential like engineering. And, as we'll talk about in Chapter 3, the result of this view is a society that accepts, as normal, winners and losers, demonizing working-class folk and people in poverty.

The final reason a society provides education is to promote social transformation. In this view, a society recognizes that there are long standing, stubborn problems that face our communities, and that education is a way to identify and solve those issues. This view of education is rooted in the writing of John Dewey, Paulo Freire, bell hooks, and countless others. Dewey (1916) said, "But in general it may be said that the things which we take for granted without inquiry or reflection are just the things which determine our conscious thinking and decide our conclusions" (p. 18). In other words, the problems that face society will continue to do so if we don't take the time and effort to reflect on our biases, overcome our prejudices, and maintain a sense of justice. Societies need to change and adapt to thrive, and education is a way that folks can learn how to better serve their communities—to imagine and pursue a society free from hunger, poverty, and want.

This ethic in education puts a great deal of emphasis on both the process and product of education. As process, education should foster the types of thinking that will help students cultivate a view of social ills as shared community problems. So, classes should be less focused on lecture, memorization, and standardized tests, and instead become an intellectual laboratory where people experiment with new ideas and solutions. As a product, education should produce people who are capable of being autonomous, self-motivated change agents who are interested in social and economic justice. We know that we live in a society that is structured in ways that harm some folk while privileging others. Take our example of wheelchair access from earlier—it doesn't take society that hates people with disabilities to create this system, it only takes a society that ignores them. Within this tradition, it is precisely these types of problems that call us to re-evaluate our assumptions and restructure ourselves and society toward justice and harmony.

Figure 1.6

We acknowledge that these three aims, and others (e.g., finding friends/ romance, developing adulthood, and establishing networks), will always be a part of education in the United States, and that your time in college will be characterized by navigating the push–pull tensions among the different perspectives. However, we wish to be upfront with you about our motives—we wrote this book with the belief that the social transformation goal is both underemphasized and sorely needed. We feel that as our (global) society moves ever closer to political, social, and ecological disaster, stripping education from its social transformation aim does not serve your or society's best interests. Thus, our desire is for you to seriously consider your place in the world. Take a minute to think of the problems that face our society and the world—the big ones, the ones that have or will have far-reaching, negative impacts. Maybe you thought of problems such as global climate change, racism, disability issues, wealth inequality, corporate greed, government surveillance, or growing ethno-nationalism. Now answer this question: How much did your education explicitly and intentionally teach you about these problems or how to overcome them? If you are like us, then the answer is probably quite distressing! Students and teachers, in recognizing a shared future, must come together to identify and overcome the problems that face our society and planet. Our communities deserve, and need, nothing less.

Navigating Higher Education: Connecting the Personal With the Political

Like many of your parents and grandparents, I (Katherine) am a baby boomer and, as such, a direct beneficiary of critical social movements in this country during the 1970s—the Civil Rights and Women's Rights movements and the Vietnam War protests. I am the sixth and youngest child of African American parents (Samuel and Lizzie Mae) who moved from Alabama to California in the 1950s for more economic security and to ensure a strong education for their children. My Dad was a beekeeper and my Mom a homemaker who many women in the neighborhood relied on to keep an eye on their children—especially the boys—after school while they were still at work.

I was active in individual events (e.g., oral interpretation and persuasive speaking) and debate during high school. My performance in such events caught the eye of several professors teaching at California State University–Fresno. These young, White male assistant professors (never judge the heart of a person by their outward appearance), like my parents, recognized education as a door that would expose me to a new world far outside my local neighborhood. An education would provide a better existence for me and create a path for others to follow. Those professors—Diestel, Cagle, Ullman, Bochin, Quadro, and Hennings—saw *me*. They saw *me* as an individual, appreciated my intelligence, and guided my career—providing a safety net—from BA to MA to PhD.

These White men, even with all their inherent privilege, were savvy enough and tuned into societal ills enough to recognize the prejudice and racism that I would face as a young African American woman. Consequently, they actively invested in guiding my career. My siblings and parents were (and still are) staunch supporters. My sister Arzell and my brothers Sammie, Mearns, Roy, and Robert all contributed financially so I could dress like other students (you may understand how important this is), buy my books and supplies, and have a little spending money. One of my brothers sent money home from Korea and two from Vietnam. I contributed as well as a work-study student.

My degrees are not my own. They belong to my family, my neighbors, and my professors. Remember the movie *Akeelah and the Bee* (2006)? I had that kind of support system. Yes, there was prejudice (still is). Yes, there was racism (still is), but you cannot give up when everyone is counting on you. Sometimes you cry, get mad, and even want to slap somebody. Sometimes you want to give up, but you don't. You press on.

You cannot judge someone based on their exterior. That lesson manifests itself over and over in my life. As a result, I understand that some of my White students have come from a tough environment, whether it be an abusive family, economic hardship, being a first-generation college student, or something else. As my professors did for me, I try to do for *all* of my students—to see their potential and offer a bridge to a better life. Acts such as these are highly personal forms of political activism.

Figure 1.7

As you attempt to navigate the opportunities for activism, it's not uncommon to find yourself lost. One of the primary problems with the national economic development and personal investment aims is that both perspectives assume that the political and economic systems of our present moment are neutral, normal, or natural. As such, when there are failures in the system, many people who adhere to these beliefs are more likely to blame individuals than to do the hard work of identifying and transforming our society. For example, racial/ethnic minority students, students with disabilities, English language learners, first-generation students, and students from poverty are often labeled as "at-risk for failure" or "special needs" populations. Notice how both categories make the lack of equal access and treatment seem like it's the students' problem, and not the university's or society's fault. These ways of casting blame on students for the institutional and societal failures are called a *deficit view* of education. This view incorrectly categorizes students as lacking or wanting in their skills, knowledge, or dispositions, and clouds the true issues that lie at the heart of problems.

We cannot hope to build a just society if we do not correctly diagnose the problems that afflict it. Even if we are doing something about the problem, those actions may not help and, in fact, may even make the problem worse! For example, we wouldn't want a medical doctor to misdiagnose a common cold for cancer and begin chemotherapy—such a treatment runs the risk of killing the patient. Likewise, thinking that some students don't have the correct skills, knowledge, or dispositions to succeed would suggest that they, and their families, should simply work harder if they want to be economically successful and productive citizens. We wish to be clear; you will need to work hard to be successful in college. You will encounter a range of ideas, texts, problems, and issues that probably didn't characterize your high school education. And, you'll be required to read, write, calculate, and experiment on a variety of assignments (some that will feel meaningful and others, not so much), and manage a social and work life. You'll be busy, you'll work hard, and will have many questions. But, the challenge of education should be a challenge of growth, self-exploration, and development, not based on (mis)perceptions of your abilities or your family's wealth. We should strive for a society where our institutions, within and beyond higher education, support all people to fulfill their potential.

When you consider problems that face you as part of a community, rather than individual, then better conversations and stronger solutions can emerge. This type of conversation reminds us of the old saying, "Give a person a fish and they eat for a day. Teach a person to fish and they can eat for a lifetime." The lesson of the saying is clear—showing a person that they require help and instilling them with personal responsibility and education will solve problems. However, we argue that sometimes a person needs a fish—direct and temporary

Figure 1.8

relief from the problems they face. In those instances, it is important to recognize that society should be structured in ways to provide immediate aid for those who do not have access to essential goods and services. Other times, a person may need to learn to fish—to understand how to navigate systems to provide for themselves. A great deal of this book will be devoted to offering you tips about the resources and groups that will help you navigate higher education and society. However, we will also challenge you to explore two important questions: (1) Why did the person not know how to fish in the first place? and (2) What if there are no fish in the pond? These two questions call us to explore how social problems are more than just a matter of changing individuals' circumstances, attitudes, or behaviors, and demands that we explore and change the social aspects of problems.

Organizing people for social and economic justice while you're in college will not be easy. You'll need three things in your toolkit: (1) a knowledge of and skills to identify/navigate the system of higher education, (2) a language for understanding the social dimensions of problems, and (3) a democratic ethic of collaboration and advocacy. We hope this book provides these tools for you. Your job, as a person who wants to see the world become more just and humane, will be to ensure that you model and pursue the type of world you want to realize. We won't lie to you—you will face a lot of obstacles along the way. There will be fellow students who say you are too radical or angry, instructors who will not respect you or your passion, administrators who will try to delay your advocacy until you graduate and are "out of their hair," community members who will call you entitled or ill-informed, and media outlets that will ridicule and dehumanize your generation and movement. But, and this is important, you can overcome these barriers by creating coalitions with other students, instructors, administrators, community members, and media outlets who will want to be a part of a movement for social transformation. Because the personal is never just personal—it's political. In other words, the things you can do for yourself and community—today, right now—can have effects far beyond just yourself. Some projects will have an immediate effect while others will come to fruition long after you have graduate college. And, therein lies *your* power, you can organize and network with others to amplify your voice and mobilize people for positive change. We can't guarantee that movements for justice will always be successful, but we can promise you that you will never have a better chance than right now to start advocating for a better world.

****

The purpose of this chapter was to introduce you to us. We were once like you and, in many ways, still are just like you. We care deeply about education, families, and friends; we have hobbies, hopes, and dreams; and we have experienced failures and setbacks. Another purpose was outlining the stakes in conversations about the aims of education, goals of advocacy, and your life, and to challenge you to see your work as the key to addressing social ills. We want to be honest with you about our intentions with this text, to show you how our experiences have shaped our advocacy and to invite you to join us in identifying and overcoming the challenges that face higher education, society, and our shared futures. We can think of nothing better than forming strong collaborations with our students and jointly realizing this dream. And to those ends, we promise to never insult your intelligence or make recommendations that will waste your time. The choices on how to engage, activate, and navigate higher education and beyond are yours to make.

College life can be fun. You can party, make friends, find romance, laugh, and genuinely enjoy many aspects of your time. But, there will be times when those positive things are going to be overshadowed by the difficulty associated with acquiring what will most likely be a completely different way to look at the world (i.e., evidence based) and the pressures to meet (sometimes impossibly) high standards. There will be times you are watching TV and feel an odd, slumping feeling in your chest. That's guilt, because you probably should be doing your homework or reading for your class. College can be a challenging, difficult, and stressful experience, no doubt. But, when it's over and you walk across the stage for your diploma, you will know that you have done something that truly—and maybe even for the first time in your life—challenged you to deeply and meaningfully work with others to change the world around you. And, that journey to building a sustainable and shared future begins today.

Discussion Questions

- What are your thoughts about being able to transform society as an individual?

- Where do you agree and disagree with the authors about the three aims of higher education?

- What do the terms *social justice* and *economic justice* mean to you?

Student Challenge

- Each author shared a story about how they began college. Share your story about your journey to college.

CHAPTER 2

Reflective Practice
Building a Vocabulary for Justice

CHAPTER OBJECTIVES

By the end of the chapter, you should be able to:

- Identify the reason for a social justice approach to community and global problems

- Identify the important aspects of racism, sexism and gender discrimination, heterosexism, and capitalism

- Describe how privilege and oppression manifest in your life

- Connect how the systems of oppression shape the culture of higher education

ORIENTING QUESTIONS

As you read the chapter, try to answer the following questions:

- What does the term *social justice* mean?

- What do people need to realize their full potential?

- Where can students enact change?

A common refrain from many parts of society (e.g., media, families, and religious institutions) is that the youth of today are apathetic, lazy, and politically unengaged. Take, for example, the pejorative term *snowflakes* used primarily by right-wing outlets such as Fox News, the Drudge Report, and Breitbart to describe youth as having an overinflated sense of importance that can melt at the first sign of resistance. Or, the slew of television shows, books, and newspaper articles and editorials that decry youth as soft, weak, or spoiled. It doesn't take much effort to find someone writing about how the "kids today" just aren't as good as they used to be.

Although many might believe there is a crisis of youth today, the fact is that the same negative descriptors used to label youth today are the same as those used by virtually every group of elders to describe youth for hundreds of years. And while it may sell books or advertisement space on television to perpetuate one-sided and negative labels, the truth is that every cohort of youth is complex, multifaceted, and changing. The political-economy that youth are entering as they graduate high school or college has evolved from their parents' time and continues to change rapidly. Manufacturing jobs are disappearing to automation and overseas relocations (DeSilver, 2017); wages are stagnant even as corporations report record profits (Schwartz, 2013); and under- and unemployment for youth continues to be a problem, particularly for youth of color (Ross & Svajlenka, 2016). These issues, as well as student loan debt, unpaid internships, lack of meaningful health insurance, and the rise of the "gig" economy have resulted in a generation that continues to struggle to find their place in society.

But, find it they will. What others may label as whining or entitlement, we see as the struggle of young people to create a society that meets the needs of the many, not the few. Youth are not passive, nor are they coddled; rather, they have the energy, intelligence, drive, and, above all, the heart to see that the world as it currently is simply isn't the world as it should be. This drive to see a better world manifests in their political and community involvement. For example, youth are more involved in community service now than in the past 30 years (Syverston, Wray-Lake, Flanagan, Osgood, & Briddel, 2010). And, even though media outlets state that youth lag in their voting participation relative to other generations, the truth is that youth vote at similar rates as previous generations when they were the same age (Fry, 2018). From Rock the Vote, Occupy Wall Street, and Black Lives Matter, to the Women's March and the

> ## Student Voice
>
> My first feeling of making a difference was in my family by going to school. I recognized that I had an opportunity to be the first one to finish school. From there, that attitude went with me to school, where it made me understand trusting the process and staying the course. Like anything, there are uncertainties going into it [school], but it isn't until you're there you start to see all the parts. —*Simone*

Climate March, youth are rising to the challenges of our increasingly polarized and unequal society. In short, youth aren't whining—they're winning.

As you think about what kind of world you wish to live in, we encourage you to develop a vocabulary that helps you name the problems, and solutions, to the persistent, stubborn issues that face society. To that end, we have developed this chapter to provide you with some basic vocabulary for viewing social problems. Remember, we don't think that viewing the issues that face society as only individual problems is necessarily the best approach. Rather, we think that the problems that face society are social, and it's only when we all work together that true and lasting change will happen. We begin this chapter with a section on social justice—what the term means and why we think it's important to strive for in society. We'll also discuss some of the common misperceptions about social justice, so you'll be ready when others call your goals and methods into question. If social justice is what we are *for*, then what do we think the problems are? To answer that, we'll address four areas that those who wish to change the world should address: racism, sexism and gender discrimination, heterosexism, and neoliberal capitalism. As we'll talk about throughout the book, these problems intersect, combine, and work against each other in a variety of ways that affect your daily life, and prompt you to both be personally (as a student navigating college) and politically (as a citizen in a democracy) savvy.

Social Justice

Building a Vocabulary

Social justice is a term that is becoming increasingly mainstream within society. Although, on the one hand, we are glad that more and more people are talking and thinking about justice, we know that its ordinariness in popular culture can lead to competing, and even contradictory, definitions of what it is and why it's important. As a result, there are people who are doing social justice work, but who don't explicitly espouse the term, whereas others who do claim to work toward social justice fail to uphold its principles or goals. This confusion, in turn, makes it difficult to ascertain exactly what people mean when they say they are *for* social justice.

> **Student Voice**
>
> The first time I heard the term social justice was in elementary school and thought it was supposed to be "justice for all." And then you get into the real world and realize the justice system is not fair. —*Debra*

> **Student Voice**
>
> It is commonly understood that social justice is the act of defending or speaking with or in defense of a group of people or individuals who are viewed as the other or lesser than what popular culture deems to be correct, normal or "right." —*Ronnie*

Although there are many approaches to social justice, we prefer the work of Nussbaum (2002, 2011) who defines social justice in terms of a **human capabilities approach**. To Nussbaum, human life is characterized by a profound need to realize one's potential—economically, socially, relationally, personally, and politically. However, needs can be unmet when a society does not create the systems necessary for people to flourish. Take, for example, two children, of equal ambition and upbringing but who go to two different schools; the first goes to a well-funded school, equipped with a host of extracurricular activities, and the second does not. Unsurprisingly, the first student scores higher on the ACT/SAT, goes to a better college, gets a better job, earns more money, lives longer, and has fewer health issues throughout their life. Is it fair to say that the second child's inability to reach their potential was their fault; that they should have simply worked harder? We, along with Nussbaum, would say that this situation is extremely unfair, and yet it characterizes far too much of U.S. society. Although there is no perfect society, we believe that, together, we can all work to create a world where people have the opportunities to imagine possibilities and realize the full extent of their capabilities.

But, just what do people need in order to realize their full capabilities? Pyles (2014), working from Nussbaum (2011) and the Center for Popular Economics (2012), identified 10 central human functioning capabilities:

1. Life: Being able to live a human life of normal length; not dying prematurely.

2. Bodily health: Being able to have good health, nourishment, and shelter.

3. Bodily integrity: Being able to move freely and to be secure against assault; being able to have opportunities for sexual satisfaction and to have choice in reproductive health.

4. Sense, imagination, and thought: Being able to use one's mind and senses in matters of expression both politically and artistically.

5. Emotions: Being able to be attached to and love others; not having one's emotional development thwarted by fear and anxiety.

6. Practical reason: Being able to conceive of what is of most value and to critically reflect and plan for one's life.

7. Affiliation: Being able to live with others and engage in social interaction and to have the social bases of dignity and to be free of humiliation and discrimination.

8. Other species: Being able to live with and be concerned for animals, plants, and the world of nature.

9. Play: Being able to laugh, play, and recreate.

10. Control over one's environment: Being able to participate politically and have free speech protections; being able to hold property, seek employment on an equal basis with others. (p. 7)

The list provides a few important features and caveats. Perhaps most important, Nussbaum argues that all of the capabilities are unique. In other words,

Figure 2.2

each capability must be addressed on its own; for example, securing a high amount of life doesn't justify a low level of bodily health. At the same time, all of the capabilities are intertwined with the others. One cannot, for example, be free to create relationships with others if one doesn't have bodily integrity. All capabilities must be met in order for humans to be able to flourish.

Another important caveat is the difference between having access to capabilities and how people realize their capabilities in their day-to-day lives (Nussbaum, 2011). In other words, social justice advocates are concerned with making sure that people have access to the things that secure their capabilities, but they do not advocate that those capabilities must be enjoyed or experienced in the same way by all people. Consider what it might mean or look like if we explore the differences between equality and equity. A contemporary example would be Muslim women who wear the burka. To say that the burka is inherently dehumanizing and forcing all Muslim women to remove it would be to ignore the millions of Muslim women who find that it is an important part of their spiritual and cultural identity. Any type of clothing—whether burka or bikini—can be dehumanizing if it is used to curtail someone's capabilities. Thus, treating everyone the same (equality) isn't a route to justice; instead, we need to ask tough questions about choice, spirituality, and tradition, and then make decisions based on this complex web of information (i.e., equity). In short, whether forced to wear a burka or bikini, women shouldn't be forced to do anything because that would be a violation of their bodily integrity. Rather, social justice advocacy is founded on the respect of people's autonomy while ensuring that individual actions are made in a system that is open and without coercion.

This idea, in turn, leads to the final and most sticky part of a capabilities approach. Making determinations of what does or does not enhance people's capabilities must be done in consultation with, but not wholly rely upon, the people at the center of the controversy. For example, millions of young girls are married without their consent to men as a form of monetary transfer, to consecrate a business deal, or to curry favor (i.e., human trafficking). If someone were to ask some of these girls if they objected to this practice, many may not—because they have been told it's their duty, that they are helping their family, that they would be selfish for not acquiescing, or due to the threat of violence. Thus, if a 6-year-old girl were to assert that she wanted to get

Student Voice

Making a difference is solely about intent and passion. Nothing will get done unless you truly care, and people will be able to tell if you genuinely care about a topic versus you doing it just to impress. In my life, I plan to use my intelligence, empathy, and sense of self to try to bring people together, even if just for a moment. If I can bring our population or even just one person to the understanding that no one is better than anyone else or that everyone means just as much to the world as the next person, I will have created change that I can be proud of. —*Jonesy* married, we must be humble, but clear-eyed, in acknowledging that she is ill-equipped to advocate for herself. For her to do so may result in her abandonment, rape, and/or death. This kind of example is why it is important to have a social, rather than individual, lens in which to view social problems. Only when we look at the aggregate of experiences in relation to a problem, and the systems and institutions that shape those experiences, can we possibly make determinations about how, or even if, to act.

The capabilities approach gives us a language for understanding what social justice activists mean when they talk about oppression and privilege. **Oppression**, in this framework, refers to systems that bar humans from realizing their capabilities based on social group memberships and political-economy (Rudick, Golsan, & Cheesewright, 2018). When people are not able to realize their capabilities due to race, gender, sexuality, or family income, then we have a society that is fundamentally unfair and must be changed. Everyone participates in the systems that make it difficult for some to access the resources (e.g., rural folks' difficulty accessing quality health care) or break from social group stigmas (e.g., racist stereotypes), which adversely affects their ability to realize their capabilities. For example, when there is little national outcry to prosecute those responsible for poisoning the water supply in Flint, Michigan, and little progress after many years in fixing the situation or providing recompense for the economic or health ramifications (Sanburn, 2017), then we have all participated in a system that has harmed some peoples' chances to realize their full capabilities.

Conversely, when we talk about **privilege**, we mean systems that provide unearned access (whether social or material) to goods, services, or resources (Rudick et al., 2018). Note that privilege doesn't mean a person didn't work or work hard for the access they enjoy, it simply means they are rewarded disproportionately to the effort of others who strive for the same goal. For example, a White man has to study hard, meet deadlines, and pass all of the tests to become a medical doctor; however, a Latina will have to meet those criteria in addition to overcoming sexual and racial stereotypes about her intelligence and work ethic. To ensure an equitable society, it is incumbent on all of us to ensure that the systems fairly and humanely provide the resources necessary so that people can reach their full capabilities.

In striving for social justice, advocates recognize that oppression and privilege operate "intentionally and unintentionally,

> **Student Voice**
>
> In my eyes, privilege is a gift that no one should be ashamed of, but everyone should be cognizant of. The example that comes to mind for me is the very idea that people treasure the idea of heterosexual love more than LGBTQ love. In some cases, people can even believe that LGTBQ love is wrong, as if it isn't love at all but some sort of perversion of the soul. Not being cognizant of how that hurts people—that's privilege. —Darlene

on individual, institutional, and cultural levels" (Hardiman, Jackson, & Griffin, 2007, p. 58). Said differently, we must all recognize the ways that privilege and oppression manifest at all levels of society, to see the various instances of injustice—from the everyday to the egregious—as interconnected. For example, although it may be easy for some to say that **microaggressions** aren't a big deal because it's just a person's feelings that get hurt, the truth is that oppressive talk lays the groundwork for, and eventually justifies, oppressive behavior. For example, the stereotype that Black men were sexually promiscuous and out to steal White women's virtue was so prevalent in the United States that in 1921 the accusation against a Black man of raping a white woman in Tulsa, Oklahoma, resulted in the burning of the Black district (known as the "Black Wall Street"), resulting in 10,000 homeless Black people, tens of millions of dollars in damage, 39 deaths, and untold harm to future generations of Black people (Gates, 2003). Our argument here is simple—it is a short step from oppressive labels or stereotypes about groups of people to enacting violence, whether through implicit bias, legislation barring equal participation society, banks barring access to secure loans for homeownership, or targeted killing of traditionally oppressed groups.

Social justice, conceived within a framework of human capabilities, gives people a goal to strive for in their activism rather than just being "against" something. As the famous labor activist Samuel Gompers wrote:

> We want more school houses and less jails; more books and less arsenals; more learning and less vice; more constant work and less crime; more leisure and less greed; more justice and less revenge; in fact, more of the opportunities to cultivate our better natures. (as cited in Greenhouse, 2019)

We can think of nothing better than to realize this goal for ourselves and our communities. We hope that you wish to take this journey with us to realize a more hopeful, humane, and equitable society.

Student Voice

I have met a multitude of men who have completely disregarded my affections or even attempts at friendship because of my queerness. There are lots of reasons for this but the most popular was the excuse that they were afraid that I would develop a crush on them. They seemed to think that just because I am gay that I, by association would find any and every man attractive and develop feelings for them which if they looked in the mirror was most definitely not the case. —*Casey*

Student Voice

Most people I have met in my life or come into contact with make assumptions about my identity just because of stereotypes or generalizations which isn't necessarily a bad thing but that doesn't make it any less irritating. An example would be people not caring to ask how I feel about a political issue relating to LGBTQ policy and laws rather they lead the statement with the assumption that I stand on the same side as every other gay person which isn't always the case. —*Joe*

Student Activism and Systems of Oppression

In the previous section, we talked about what social justice advocates are "for" in their work. Here, we want to address four interlocking systems of oppressions that block humans' ability to realize their capabilities. A recurring theme in each of these areas is that each issue is also a social, and not merely individual, issue, and therefore requires a community response to remedy. We also detail some of the recent student activist work that has been done to address these problems to show you the ways in which everyday students are striving to make a difference in their communities.

Student Voice

The first time I got to a community college campus I realized that most of my instructors and peers were White. I have moments where I can see what I want or the relationship I want to have with people or my major, but it's hard because they can rarely address the sensitivities of my lived experiences as a person of color. —*Simone*

Student Voice

As an African American you truly have to rely on how your ancestors would react. You have to take the high road because you know that people are going to hit those scars that are shared generationally. You see within the classroom or college spaces who are willfully ignorant of the historical context I have lived. I am confronted with having to choose my moments of keeping others accountable and my own safety. —*Jalen*

Racism

When most people talk about **racism**, they often think of it as a matter of an individual's overt prejudice against a person from another race. This understanding of racism calls to mind the obvious components of racism within U.S. history: slavery, Jim Crow laws, segregation, and the Ku Klux Klan. Our argument is that, even though most forms of overt racism are frowned upon in society, there are many subtle and covert ways in which racism achieves the same goals of barring people of color from realizing their capabilities. For example, even though practices such as lynching are no longer widely practiced in the United States, people of color are sentenced to death, are shot by police (even when unarmed), and are given longer prison sentences than their White counterparts, even when they commit the same crimes (or are innocent!) (ACLU, 2014, n.d.; *The Washington Post*, n.d.). In other words, much of the so-called progress on overcoming racism in the past century has less to do with the effect of racism (i.e., people of color are still disproportionately, and negatively, targeted), and more to do with how overt or mainstream such actions are. In short, although there are certainly behaviors, laws, or groups that are overtly racist, we fear that over focusing on them is to the detriment of truly combatting all types of racism.

To address racism, we first have to define what we mean by race. We identify four ways that people normally understand race within contemporary U.S. politics and everyday life (Bonilla-Silva, 2006; Leonardo, 2009, 2013). First, the

biological perspective on race argues that there are physical and/or genetic markers that make some races better than others. This idea has its roots in the eugenics movement of the late 19th and early 20th centuries, which perpetuated the belief that skull size, skin color, and/or hair texture were markers of racial purity and strength. In a more contemporary sense, the U.S. Alt-Right movement, which espouses its views on 4chan, Reddit, and Twitter, typically perpetuates the idea that people of color are biologically inferior to White people.

Although we might like to think of hate groups as occupying the fringe of society, the truth is that there are many people who espouse these beliefs. For example, President Trump described Latinx people as "bad hombres" and "rapists," asserted that Nigerians should "go back to their huts," and defended neo-Nazis in the Charlottesville protests. In fact, when President Trump described Haiti and other African countries as "shitholes," the prominent Alt-Right White supremacist Richard Spencer (2018) wrote:

> I must come to the defense of #Haiti. It's a potentially beautiful and productive country. The problem is that it is filled with shithole people. If the French dominated, they could make it great again. #MakeHaitiGreatAgain

In short, there are prominent people in society who believe that phenotype (e.g., skin color, facial structure, and body build) predicts or directly influences a variety of outcomes, and that skin color is therefore a useful tool for establishing a hierarchy of races (where, unsurprisingly, White people always put themselves at the top). These assertions are made in the face of overwhelming evidence that skin color has no direct relationship with drug use, propensity for crime, productivity, intelligence, or violence (Sussman, 2014).

The second way that people understand race in society is through the **socio-cultural perspective**. This framework shares many of the same assumptions as the biological understanding; that is, it supports the idea that some races are simply better than others. Where it departs, though, is its reliance on cultural rather than genetic reasons. To these people, Black, Latinx, and Native American people have less wealth or are incarcerated disproportionally because they have cultural deficiencies that make them unsuccessful. Asian people from countries such as Japan, South Korea, and China are touted as "model minorities" because their groups' economic gains are on par with White people's, even though these gains are not true for all Asian people (see, for example, the economic plight of Hmong, Thai, or Laotian people), nor are they immune from other forms of racism (e.g., redlining neighborhoods, internment camps, or workplace discrimination). In this understanding, White people and White culture are either explicitly or implicitly viewed as normal, natural, or desirable, and it is up to people of color to assimilate to those standards. Failure to do so is not seen as a virtue or as preserving a unique cultural history, but rather as a failure to recognize and adopt to the superiority of White norms and habits.

The third, and perhaps most dominant, way of talking about race in the United States is the **race-evasive perspective**, or the notion that to eliminate racism people should stop talking about race altogether. There are two parts to this understanding. On one hand, **normative race-evasiveness** refers to the idea that racism is no longer a problem, and that most people don't see or act upon race. This notion perpetuates the belief that claims of racial discrimination or violence are unsubstantiated illusions that people of color use to gain unearned advantages (e.g., "pulling the race card"). On the other hand, **idealistic race-evasiveness** refers to times when a person argues that while we might not be past race right now, we could be if individuals would start looking "past" or "beyond" race to see a person as "just" human. To these people, trying to address racism is, in fact, racist, because doing so names racial categories in order to understand if there are systemic disparities among different racial groups.

Figure 2.3

Although the idea that "race" could be removed from the public imagination and that society could return (or has returned) to a time when racism did not exist might be appealing to some, there are compelling reasons that this way of thinking is problematic. First, if we believe that racism is truly over and that race plays no part in organizing peoples' experiences or their economic circumstances, what other reasons can be offered for the vast disparities of wealth and access along racial lines in contemporary U.S. society? The answer to this for some people is that there are deep-seated genetic and/or cultural traits that can account for these disparities. In other words, people who espouse race-evasive rhetoric inevitably rely upon the overtly racist biological or socio-cultural frameworks when faced with the overwhelming evidence showing that race and racism are significant organizing forces in the United States (Bonilla-Silva, 2006; Leonardo, 2009). Second, the idea that people should stop seeing race relies on the idea that they *can* stop seeing race. However, there is no evidence that any human society has simply ignored or forgotten a belief system as widespread and ingrained as race and racism has become in our society. In other words, we shouldn't try to ignore the historical weight of hundreds of years of racism. Rather, we should strive to create a society where we all recognize that racial histories—both good and bad—have shaped, and continue to influence, our society.

This imperative leads us to the final way to understand race—a social justice perspective. This framework argues that race does not determine one's biology or culture; rather, race is a social construction that was created and is currently maintained because it provides psychological and economic benefits (i.e., privilege) to some groups based on perceived racial group membership. Historically, White Europeans invented the concept of race in the late 14th and early 15th centuries as they began to make more contact with people of color around the world. The concept of race was used to cast people of color as subhuman, and therefore as undeserving of universal human rights. This idea, in turn, justified their desire for colonization and imperialism—what Rudyard Kipling would later call the "White man's burden" of ruling people of color because White people believed they were spiritually, technologically, biologically, and culturally superior. These ideas formed the foundation for the U.S. view on people of color, leading to a host of oppressive practices. For example, African people were abducted to be used as chattel slaves, Native American people were almost wiped out, Latinx people had their land stolen through conquest, and Asian people were subjected to inhumane laws such as the Chinese Exclusion Act.[1] The legacy of this oppressive history is still present in U.S. society, continuing to harm the social and economic life of people of color.

In contemporary times, a social justice perspective on race calls us to see the often invisible, and sometimes egregious, ways that systems of racism continue to privilege White people and oppress people of color. Here, we define racism as the beliefs, norms, attitudes, and behaviors, operating at all levels of society and with(out) conscious intent, that reinforce the subjugation of people color and perpetuate **White supremacy**. In the words of Simpson (2003):

---

1. The Chinese Exclusion Act was a U.S. federal law signed by President Chester A. Arthur on May 6, 1882, prohibiting all immigration of Chinese laborers. The Chinese Exclusion Act was the first law implemented to prevent a specific ethnic group from immigrating to the United States. It was repealed by the Magnuson Act on December 17, 1943.

Racism occurs in courts, classrooms, grocery stores, religious conventions, all-white suburbs, in the media, on the job, at fast food and fine restaurants. It is routine and often subtle, especially to white eyes. Racism engages ideologies and structures, depends on both ideas and behaviors, and "is all around us." (p. 15)

Unlike the biological or sociocultural perspective, which holds that people of color are inferior and casts them as responsible for their own plight, or the race-evasive framework that argues that race should be ignored, a social justice perspective maintains that "ultimate solution to racial oppression involves far-reaching changes in social institutions" (Doane, 2006, p. 268). This perspective requires recognizing the ways that racism has been used to oppress people of color while privileging Whites and working to undo the ways that racism has restricted our abilities to recognize our full capabilities. In short, although people can't eliminate the concept of race, they might be able to realize a society where institutions (e.g., government, corporations, or families) don't act on race in oppressive ways. As college students, you have the opportunity to address racism on university campuses, and begin the work to realize a society free of racist institutions.

Important Moments in Student Activism

Student activism about racism played an important role in changing the culture of University of Missouri. Between 2010 and 2014, numerous documented incidents of racism were reported to university officials, such as putting cotton balls outside of the Black Culture Center, White students yelling racial slurs at students of color from vehicles, and swastikas being drawn in feces on a residence hall where Black students lived. After repeated charges that the university's administration had not done enough to address the culture of racism on campus, the student group Concerned Students 1950 (named to address the fact that Black students had only been able to enroll at the university since 1950) launched a campaign to change the culture of the university. An African American student leader, Jonathan Butler, went on a hunger strike, going so far as to write a will and do-not-resuscitate order. The university football team, supported by coaches and staff, went on strike, refusing to play until the administration had taken steps to correct racism on campus. In the end, student activists were successful in forcing the university administration to address the university culture and removed administrators who had failed to uphold their responsibility to create an equitable campus climate. The story of Mizzou is one that shows that when students act together, and work with those beyond the campus community, they can create systemic changes.

Sexism and Gender Discrimination

Sex and gender are two terms that can help us unpack the complicated ways in which biology, culture, and history intertwine (Palczewski, DeFrancisco, & McGeough, 2019). Unfortunately, many media, academic, and nonprofit organizations conflate these two terms, making it difficult to understand the unique contours of privilege and oppression. Traditionally, **sex** is understood as biologically determined, and used to denote two categories—males and females. Sex is often linked to genitalia, chromosomes, hormones, or other biological markers. In popular culture, the idea that there are deep, intractable differences between men and women is perpetuated by television shows (e.g., *How I Met Your Mother*), books (e.g., *Men are from Mars, Women are from Venus*), and movies (e.g., the Twilight series). Men are supposed to be strong, non-emotive, controlling, sexual, and aggressive, whereas women are thought of as weak, overly emotional, nurturing, nonsexual, and passive. Importantly, the traditional view on sex asserts that differences between males and females are the product of biological makeup; that is, they are hardwired into humans' brains and bodies.

> **Student Voice**
>
> Fortunately, I can't recall a moment where I have struggled with sexism on campus. In this realization I am struck by my own privilege as a cis man. —*Jonesy*

Gender, on the other hand, traditionally refers to the cultural, rather than biological, values, beliefs, and norms that guide peoples' communication about, and performances of, sex. Gender is viewed as an expression of one's self, which can include clothing, hairstyles, jewelry, or make-up. Traditionally, gender is viewed as a continuum between masculine and feminine, with the term *androgynous* denoting a person who is a mixture of both. Masculine and feminine behaviors are, for the most part, the exact same as those thought to be male versus female behaviors. However, the inclusion of androgyny is meant to show that people may perform gendered behaviors that do not correspond to biological markers (e.g., a man who is nurturing or a woman who is nonemotive).

We believe that traditional understandings of sex and gender are inadequate to address the full range of issues at stake in conversations about sexism and gender discrimination. A social justice approach to these terms provides a clearer picture for those interested in addressing sexism and gender discrimination. First, as the astute reader may have already noticed, traditional thinking on sex and gender relies primarily on **binary thinking** (e.g., male vs. female; masculine vs. feminine). However, this dichotomy is not empirically supported by research in biology, anthropology, sociology, communication, or psychology, nor is it historically/culturally supported (i.e., there are many nations and cultures that recognized more than two sexes or genders; Carothers & Reis, 2012; Khaleeli, 2014; Lacey, 2008). In fact, the primary question in these disciplines is

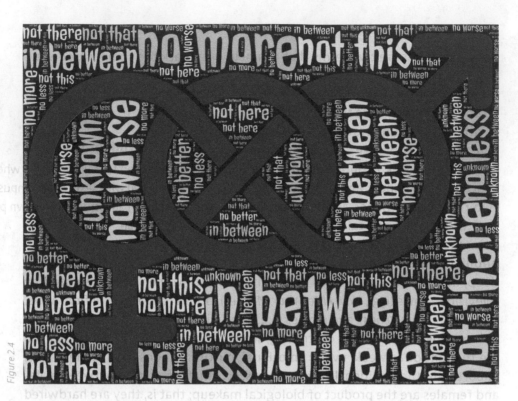

Figure 2.4

not "are there only two sexes or genders?" but rather "how many more sexes or genders are there than only two?" Three? Five? Twenty-three? More (Davis, 2015; Henig, 2017; Kelly, 2016; Palczewski et al., 2019)? What all the studies and cultural/historical examples point to is the notion that sex and gender are deeply intertwined, and that peoples' sex and gender are changing and fluid dynamic representations.

Take, for example, a person who is born intersex (i.e., they are born with multiple and/or ambiguous genitalia or secondary sex organs). In the United States, it was common for doctors to advocate for parents to choose the sex of their child. The doctor then performed surgery to make the baby's genitalia match the assigned sex. However, as the Human Rights Watch (2017) reports, this procedure is based primarily on the appearance of external genitalia, social expectations, and parental wishes, and does not take into account the fluid-ity of culture and invisible markers, such as chromosomes or hormones. As a result, children who are subjected to this procedure often face social stigma and develop mental stressors based on feeling disconnected from their assigned sex identity. In short, traditional notions of sex are so strong that our society is willing to perform surgery until a baby fits into one of the two boxes we think of as normal sex identity.

The realization that sex and gender are more than just a binary lead to the second implication, which is that sex and gender are actually better understood as **gender/sex** because we cannot know where biology begins and culture ends

(Palczewski et al., 2019). All efforts to create categories along the continuum of sex/gender are, in fact, society's attempt to impose groupings that have mixed empirical support. We assert that sex is an assigned category and that our gendered expectations are culturally and historically informed. For example, even though we now think of pink as a feminine color, in the 19th century, pink was considered masculine. There is no true, objective, or natural way for people to present or perform their sex/gender—there is only what is viewed as appropriate or normal in a given time and context.

A Nonexhaustive List of Sex/Gender Categories

Agender. Not identifying with any gender. Sometimes referred to as being *genderless* or *gender-void*.

Androgyne. This term overlaps a lot between gender identification and presentation. It can be used to describe others and as an identification. This term is used to describe people who are neither male nor female or are both male and female. Basically, it refers to anyone who does not fit into a binary gender category.

Aporagender. Person with a strong gender identification of themselves that is nonbinary.

Bigender. Identifying as two genders, commonly (but not exclusively) male and female. Sometimes the person feels like both genders at the same time, and sometimes they fluctuate.

Butch. A person whose gender expression is more masculine than feminine.

Cisgender. A person who has the feeling of being the gender they were assigned at birth all the time (assigned (fe)male/feeling (fe)male).

Demigender. A person who feels as if they are one part a defined gender and one or more parts an undefined gender. Terms can include demigirl, demiboy, demiagender, etc.

Female-to-male (FtM). A person assigned as a female at birth but who identifies as a male.

Femme (fem). A person whose gender expression is more feminine than masculine.

Gender apathetic. A person who does not really identify nor care about any particular gender. They are fine passing off as whatever and do not really have an opinion toward their own gender.

Genderqueer. Originally used as an umbrella term for nonbinary individuals. May be used as an identity. Describes a nonbinary gender regardless of whether the individual is masculine or feminine leaning.

continues

Genderfucked. Term meant to convey the frustration with, and a disidentification from, gender labels.

Greygender. A person with a weak gender identification.

Intergender. A person whose gender is somewhere between male and female.

Intersex. A person born with genitals, gonads, and/or chromosomes that do not match up exactly with male or female.

Male-to-female (MtF). A person assigned as a male at birth who identifies as a female.

Maverique. A nonbinary gender that exists outside of the orthodox social bounds of gender.

Pangender. A person who has the feeling of having every gender; this is considered problematic by some communities, and thus has been used as the concept of relating in some way to all genders as opposed to containing every gender identity; only applies to genders within one's own culture.

Trans man. A person who is assigned at birth as a female but identifies as a man.

Trans woman. A person who is assigned at birth as a male but identifies as a woman.

Transgender. A person who identifies with a gender different than the one they were assigned at birth.

Source: Trans Student Educational Resources, http://www.transstudent.org/definitions; G. Kelly, "A nearly complete glossary of gender identifies for your next census," https://www.telegraph.co.uk/men/the-filter/a-nearly-complete-glossary-of-gender-identities-for-your-next-ce.

A social justice approach to sex/gender offers a clear language for understanding how sexism and gender discrimination curtail peoples' capabilities. **Sexism** refers to the beliefs, norms, attitudes, and behaviors, operating at all levels of society and with(out) conscious intent, that reinforce the subjugation of people not viewed as male and perpetuate patriarchy. The term **patriarchy** refers to the systems that privilege people viewed as male and supports **toxic masculinity** (i.e., the traits assigned to males that encompass dominance, devaluation of other, self-reliance, and emotional suppression). People who are viewed as women or intersex are the ones who are the most negatively affected by systems of sexism. For example, nearly 90% of all sexual violence is directed to those who are not viewed as male (RAINN, n. d.). This system of violence makes it difficult for nonmales to feel free of threat in workplaces, romantic or familial relationships, or education. As such, it harms their ability to realize their human capabilities because it makes connections, intimacy, economic prosperity, and physical health harder to build and maintain.

Gender discrimination refers beliefs, norms, attitudes, and behaviors, operating at all levels of society and with(out) conscious intent, that reinforce the subjugation of gender nonconforming people and perpetuate **cissexism**. Cisgender people are those who identify with the sex they were assigned at birth, and cissexism is the belief that cisgender people are normal, natural, or good. Gender roles and expectations strongly regulate a person's capabilities. For example, if a people view as male starts crying at a romantic comedy, what would we call that person? Or, what about a person people view as female acting very aggressively in a meeting? Or, what if a person with an ambiguous body type and very short hair wore a dress? Cissexism is the belief that those people who identify with their designated gender/sex are normal, natural, or desirable, whereas those who do not are aberrant or abnormal.

The system of sex/gender, and people's understanding of its arbitrariness and the harm caused by binary thinking, has given rise to terms associated with gender/sex nonconforming people. **Transgender** refers to people who do not identify with their assigned sex. The term *transgender* is also an umbrella term for a host of other labels a person who rejects sex/gender binaries may adopt, such as *gender fluid*, *genderqueer*, *genderfucked*, and *trans*. Overall, a social justice perspective on gender recognizes how society maintains a system of language, laws, and norms to dehumanize people by forcing people to conform to sex/gender expectations, regardless of personal harm or identity.

Important Moments in Student Activism

Student activism about sexism and gender discrimination changed conversations about sexual violence and consent at one university. Sofie Karasek claimed she was sexually assaulted by a male student at an off-campus event. At first, she didn't feel comfortable bringing her story to university officials. However, she later learned that three other students stated that they had been assaulted by the same student. She and two other students brought their stories to campus officials, but later found out that even though he had been found in violation of the student conduct code, he would not be expelled or suspended; rather, campus officials were going to allow the student to graduate early. Sofie, along with eight other students at various universities, filed Clery Act complaints against their universities for failure to provide a safe environment for them based on sex/gender. Many of the complaints resulted in policy changes at the universities, including Sofie's UC–Berkeley campus. Sofie went on to cofound End Rape on Campus, a nonprofit organization that has helped dozens of students navigate the cultural, legal, and political dimensions of sexual violence on campus, providing a campus that supports students' rights to be safe from sexual assault.

Heterosexism

Sexual attraction is another system by which people are classified and dehumanized. **Heterosexism** refers to beliefs, norms, attitudes, and behaviors, operating at all levels of society and with(out) conscious intent, that normalize **monogamous**, opposite-sex desire, affect, and relationships and reinforce the subjugation of nonopposite sex desire, affect, and relationships. Until relatively recently, relationships that were not monogamous and opposite sex were considered aberrant or deviant behavior by psychologists. In fact, the term *homosexual* is the medical term for opposite-sex attraction and was considered a form of mental illness. Many states still have laws that directly criminalize same-sex relationships (i.e., so-called anti-sodomy laws) or that bar same-sex partners from adopting children. And, even though the U.S. Supreme Court ruled that opposite-sex couples could marry (*Obergefell v. Hodges*, 2015), they recently upheld a decision that maintained that same-sex couples did not have a legal right to share their partner's employment benefits, even though opposite-sex couples benefits are protected (*Jack Pidgeon and Larry Hicks v. Mayor Sylvester Turner and the City of Houston*, 2017). These types of legal decisions continue the trend that people who do not fit the mold of traditional heterosexual relationships are second-class citizens.

> ### Student Voice
>
> There have been times where professors I've had have spoken to the men in the class and said phrases such as, "boys, think of your girlfriend or your wife and ..." this kind of language only excluded me as a gay person. Although I haven't encountered heterosexism on campus a lot, in the times that I have experienced it, it has left a lasting impression on me in regard to my thoughts on that professors own understanding of what normalized language and culture is and how toxic and widespread it truly is. —*Robert*

> ### A Nonexhaustive List of Sexual Attraction Categories
>
> **Androsexual.** Being attracted to masculine gender presentation.
>
> **Aromantic.** A person who does not experience romantic interest in others.
>
> **Asexual.** A person who does not experience sexual attraction (asexual doesn't necessarily mean a person is aromantic).
>
> **Bicurious.** A person who is open to experiment with genders that are not only their own, but do not know if they are open to forming any sort of relationship with multiple genders.
>
> **Bisexual.** A person who is attracted to two or more genders. This term is generally used to describe being attracted to men and women, but can apply to being attracted to any

continues

two or more genders. Note that a person does not have to be equally attracted to each gender.

Demisexual. When a person only experiences sexual attraction after forming a strong emotional or romantic bond. The emotional bond is often not connected to sex/gender presentation.

Grey asexual. A person who experiences attraction only rarely, on a very low scale, or only under certain circumstances.

Gynosexual. A person attracted to feminine gender presentation.

Heterosexual. The attraction to a gender different from one's own (commonly used to describe someone who is gender binary [female or male] attracted to the other binary gender).

Homosexual. The attraction to a gender the same as one's own (commonly used to describe someone who is gender binary [female or male] attracted to the same binary gender). Sometimes referred to as *gay*.

Lesbian. Women who are attracted only to other women.

Monoamorous. People who have or open to have relationships with only one other person at a time. The term *monogamous* is also sometimes used.

Pansexual. A person attracted to all genders and/or does not concern gender when they are attracted toward someone.

Polyamorous. An umbrella term referring to people who have or are open to consensually have relationships with multiple people at the same time.

Polysexual. A person who is attracted to many genders.

Questioning. A person who is debating their own sexuality/gender.

Varioriented. When a person's sexual and romantic orientations do not target the same set of genders (e.g., being heteromantic and bisexual or being homoromantic and pansexual).

Source: The PBHS Closet, "List of genders and sexualities," http://thepbhscloset.weebly.com/a-list-of-genders—sexualities-and-their-definitions.html

Typically, when people talk about discrimination against nonheterosexual people they use terms such as **homophobia**, **panphobia**, and **biphobia**. Although we are happy that there is a vocabulary emerging that directs attention to the harms some people face due to their sexuality, we think the suffix -*phobia* (i.e., "the fear of") sometimes does a disservice to truly understanding the stakes in conversations about sexuality and discrimination.

Sometimes, it is not simply fear that motivates a person to harm another (e.g., fear could motivate a person to reach out to get to know someone). Rather, hatred, along with fear, motivates a person to out a gay man, sexually assault a lesbian woman, or tell a bisexual or pansexual person that their sexuality is just a fad and doesn't really exist. Therefore, we believe terms such as **homo-hatred**, **pan-hatred**, and **bi-hatred**, are important because they recognize that the intent on the part of the perpetrator is to damage the capabilities of another human being.

Figure 2.5

Heterosexism often intersects with sex/gender, which is why you may see group names, such as LGBTIA. Lesbian, gay, bisexual, and asexual typically refer to sexuality, whereas transgender and intersex denote sex/genders. One of the reasons for this is because sex/gender and sexuality are deeply intertwined in our culture and everyday life. For example, a heterosexual, cisgender man who does not perform his sex/gender in ways that support traditional gender roles would most likely be called demeaning names about his sexuality (e.g., fag) and sex/gender (e.g., pansy). Additionally, a gay man, even if he meets sex/gender norms, may still be attacked about his sexuality and sex/gender because his romantic interest in other men is also understood as a break from toxic masculinity. As a result, it is sometime difficult to see where sex/gender and sexuality begin and end. However, this realization prompts us to be clear in our understanding of how the systems of privilege and oppression operate within these domains.

A social justice perspective on heterosexism demands that we stop thinking that there is a normal or correct way to express love, build romantic relationships, or find happiness with others. For some people, the type of person someone is attracted to is something that they are very sure of throughout their life. For others, their preference may evolve to include more or less of other types of people. And, for some others, they never feel inclined to be sexually involved with other people. What is important from a social justice perspective is that all people are free to realize their capabilities by meeting their needs for intimacy, relationships, and love freely. Anything less than this goal creates an arbitrary hierarchy where some types of human relationships are viewed a more important than others. When those systems are backed by the power of corporations that wish to reserve the right to not provide services to LGBTIA people or government officials that use the power of the state to make LGBTIA folk second-class citizens, then it we must stand up, be heard, and intervene.

Important Moments in Student Activism

Although Chris Armstrong, an openly gay male student, hadn't planned on being politically active when he enrolled, he soon found a passion for supporting LGBTQIA students on campus. After years of working with other LGBTQIA student groups and serving on the LGBTQ commission on the Student Assembly, he decided to run for the office of the president of the Student Assembly. However, during the campaign and after winning the election, Armstrong was the subject of a coordinated smear campaign through one of Michigan's assistant attorney generals, Andrew Shirvell. Shirvell wrote in a blog he created called "Chris Armstrong Watch" that Chris promoted a "radical homosexual agenda" and was "Satan's representative on the student assembly." He also monitored Chris's movements, posted photos of where he and his family lived, and made him the subject of numerous other forms of harassment. Chris, who knew that online harassment and bullying are major causes in LGBTQIA youth's reasons for committing suicide, decided to fight back and took his story public. The University of Michigan's student body rallied on Chris's behalf, holding demonstrations of support and calling for Shirvell's removal from office. In the end, Shirvell was fired from his governmental post and his harassment came to an end. Chris's story shows how even when traditionally oppressed groups gain victories, powerful interests who wish to maintain an unequal status quo will try to dehumanize them. However, hard work, courage, and love can win when we all stand together and fight to remove bigotry and hatred.

Neoliberal Capitalism

Historically, Western society has based its economic systems on capitalism. Some forms of capitalism have very strong protections for the public on issues such as fair wages, workplace safety, and environmental laws and strong support for services such public transportation, education, and social services (e.g., law enforcement). The notion that there is such a thing as the "public good" or "public interest" and passing laws to protect those ideals are a central tenet of socialism (i.e., the idea that sometimes public concerns outweigh for-profit interests). Economies that mix capitalist (i.e., privileging for-profit concerns) and socialist (i.e., privileging public concerns) systems are called social democracies, and contemporary examples include Western countries such as Norway, Denmark, and Sweden. For example, until the 20th century, many U.S. firefighting services were for-profit systems in many cities. If your house caught on fire, but you hadn't paid your dues to the firehouse, or had paid them to an inefficient one because it was the only one that would service your area, your house may have burned down. Or, if there was a large fire, the firefighters would address the wealthy neighborhoods first and, if there was anything left of middle- or lower-class homes, they would then deal with those structures. It wasn't until the 1900s that people recognized that when everyone paid for the service not only was it cheaper per person because there was a greater pool of money, but then firefighters were obligated to protect everyone's homes equally. In this instance, people concluded that for-profit concerns were outweighed by an obligation to ensure the public was protected equally.

The United States was a strong social democracy in the mid-20th century. Social Security, Medicare, and Medicaid were programs meant to ensure that people had access to food, medicine, and shelter, regardless of their economic plight or disability. The G.I. Bill offered free college to veterans, and the Department of Veterans Affairs oversaw education, health care, and job training for those who had served in the military. Labor programs were available for those who could work and ensured people worked for a fair wage. Hundreds of new public universities and schools were built, becoming factories of innovation and development. The federal highway

> ### Student Voice
>
> The science and math department on campus are guilty of forcing students to purchase course materials that require: computers, fast internet connection and, most importantly, large sums of money. What makes this worse is when students tell the professors that they lack some of the requirements and the professors retort that there's a computer lab on campus. This reply doesn't help since some of these students may lack transportation required to get to campus. The worst part of this unfortunate situation is if these students are simply unable to satisfy these professors wants, some professors will drop the student from the course without giving them proper attention or alternatives which is not the right way to go about handling these types of situations.
> —Anna Marie

transportation system was created, linking major cities and allowing commerce to flow throughout the United States. Labor unions gained significant victories protecting workers' rights and compensation, while environmental groups helped push through legislation that defended clean water, clean air, and national parks. And, although there was still a great deal of inequality (particularly along racial and gender lines) between the wealthy and the rest of society, there were more opportunities for people to obtain an education, a job, and a living. These accomplishments, and more, were attributable to people's belief that there were some aspects of society (e.g., healthcare, the environment, education, or public safety) that were so important or essential that they could not be left to corporations to decide whether or how to manage them. Instead, they felt that everyday people, through voting, governmental service, and civic engagement, were the best stewards of these essential programs and services.

In the 1980s, many people started to turn away from the idea that some concerns should always be public issues. People changed their beliefs for two primary reasons. First, the civil rights, feminist, labor, and other social movements had gained influence, and people of color, women, the working class, and other traditionally oppressed groups were starting to wield power. This development threatened the power of traditionally dominant groups—White, wealthy, straight, and/or male—who ran the legislatures, corporate board rooms, and banks. By attacking the institutions that helped everyday citizens, these traditionally dominant groups sought to maintain their hold on society. Second, between 1950 and 1975, most other countries couldn't compete with the United States because their economies

Figure 2.6

had been devastated in World War II. However, by the late 1970s they began to gain market edge over U.S. businesses as their economies recovered, which meant that the "pie" of profits started to shrink. Business leaders and government officials began enacting policies that would ensure that shareholders and CEOs would enjoy record profits even as their market shares declined by attacking the most malleable costs of doing business: labor protections, wages, and environmental regulations. These policies were based on the premise that stripping workers of their right to fair compensation or removing environmental regulations would unleash U.S. business activity and provide an overall better economy for everyone.

These policy shifts, collectively, are known as **neoliberal capitalism**, which is the belief that for-profit interests are more important than public interests. *Neo-* means "new" while *liberal* refers to "unchecked" or "unregulated." In other words, neoliberal capitalism means a "new form of unchecked or unregulated capitalism" and is based on the belief that social, economic, and political problems are best solved by the marketplace and without public oversight. In addition to removing work and environmental protections, marketplace solutions now influence almost every aspect of society. There are for-profit schools and universities so the wealthy can access special educational resources; the internet is viewed as a commodity to be managed by corporations rather than as an essential service; health insurance companies make billions of dollars while tens of thousands of people can't access health care; and businesses move jobs and plants to other countries to avoid paying workers, paying taxes, or complying with U.S. environmental laws.

These new developments, in addition to a host of others, have created one of the most unequal societies in the past 30 years. From 1980 to 2016, the Economic Policy Institute (2018) estimates that the average U.S. worker became nearly 175% more productive; that is, people are producing more goods and services for their employers now than ever before. However, wage increases have not matched this rise in worker productivity. Over the same period, the average worker saw only a 12.5% wage increase. Furthermore, as Ingraham (2017) reports, although those in the upper middle class (i.e., households earning between $121,000 and $423,000) saw their overall share of wealth remain the same, the bottom 90% of U.S. society (i.e., households that earn less than $121,000) saw their share of wealth decline nearly 20% between 1970 and 2016, whereas the top 1% (i.e., households earning above $423,000) saw an increase from about 10% to nearly 20% of all annual income. He goes on to point out that the top 1% owns nearly 40% of all wealth in the United States—more than the total wealth of the bottom 40% of all Americans (see also Kochhar & Cillfuo, 2017; Wolff, 2017).

The problems with neoliberal capitalism go beyond wealth inequality and wages to a larger impact on American culture. A central belief of neoliberal capitalism is that people should see themselves as self-interested economic actors who should believe that their success or failure is simply a matter of their individual choices. For example, as an economic actor, your success in obtaining professional employment will come down to going to the correct high school, attending the correct college, picking the correct major, networking with the correct professors and administrators, obtaining the correct internships, and performing the correct interview. This type of thinking has many downsides. First, many of things that may affect a person's success—where a person lives, their family's economic circumstances, or their talents—are simply beyond their ability to control. For example, if a student's parents both work full-time jobs to make ends meet, then they may not have the time to drive their child to the best school or have the money to send them to a prestigious for-profit, private school. Second, in a marketplace society, there are always winners and losers—houses that are allowed to burn down, to return to the example about firefighters. When resources and access are artificially limited by the market, people will, in turn, see each other as competitors for scarce resources (i.e., good jobs, safe neighborhoods, or health care) rather than as fellow citizens who can achieve goals through collaboration and compromise. This type of thinking encourages people to blame each other (i.e., other competitors) for their problems, rather than see the economic system as inherently unfair and patently cruel.

Figure 2.7

The final problem with neoliberal capitalism is the way that it promotes for-profit interests over the environment. For example, petroleum companies have a strong investment in continuing to extract and burn fossil fuels, despite overwhelming evidence that burning of fossil fuels harms the planet's air, water, and atmosphere. The harms of dirty air are particularly acute in large cities, where tens of thousands of people develop illnesses due to smog and polluted air from industry and automobiles (Caiazzo, Ashok, Waitz, Yim, & Barrett, 2013). Offshore oil drilling can devastate local economies, destroy wildlife, and harm public health, as we saw when the oil rig Deep Horizon exploded, killing 11 workers and spilling nearly 5 million barrels (210 million gallons) of oil into the Gulf of Mexico. Transporting oil, too, can result in environmental harm. Harrington (2016) estimates that there have been nearly 1,300 oil spills since 2010 that have involved transporting oil through pipelines or by ship, truck, or train, resulting in nearly 9 million barrels (over 300 million gallons) of spilled oil. Despite the need to transition to renewable energies with low environmental impact, the for-profit concern of oil companies is privileged over the public's health.

Social justice advocates take a variety of intellectual and moral approaches to their critiques of neoliberal capitalism, but at their heart is the assertion that there are some aspects of society where public interests should outweigh for-profit motives. This is not to say that there are not instances when a for-profit motivation isn't warranted or beneficial. We don't believe the problems that face us are so easy as to make easy binaries of public versus profit, communism versus capitalism, socialism versus capitalism. In fact, we think that these dichotomies tend to harm, more than help, develop solutions to the problems that face society. However, neoliberal capitalism, as a particular type of capitalism, almost always values profits, corporate interests, and the wealthy above anything and anyone else in society. Social justice advocates believe that human capabilities can only be met in a political-economy that guarantees a standard of living that supports everybody's ability to be politically, spiritually, and morally active. If we are going to meet the challenges of the future, we need an economy that works to support everyone's needs and helps them realize their true potential.

Important Moments in Student Activism

In the 2012–2013 academic year, Jess Grady-Benson, Kai Orens, and Meagan Tokunaga were students in the Claremont College system. The colleges in the system, including Pomona, Scripps, Claremont-McKenna, Harvey Mudd, and Pitzer, had investments in the fossil fuel industry as part of their endowment portfolios. The students, knowing that the long-term economic and environmental impacts of supporting the fossil fuel industry far outweighed the short-term profits, began a campaign to encourage the university system's board of trustees to divest from the fossil fuel industry and reinvest that money into companies that had better social justice records. The movement started with

continues

a few dozen supporters, but eventually garnered hundreds of students and community members and national attention. After months of debate, negotiation, and compromise, Pitzer College led the way by divesting its stocks in petroleum companies. Their actions, as well as efforts to reduce fossil fuel consumption and pollution on campus, sent a strong message to the rest of the higher education community that the public's right to health and safety are more important than corporate profits.

****

As you work to identify and change the systems that bar people from reaching their capabilities, you will need to do so with a humble, but courageous spirit. You will need to stay in constant contact with fellow organizers, be open to criticism and change, and be willing to put yourself at risk when advocating for change. An important part of this ethic is recognizing that people are all enmeshed in the five systems that limit our capabilities. The idea that people inhabit multiple **positionalities** in society and navigate the political economy in a variety of ways should encourage you to adopt an **intersectional** approach to **identity** (Crenshaw, 1991). In other words, everyone has areas in their lives where they are oppressed or privileged, and it is important to recognize that people's identities are shifting, fluid, and changing. An intersectional approach suggests that positionalities are multiplicative, not additive. For example, Asian, Black, Hispanic, and White females are not just females that have different races; rather, their identities are different in dozens of small and large ways because of the ways that race and sex/gender cannot be separated from each other. As such, it is important to respect people in all their complexity while being open and honest about how your identity may shape and constrain the way you view the world.

Intersectionality doesn't mean that everyone is equally oppressed or privileged or that everyone should have an equal say on every topic of advocacy. There will be times when you will find yourself in situations where you are privileged in relation to the topic of advocacy. For example, many men support women's reproductive rights, equal pay, and wish to combat sexual assault. However, men who engage in this activism, no matter how involved or helpful, do not have the women's lived experiences of oppression. As such, it is crucial that men who wish to advocate for feminist beliefs to ensure that they are supporting, not stepping on, the people that they purport to serve. Here we believe it is important to mark a difference between someone who says they are an **ally** as opposed to a **person who allies with others**. Our experiences lead us to believe that people who claim they are an ally all too often use their perceived identity as an ally as a cover or shield for bad behavior. They often forget in their zeal for advocacy that social justice is not about their needs or desire for approval/fame, but about addressing issues that face our communities and society. Instead, we encourage you to think of yourself as a "person who allies with others" to remind yourself that your behavior is what is important—not what you believe you are, but what you are doing, right now, with other people, to make the world better. Your role, as someone who allies with others, should be to amplify the voices and those who are affected by the problem—be the megaphone, not the announcer. You'll find that when you create a space for others to fulfill their potential in a community of activism that there is nothing that can stand in your way!

Discussion Questions

- What are some of the different forms of capitalism?

- After reading this chapter, what recent events in the United States help you to see racism, sexism, and gender discrimination?

- What important moments of student activism have occurred on your campus? What needs to happen?

Student Challenge

- Research the case of South African female athlete Caster Semenya. Compare and contrast her treatment with that of U.S. athlete Michael Phelps.

- Interview five strangers on campus and ask if they know of student activism efforts on your campus or a different campus. Also, ask them what they think are the key issues affecting students on your campus. Come together in small groups to discuss your findings. Determine which student activism efforts are realistic. What should you do next?

CHAPTER 3

Authority and Cultural Capital
Demystifying the
Institutional Culture

CHAPTER OBJECTIVES

By the end of the chapter, you should be able to:

- Define *cultural capital*

- Describe the organization of higher education

- Explore how people within a group enforce the mythic norm by using subtle (and sometimes not-so-subtle) putdowns and verbal attacks to make a person feel out of place, unwanted, or unwelcome

- Navigate higher education, including interactions you will likely have with faculty and various parts of academic institutions

- Connect activism through student organizations to build stronger campus communities

---

ORIENTING QUESTIONS

As you read the chapter, try to answer the following questions:

- If you have a personal problem, what campus resources are available to you?

- What is the meaning of the term *cultural capital*?

- What are appropriate ways to communication with your professor, both in person and online?

Think back on your education before arriving in college. What authority figures did you interact with the most? Unless you were homeschooled, you probably worked the most with teachers on a day-to-day basis. You probably referred to them as Mister or Missus or Miss So-and-So, and maybe they seemed cool because they let you call them by their first name. Most provided guidance on both content (e.g., math or language) and behavior (e.g., raising hands to speak in class). Teachers, unless they are volunteer or substitute, have a degree in education and have passed several state-mandated tests for certification. After many years of exemplary teaching and service, they can apply for and be granted tenure, which is the idea that an employee must have a documented history of poor performance before they are fired (rather than most jobs, where employees are "at-will," which means they can be fired for any reason, at any time). Unless you were in trouble or had a community-driven school, you most likely never interacted in a meaningful way with the administrators of your school. Think of your school superintendent, principal, or school board members: Do you remember their names? Do you know what they do, or how they fit into your education? Did they seek out your perspectives or get to know you? Did you ever know them in the first place?

> **Student Voice**
>
> I often found that there were moments that the question I thought I had wasn't the question I should have been asking. So, make sure that when you talk with a professor (preferably during office hours) you can demonstrate you've tried to use the basic tools of the course to understand expectations and keep yourself on track. —*Jacquelyn*

Figure 3.1

Similarly, in college, you'll find that you interact the most with instructors. We use the term *instructor* very intentionally here, because not everyone who teaches in college is a professor (which is a rank) or a doctor (which denotes a degree held). Instructors can be graduate students who are enrolled in master's- or doctoral-level classes and are entrusted by the institution to teach classes (often they are called teaching assistants or graduate student teachers); people who may have a graduate degree and were hired as a contract employee rather than as a full-time employee (often called adjuncts, contingent faculty, or term/temporary faculty); people who have no degree or only a bachelor's but have life experiences that make them an authority (often called visiting professionals); or people who have obtained their doctorate and who have been hired full time (which is the traditional idea of a professor). Like teachers, in most colleges and universities a professor must demonstrate anywhere from 5 to 7 years of excellence before obtaining tenure.

Also, much like in your high school, you probably don't know all the layers of the institution's bureaucracy beyond the instructors you meet almost every day. There are department chairs, deans, provosts, chancellors, presidents, and a host of other administrators who deal with the policies and regulations of the institution. There are also student service workers, administrative assistants, custodians, groundskeepers, campus police officers, and maintenance crews who ensure that students, faculty, and staff can do their jobs effectively and safely. So, while instructors have a say in how a college or university is organized and run, their voice is only one of many (and often a minor one at that) when it comes to how a university or college chooses to allocate resources, create policies, or address issues.

This chapter, then, is meant to help you navigate the organizational flow of your university or college, where to find resources when you need them, and when or how to ask questions. This includes how to traverse the map of unwritten rules and codes that guide both everyday life and the bureaucracies of colleges and universities. For example, if you have a documented disability, do you know how to bring up the subject with your instructor, what organization can help you fill out the paperwork, or when to ask to get tested? Not knowing this kind of information can result in not reaching your full capabilities within and beyond college because you didn't get the resources you needed to achieve excellence. What is vital to remember is that the terms or acronyms we use are sometimes not reflective of the institution you may attend. You'll have to figure out what terms are used where you are enrolled. This is not one of those times where you can simply ignore or not read the information, like the terms of agreement for the app you recently downloaded! Most colleges and universities will have the position/office we describe (even with a different name) because they fulfill administrative or legal functions that are applicable to all institutions. We'll start first with general advice for how to navigate working with instructors and other students in higher education. Then, we detail the different people, and the roles, that you may interact with or be affected by while you are a student. Finally, we'll offer some ways for you to assert your voice within and beyond the campus to work as an advocate for social justice ethics within higher education.

The Cultural Capital of Higher Education

Think of all the organizations you have been a part of up until this point in your life. Perhaps you have a part- or full-time job, attend a religious institution, or maybe you have a club that you have been active in, such as student government, a gay–straight alliance, gaming group, or hobby. Think on your first few weeks in that setting. Did you feel a little intimidated by other members of the group because they seemed very comfortable and you were an outsider? Did they use terms or have rituals that seemed strange or weird to you? And, after weeks, months, or years, did you start to feel like "one of the group" and start saying or doing the things you thought were odd when you began?

If this has ever happened to you, then you should know that you are not alone. Humans, generally speaking, are social creatures—they thrive with social interaction (although the level of frequency can vary widely) and will become sick, depressed, or even suicidal if isolated for long periods of time. One way that humans maintain social bonds within groups is to create habits, rituals, or sayings that become understood as the "in" language or "normal" practices for people in a group. These instances also show who is "out" or "abnormal." You probably had a few instances, early in your participation in a new organization or club, where you said or did something that everyone else thought made you rude, odd, or other kinds of negative attributions. Perhaps, you are not a part of the "in" group and often feel like an outsider. Or, maybe you roll your eyes and sigh in exasperation when someone new doesn't "get it." Whatever the case, the tendency for humans to create groups and (often arbitrary) criteria for inclusion/exclusion is very common and requires analysis to identify and understand.

Bourdieu, and other scholars after him, have labeled the types of communicative practices that constitute the in/out binary as cultural capital (Bourdieu, 1984, 1999; Bourdieu & Passeron, 1990; Navarro, 2006). Cultural capital refers to the habits, rituals, sayings, or practices that a person performs in order to be understood as normal, natural, or desirable within an institutional culture. Higher education, as with most institutions in the United States, are characterized by a culture that is based on the mythic norm (Lorde, 1984). In other words, the culture of higher education reflects the desires and preferences of privileged groups of people, such as those who are White, heterosexual, middle class, and able-bodied, making it less supportive for students who do not come from those backgrounds. For example, it may be viewed as perfectly normal to have a public display of affection between people of the opposite sex; however, if a same-sex couple were to kiss or hold hands in public, then they might get stared at, called out, or even

Important Concepts

Microaggression are ways that people within a group enforce the mythic norm by using subtle (and sometimes not-so-subtle) putdowns and verbal attacks to make a person feel out of place, unwanted, or unwelcome. Microaggressions can take the forms of assaults, insults, and invalidations.

Microassaults. Intentional, explicit attacks on another person due to their identity; for example, calling a gay man a "fag" or a lesbian woman a "dyke."

Microinsults. Unintentional, often implicit messages that demean or undermine a person due to their identity; for example, a male expressing shock or surprise that a female is good at math, sports, or video games.

Microinvalidation. Unintentional, often implicit messages that make a person from an oppressed group feel that their concerns are not valued or taken seriously; for example, a White person telling a person of color that "everything isn't always about race" when the person believes they have been the target of racism.

These types of communication, whether intentional or not, sustain a university culture that can make people from targeted groups stressed, angry, frustrated, or depressed (Sehgal, 2016; Sue, 2010).

subjected to physical violence. Your familial background, socioeconomic status, race, sex/gender, and a host of other roles and identities will push, pull, and pinch as you figure out how to navigate your institution. What's important is not that you lose yourself, your culture, your background, or your heritage, but rather that you can identify what rules and norms characterize higher education so you can make an informed choice about how and when to follow or break from those guidelines. Practicing this skill now will be invaluable as you navigate other institutions in the future (e.g., the workplace).

Higher education is the context you currently find yourself in, and your ability to correctly match your actions to the culture will in many ways determine your success within it (beyond, that is, your ability to learn information and perform well on tests). For example, if you're in a class and the teacher asks a question, you probably shouldn't sing the answer at the top of your lungs (even if it is the correct one). Instead, the proper response would be to either raise your hand to ask permission or to answer the instructor using normal volume. You may want to impress an instructor and "get on their good side" because you hope they will think positively about your work in the course, cut you some slack if you slip up, or write you a letter of recommendation one day (especially if that person teaches classes in your major). In this instance, your communication is contextual to the person you are addressing (i.e., one in a higher societal position) and the resources they can share with you (i.e., aiding your postgraduation career options) based on your role within the institution. Whatever your motivation (e.g., respect, friendship, or deference), the fact remains that your ability to communicate those feelings adequately relies on your being able to identify and mimic/internalize those practices. Think of cultural capital like a bank where you'll make deposits, withdrawals, and transfers. The money in this case is cultural capital, which earns value based on what you say, what you do, and how you say it. Here we list some of the most important aspects of cultural capital so you can make an informed choice about how to interact with others as a student in higher education.

Types of Cultural Capital

Syllabus. The syllabus is the single most important document you will receive in any class. A syllabus should contain information about the instructor (e.g., contact information), the course objectives, materials (e.g., textbook) you will use, attendance policies, assignments, and the day-to-day schedule. On the first day in almost every class you take, your instructor will go over the syllabus and the expectations for the course. Make sure to attend this class! We know many students think that this is a wasted day and that they don't have to show up for it. We also know that many of those students will be the first ones to struggle in class because they didn't read or understand the syllabus. Keep the syllabus in a place where you can always reference it, and once you have the syllabi for all your classes, mark down on a calendar when things are due in each of your classes. You don't want to be taken by surprise when three of your classes have tests on the same day. Part of your ability to be successful in college will be your ability to juggle all of your responsibilities, and the syllabus provides you an explicit roadmap for how to manage all of your obligations. We cannot stress this enough: reference your syllabus early and often during the semester!

> **Student Voice**
>
> Read the syllabus and refer back to the syllabus. Use those first couple of classes to actually ask questions about things that aren't clear to you. Many instructors have been doing this type work for years and what is clear to them may not be clear to you. Face to face always works best for course clarification. —*Leslie*

Honorifics. One of the first issues you might face is what to call your instructors: Mr., Mrs., Ms.? Doctor? Professor? First name? And, it might be even more complicated because the title of the person depends on their degree held and their position—not every person teaching in higher education is a doctor. We suggest that unless an instructor tells you otherwise, you should refer to instructors as "professor" and then their last name. Although this term may not always be technically correct, your instructors will most likely appreciate your attempt to recognize the work they have completed in order to teach at the college level (which is a lot!). This gives your instructor the opportunity to let you know what they would like to be called, which may be very formal or very casual (i.e., their first name). Remember, though, that instructors vary in their preferences for address, and if someone tells you they prefer to be called "doctor" they are

Student Voice

I used to make a lot of assumptions about my professors. Getting to know simple preferences demonstrated to them that I saw them as more than a person in classroom but someone who dedicated themselves to something. Knowing their earned title or preferences often led to meaningful conversations that helped me to understand that they didn't see themselves as better than me, however having only done academic work longer. Showing a sign of respect through title also opened doors for professor to see me as more than just another student. —*Lydia*

Student Voice

Make sure to do a little internet sleuthing on your professors. Have they done research? Do you share a hobby or interest? Office hours are amazing times to look at their office walls or bookcases, which tell stories they may not share in class. Also, talking to professors in-between classes isn't really effective because they're packing up, prepping for the next thing they need to do, so going to office hours becomes another way to demonstrate understanding their preferences. —*Jasmine*

not necessarily stuffy or mean. Rather, it could be that they are justifiably proud of the immense amount of work they completed to earn their doctorate (typically 5 to 7 extra years of graduate school and writing an approximately 300-page dissertation on an aspect of the subject they are teaching). This is especially true for instructors from poverty, instructors of color, instructors with disabilities, and other traditionally marginalized groups because it wasn't long ago that many of these people were barred from the chance to earn a doctorate. If all else fails, feel free to ask your professor how they prefer to be addressed. Most will appreciate your thoughtfulness and candor.

Office Hours. Now that you are an adult, instructors expect you to interact with them as an adult. This ethic means, among other things, that you might go to your instructor for advice, help, or just chatting in the same way you might coworkers in a professional setting. Doing so can establish a relationship or, at the very least, help them put a name with a face (which can be helpful if you are in a large lecture class). Of course, not all instructors want to have this sort of relationship with students. And, students sometimes abuse this relationship, and ask for too much emotional support, forgetting that instructors are not therapists or psychologists. These problems are especially true for female faculty and faculty of color, who are disproportionately overburdened with caring and providing emotional support for students (in comparison to their male and White counterparts). Walk the fine line between getting the support you need and not being a burden or a nuisance. However, you should take advantage of the informal interactions and mentoring that can occur just by stopping by your instructor's office and chatting with them. Even if faculty have posted office hours, because many instructors have committees, meetings, and other obligations that may pull them away from their regularly scheduled hours, it might be wise to alert your instructor of your plan to drop by for a chat. For more serious matters, we suggest you first review your syllabus for how to do office hours and make sure when sending an email to your instructor for an appointment you provide the context for the meeting. Lastly, make at least one appointment with your instructors during the semester to talk with them. You may be surprised by how rewarding you find the experience.

Attire. We get it. You stayed up way too late last night partying—we mean, studying! You roll out of bed at 8:50 a.m. for your 9:00 a.m. class. You run across campus, sit in your desk, still panting from the run, and open your book. You look down. You realize you're still wearing your pajama pants and the oversized shirt you wear to bed every night. "No worries," you think to yourself, "I'm paying for this class. I'll wear whatever I want." This sentiment is technically true—no instructor will throw you out of class for what you wear (unless it is egregiously offensive). However, what you are wearing violates the expectations of higher education, which operates with the idea that students are adults who should at least look prepared to learn. This means that, minimally, you should wear clothes that are appropriate for the time of day—no jammies and a nightcap. Your instructor may never comment on your choice of attire; however, believe us when we say that they do notice. And, if you continually look like you're hungover or act ill-prepared, then they may not think you are taking your role as a student seriously, which can affect your participation or per-formance grades. This is especially true if you are teetering on the edge between two grades (e.g., B and B–).

> **Student Voice**
>
> I mean it's one thing for me to look like a person when I go to class. I would never rely on my pajamas to class or anything. Or at least like comb your hair. Like give some effort so like you didn't just look like you just woke up. I think that's me. This is important to me. I don't know but it's just another thing with you. You look like you want to be there. —*Wanda*

Intentional Effort. Maybe you are the type of person who is used to making all As in your classes. Maybe you're used to a little more variety on your report card. Whatever your accomplishments in high school, you might find that it is a little more difficult to achieve a 4.0 GPA every semester in college. This may be especially true if you balance a job, relationship, children, or are returning to college after years in the private sector or military. We certainly want you to be successful in higher education, hope you meet all your goals, and earn the grades you want in all your classes. However, we also know that (for a variety of reasons) this is not always possible. In these instances, it might make sense to target your energies in some classes rather than others. For example, if you haven't attended a class in 6 weeks, and have missed the last two tests (which, we should add, is not a good choice), there is probably very little you can do to salvage your grade (even if your instructor is willing to help you). It may be better, in that instance, to focus your attention on the classes where you can be successful and consider an incomplete, retaking the class, or obtaining academic forgiveness for a bad grade. Being intentional about your effort is also important when thinking about classes that you have an aptitude and passion for as opposed to those you don't. First, although it may not be obvious, all courses do interact with each other regardless of the discipline. You might be asking yourself, seriously? Yes, you, your interests, and your immediate and long-term goals are that constant. So, making sure that you put specific effort into major courses is vital to your success, because when a mistake happens or you need guidance on how to manage things when they get overwhelming, those professors can help you navigate institutional processes. You are never alone in your journey through higher education. Professor and older class members have been there before. Your experiences are not likely to be new. It may not make sense for you to spend all your time trying to get an A in biology if you don't like the subject matter and have difficulty seeing how it fits into your life. Instead, focus your energy on your calculus class, because you are enthusiastic about math, see a future for yourself in that area, and are making connections with peers and professors. Please do not mistake us—we want you to challenge yourself to learn everything you can while in college. We are not saying you should not give attention to your biology class or other courses that may not immediately interest you; rather, we are saying that you must determine the appropriate amount of time and energy to devote based on your schedule and time management (see Chapter 4). We often see students who try to do everything perfectly or expect college to be an extension of their high school experiences. There are ways you can "get by" in college; however, those who try to simply "get by" end up doing poorly in their classes. Be smart and specific about where to put your efforts.

Student Voice

In high school you could get by with not really caring in the class, but when you go into major classes you had to pay attention if you want to be successful in your career, and so everything's a little higher stake. *—Dorothea*

Participation. One thing you can do to demonstrate a commitment to being a good student is to participate in class discussion, answer questions, or volunteer for activities. You may think doing so makes you seem like a suck up; however, doing so will not only give your instructors a way to notice your good attitude, but your learning will improve through your active engagement. For instructors, these activities fulfill many different functions. First, instructors want to make sure you have read and/or understood the material of the class.

Your participation demonstrates that you are keeping up with course material. Second, many instructors know that students who discuss, debate ideas with each other, and connect their experiences with their learning tend to understand and retain information better than those who simply stay quiet and let the instructor lecture. Instructors hope that you have specific questions/comments/opinions based on the reading and that your insights can spark ideas in other students in the class. Importantly, you don't have to even understand the material to contribute as long as your questions about the material demonstrate that you have made a good faith effort to understand it. Instructors will see your participation as an important component of good, professional behavior. Just make sure you have actually read the material and that your contributions aren't antagonistic, threatening, or inappropriate. Instructors do not like questions that are easily answered by reviewing the course materials they assigned or students who think debating classmates means shouting or using offensive language. Finally, asking students to participate in class allows instructors to get to know their students better; it gives them the opportunity to know your name, personality, and strengths/weaknesses. You'll want to participate in class because doing so will signal to your instructor that you have read the material, care about the class, and want to engage in thoughtful interaction with your instructor and peers. Establishing a good reputation as an engaged learner will work to your benefit when difficulties completing an assignment or personal issues arise.

Student Voice

Asking deep questions is a great way to personalize a course. It's not always obvious why a college asks you to take a course or makes a requirement. Using class time during discussions is a great way to ask about broader connections you're trying to make or even ask how the material connects to the professors outside work (like research, past scholarship, what they did when in college, or community work which could lead to an internship). All because you asked deeper questions. —*Coral*

Take Responsibility. Students, like other adults, are busy. You're trying to keep up with classes, take care of and/or keep a relationship with your family, form and break up romantic interests, have fun, relax, and figure out who you want to be for the next 10 to 15 years of your life. Instructors, too, are busy. They are preparing for their classes, grading papers, serving on committees, publishing research, working in their communities, and are trying to stay relevant to their field of study and students. Instructors, then, are not very inclined to accept a lot of excuses for late work, poor attendance, or poor performance. Their ethic in this instance is not an indicator that instructors are heartless or cruel, or that they don't care about your illness, death of a loved one, or mental health. Many of them are working with 100 to 400 students per semester, and it is simply not feasible for them to interact with each student's problems at an individual level (as much as they may want to). If you want to talk to an instructor about what you are struggling with, an important part of this process will be taking responsibility, owning your share of the work, and having that conversation at an appropriate time. Having a history of good attendance, high-quality work, and professional interactions within and beyond the classroom signals your investment into the class and will most likely be reciprocated by your instructor. Instructors are less inclined to be sympathetic if you are always making excuses for your work or showing up late (if at all). You should strive to show investment in your learning and seek their help in the context of growing toward being a responsible adult. Establish a good reputation!

Email Protocol. "Hey! I wasn't in class yesterday. Did I miss anything important?" This email, cringe worthy in its execution, is an example of what *not* to send an instructor. Instructors, as a general rule, are people who write a lot as a part of their job, and they see bad grammar, poor spelling, or unprofessional tone in an email as an indicator of a lack of respect or care. And, asking if you missed "anything important" suggests that there are days in class where nothing important occurred. Most instructors spend hours doing the research necessary to plan a single day of class lecture or discussion, and the insinuation that there are days that their efforts are unimportant can be viewed as demeaning and insulting. Make sure to write an email as if you were going to write to a hiring manager at a company where you applied for a job. Some instructors will tell you that they don't care about having formal emails, and may even communicate with you in a very casual manner. If that is the case, then let the tone of your email reflect that expectation. Using the correct spelling, punctuation, grammar, honorific, and tone may not be the criteria that your instructor uses to grant to deny a request; however, they will most likely remember your attempt at professionalism. They will, we can assure you, remember if you send a poorly written email—and that's not something you want.

> **Student Voice**
>
> I've seen a few people that I know who when they do something bad, they don't blame it on themselves. They put the blame on others. I've seen that really irritate professors and they've got a really rocky relationship with that professor in that class. —*Shen-Tao*

> **Student Voice**
>
> Best advice I got with email came from a Communication Studies professor. It was so simple. It was called the ABC. I use it for ALL my email or online interactions:
>
> A: Action, what do you want?
>
> B: Background, what info needs to be shared to understand or provide context for what you want.
>
> C: Conclusion, a simple conclusion that either thanks them for their consideration of your "A" or Wishes them a nice rest of their day. —*Omar*

Writing an Email

Hello Professor [name of professor here],

I hope this email finds you well! I am enrolled in your [give course name and time it meets]. I would like to set up an appointment to talk about [what concept or assignment you need explained further].

I looked over the notes with [person in class] to fill me in on what I missed and read [the syllabus, course reading, and/or handout]. I also drafted an outline using that information. I have attached to this email an outline to demonstrate how I'm currently understanding the [concept or assignment]. Would you please let me know your earliest convenience, so I can set up a time to meet during your office hours or by appointment?

Thank you for your understanding,

[Your name]

[Phone number to contact you directly]

Making Deferential Requests. Have you ever received a test back and, after looking at the answers marked "wrong," notice that the instructor incorrectly deducted points from your test? Did you storm into class the next day and, in front of everyone in class, call them out for their error and demand you receive the points? Hopefully not. Instructors are humans and, like all people, make mistakes sometimes. These errors are especially common when an instructor has hundreds of tests or essays to grade. Imagine the instructor for your Introduction to Writing class. If they have 100 students and it takes them 20 minutes per essay to grade, then they have to spend 2,000 minutes (or more than 33 hours) to grade the papers. It is no surprise, then, that instructors sometimes make mistakes. If this happens to you, you may wish to communicate with them in a way that isn't accusatory or demanding. For example, if you had an answer marked wrong that was actually correct, you may want to visit the instructor during their office hours and

Student Voice

I went through a couple of things in my life that affected my school work I talked to my professors about it. I explained to them what was going on and they were very accommodating. I don't remember exactly how I said it. "Hi professor, I tried to submit to turn it in last night, but it didn't go through. It's my fault." He said, "That's okay, you contribute in class. You haven't done anything else, so I'll just give you and extension. No big deal." —*Lydia* ask them to help you find out the right answer. You know that the answer you had is right, and, by asking them for this information, you know that they will review your paper and realize their mistake. In doing so, you didn't call them out for their error; rather, you offered them a space to realize their mistake, rectify it, and (hopefully) apologize for the error. Whether you take this route, or simply ask them to correct the test, we suggest that you meet them in their office (rather than in front of the class or over email) and avoid an accusatory tone. You'll find that, as with most things in life, you catch more flies with honey than vinegar.

Protocol. Maybe you emailed your instructor for help on a question and they replied with "the answer is in the syllabus" or "this is a question for your teaching assistant." Although it can feel demeaning to have someone tell you to reference material or a person, the reason your instructor told you this doesn't necessarily indicate that they are power-tripping or arrogant. Rather, many instructors put a lot of time and effort into creating their syllabus or working with their teaching assistants, and when you seek information from them, it forces them to repeat that work again by communicating it to you. This dynamic can be particularly frustrating to instructors who are very active in other activities on campus (e.g., sponsoring a student group, serving on an important committee, or advising students toward graduation) or beyond (e.g., writing research, attending professional conferences, or presenting keynote addresses) because they simply do not have the time to repeat themselves for every student they teach. If you have questions about course issues, such as when an assignment is due or how many points it is worth, you should always check the syllabus first. If you can't find the information there, or if your question goes beyond the class (e.g., you want to talk about graduate school or employment beyond college), then you should email your instructor to make an appointment to talk with them during their office hours.

> **Student Voice**
>
> One time I had to miss my biology class because of a football game. So, I told my biology professor about it and she said, "You need to give me a university excused absence form or I will count the absence toward your grade." I said, "It is a football game. You know it's scheduled. Why you need me to do so much?" But, she said that she was just following the rules by making all students do the same thing. —Ramar

There are three important takeaways from Bourdieu's research. First, if you feel weird, out of place, or intimidated by the culture of higher education or interacting with instructors, then you're probably not alone. All students, on some level, are entering into a new institutional culture and are navigating an unknown terrain. These feelings can be especially true for LGBTQ students, students of color, students from poverty, first-generation students, international students, students with disabilities, or returning students because sometimes what is "normal" for an institution is structured in ways that disadvantage these traditionally marginalized groups. Even nonmarginalized groups can feel out of place, such as rural students attending an urban campus (or vice-versa). For example, it may be normal for a campus building to have one, small, unreliable elevator to get people up and down floors, and people without mobility issues may not view it as a large concern or even be aware of the elevator's existence. For a person with a disability that affects their mobility, however, the lack of access is not only an obstacle they have to surmount to get an education, it also reinforces a culture that is threatening their sense of inclusion in the institution. As a new college student, you may be tempted to act in college the same way you did in high school—to study the same, interact with instructors the same, talk with fellow students the same. You will find, though, that sometimes this strategy will not be very successful. You will need to develop a new way of being a student, and to do that you'll need to take a step back and really study the culture that you are now a part of.

Second, the cultural capital you accrued before college will, in some ways, influence your success within higher education. Higher education administrators and full-time faculty are overwhelmingly White, male, and middle to upper class, and the culture of higher education reflects what this group of people view as normal or natural. For example, higher education is very hierarchical (i.e., everyone has a place higher or lower in an organizational chart), and those boundaries are rigidly enforced. If you had a problem with a teacher in school, your parent may have made a phone call to the superintendent and set up a meeting. However, in college, you are considered an adult, and parents cannot access your grades or other information without your written consent. And, if your parent emailed or called the president of the university, they would most likely (at best) receive a polite correspondence back from their secretarial staff asking them to have you contact someone else on campus. Your experiences up to this point with authority, structure, and bureaucracy (or lack thereof) will determine your ability to navigate this culture. If you don't have many experiences with this sort of role-oriented communication (or your experiences are predominately negative), then you need to put yourself in a position where you can watch others in these settings (e.g., student government meetings) or find the organizational chart for the college and talk about it with an instructor you connect well with. Doing so will give you opportunities to learn how to navigate the culture of higher education.

Finally, your actions within higher education (those deposits you've been making) will affect the capital you've amassed and what kinds of withdrawals you're likely to make after you leave higher education. While you were in high school, your days were largely structured by your teachers, parents, and coaches. You went to class at the same times, interacted with students similarly throughout high school, and rarely (if ever) talked as a peer with teachers or administrators. Now, in college, all of that is more or less no longer true—classes can be anytime during the day or evening, class discussion can vary widely depending on major and instructor, and there may even be times you find yourself in a bar sharing a coffee or beer (when, that is, you're over 21) with an instructor. These experiences will shape who you are, and if you are intentional and knowledgeable about how to navigate these norms in higher education, you will find yourself prepared to navigate the next step in your life: professional employment. Study after study shows that private-sector employers are looking for employees who can work in groups, maintain a professional demeanor, and work through conflict. These are all forms of cultural capital that you can begin practicing and accruing right now, which will enhance your chances for employment and success.

As you are reading this section, you might be thinking to yourself, "This sounds like a lot of nonsense and drama. Why can't I just do my work, get good grades, and graduate?" You're absolutely correct for thinking this way. Unfortunately, the reality is that humans do things that are counterproductive all the time to fulfill cultural needs. Take, for example, how some airline companies make people load onto an airplane. The most logical and efficient way to do this would be to load the plane from the back to the front, making sure that each row is filled before moving up to the next one. However, most airlines load people from the front to the back, and there is no order in how people fill the seats of a row (even if they are assigned seats, they don't necessarily load the plane in that order). This process ensures that people sit and then get up and move to allow people into the row, jostle each other's bags as they step over each other, and have people's butts in their face as they put luggage into the overhead bin. Why? Because the front of the plane has the first-class passengers, and airlines want to make sure that those people (who paid more for their tickets) enjoy getting to sit first, even though this makes the entire process less efficient. Similarly, you may find that some of the rules or codes of higher education do not make sense or are counterproductive. We encourage you, though, to learn them. Find out what is normal about the culture of higher education so you can make an informed choice about when, where, and why to either do what's normal or to diverge from it. And, if you figure out that what is considered normal harms students, instructors, staff, or community members, then you can start working within a social justice agenda to rectify those issues. However, before we talk about how to work toward creating change to higher education's culture, let's focus attention on all the different roles and jobs within the institution so you have a good idea of who to talk to if you need help or want to engage in student activism.

Who's in Charge Around Here Anyway?

At this point, you have some ideas about how to interact with others within higher education. And, most important, you're starting to adopt an ethic of studying others within college to understand how to accrue the cultural capital of the institution. However, you may still be wondering: Who do I talk to if I have a problem about this or that issue? In this section, we'll go over many of the institutional roles that characterize higher education. Again, we want

Figure 3.2

to remind you that sometimes the title of a role can vary from institution to institution; some jobs we describe may not appear on your campus, and we may miss some jobs that do appear at your institution. This section, then, provides a basic overview about the various jobs and their functions within higher education with the hope that you can (through studying the institutional culture) put together any missing pieces.

Academic Roles

Adjunct, Contingent, and Temporary Faculty. An adjunct or temporary faculty member may or may not have an advanced degree (e.g., PhD) and is hired as a contractual employee on a semester-to-semester basis. Because adjunct faculty are contractual employees, they are often paid less than their full-time counterparts, often do not qualify for health insurance or retirement, and are not protected by tenure. As a result, many adjunct faculty members teach courses in multiple universities in order to earn enough to pay for essentials rather than working at one university. Also, many adjunct faculty members are overburdened by professional and university obligations because their contractual status makes them vulnerable to being fired at will. It is important to recognize that many adjunct faculty members have similar credentials and experience as their full-time counterparts, but are put in an economically precarious circumstance because it is a cost-effective way for universities to hire faculty.

Lecturers and Term-Contract Faculty. Like adjunct or temporary faculty members, lecturers and term-contract faculty may or may not have an advanced degree (e.g., PhD) and are hired as a contractual employee. However, lecturers often have year-to-year or multiyear contracts, which provides a greater amount of economic stability. Lecturers are often paid less than their tenure-track counterparts, are not protected by tenure, are more likely to qualify for health insurance or retirement. Lecturers live in a gray area of the university where they are not treated with the respect and security of a tenure-track or tenured position, but the university recognizes the need to retain the faculty member by providing a limited, short-term contract.

Finding the Support You Need

Because the culture of higher education can be hostile or unsupportive to marginalized students, it is important to know that there are often groups or roles of campuses that may be able to help students get the resources they need for success. Almost all universities have groups, sororities/fraternities, or organizations that match the identities of students, and can offer students a safe haven to explore their identities and engage in activism. Some examples of student groups include:

African Union

Art for El Salvador

Black Student Union

Chinese Students and Scholars Association

Cultural Mentor Program

Deaf Cultural Experience

Ethnic Student Promoters

Global Business Club

Indian Student Association

International Dance Theatre Dance Company

continues

International Justice Mission

International Student Association

International Students in Business

Lambda Theta Alpha Latin Sorority Potential Candidates

Lambda Theta Phi Latin Fraternity Inc.

Multicultural Teaching Alliance

Muslim Students Association

National Association for the Advancement of Colored People UNI Chapter

Omega Psi Phi Fraternity Inc.

Pakistani Student Association (PSA)

Proud (LGBTQ group)

RISE (Refugee & Immigrant Support and Empowerment)

Young Democratic Socialists of America

In addition, some universities have an administrative position specifically directed to support marginalized students, often called the chief diversity officer or dean of equity and inclusion. This person can get students in touch with resources to help them in their everyday life, and point students toward organizations, activities, or groups they can join.

Source: University of Northern Iowa. (2014). "Student organizations." https://cgi.access.uni.edu/cgi-bin/student_orgs/student_orgs.cgi

Assistant Professors. When a person receives their doctorate, they may be hired as an assistant professor, which means they are a full-time employee who can apply for tenure. This position is also referred to as a tenure-track or probationary hire. Assistant professors are expected to demonstrate excellence for 5 to 7 years before applying for tenure. They are evaluated based on their teaching (evidenced through course development and student evaluations), research (evidenced both by the quantity of publications and quality of outlets), and service (evidenced by unpaid work for one's discipline, university, or community). After the requisite number of years, an assistant professor sends the accumulation of their work (called a tenure packet) to professors outside of their university for recommendation for tenure. If these professors approve, the tenure packet is sent to the following groups in roughly this order: department committee, department chair/head, university committee, dean, vice president of academic affairs, president, and board of regents/trustees. At any level or group, the tenure packet can be rejected, and the instructor denied tenure. If they do not obtain it, then they are fired or moved into a non-professor role. If they are granted tenure, they are awarded with the title associate professor and are no longer an at-will employee of the university (i.e., they cannot be fired without sufficient, documented cause). Tenure ensures that professors cannot be fired for producing research or teaching content that is controversial—guaranteeing they can pursue the facts about an issue without fear of reprisal from powerful groups.

Associate Professors. After receiving tenure and their new rank of associate professor, an instructor is expected to devote themselves to major projects in teaching, research, or service that will significantly contribute to their field of study. This expectation is based on the fact that they have tenure and so are protected to push the boundaries of knowledge. For example, they may completely redesign a class they are teaching, publish a book that has a major effect of their field of study, or engage in some form of service that profoundly influences their discipline, university, or community. Whatever form it takes, associate professors are an important part of the university system because they have the ability, through tenure, to change conversations in their field of study and institution.

Full Professors. After many years of meritorious teaching, research, and service, an associate professor may apply for the rank of full professor. Much like when they applied for tenure, an instructor creates a packet of their accomplishments, and it is reviewed by many of the same groups as before. Although they are not fired if they are not granted full professor status, it is extremely difficult to obtain the title of full professor. One cannot obtain an associate professor status, and simply coast into become a full professor; rather, full status is awarded in cases where an instructor has achieved, above and beyond, the expectations of their role. This is why some faculty never obtain the title and remain associate professors their entire careers. Although a person may be good at their job and fulfill the obligations and responsibilities of their role, not every associate professor desires to pursue or contribute in a way that merits the title of full professor.

Librarians. Librarians provide important teaching and learning functions, even if they typically do not have a set class schedule. Librarians can help you negotiate a wide range of resources that are at your disposal as a university or college student. Most obviously, they can help you find books, journals, magazines, and other print resources housed in the library. Just as important, they can help you utilize search engines properly, introduce you to databases that you may not be familiar with, and help you evaluate whether a source of information is credible. Librarians fulfill an important role in the university by collecting, cataloguing, and disseminating all the knowledge in order to help community members make informed choices. Make sure to visit your university library and schedule an appointment with the librarians. You'll be surprised at all the tools they offer that can help you on your path to success.

Staff Roles

Resident Assistants. Resident assistants (RAs) are often undergraduate students who are compensated either through a small stipend or reduced cost of room and board (sometimes both). RAs are the first people you should talk to if you have problems with your roommate or other members in your residence halls or dormitories. They will also be the first person who talks to you if you are being disruptive or rude to other students in the building. And, if you are looking for an on-campus job, you may talk with the resident hall director about becoming an RA.

Custodial/Groundskeeper Staff. The custodial/groundskeeper staff includes part- and full-time workers who ensure that the university is a clean, well-kept, and aesthetically pleasing place for everyone in the institution. Don't like trash bins overflowing with garbage? Thank your custodial staff! The contributions of these employees are critical to a clean, healthy environment (e.g., classrooms, student meeting areas, cafeteria, and restrooms) yet they are not always acknowledged and shown the appreciation that they deserve.

Maintenance Staff. The maintenance staff are part- and full-time workers who ensure the university's facilities are maintained and pass state/federal codes. Without these individuals, some of the most important parts of the university, such as lights, elevators, AC/heat, and toilets, wouldn't work.

Advisers. Your university may have different members fulfilling the role of adviser. Some universities have staff members dedicated solely to helping students fill out their plan of study (i.e., their schedule of class from enrollment to graduation based on their major). Other universities expect faculty members to also be advisers. And, still others have both systems, where you meet with staff members for your first year and transition to a faculty member adviser once you declare a major. Check to make sure how your university is structured.

Financial Aid Staff. These are the people who will help you navigate your Free Application for Federal Student Aid (FAFSA) form, student loans, grants, scholarships, and disbursements of financial aid (i.e., money from your grants/loans/scholarships over the amount of tuition costs that are given back to you in the form of a check). Higher education can be very costly, and you want to make sure you can obtain all of the economic aid available to you (see Chapter 9 for more help on this). These staff members can be very helpful in navigating the federal, state, and university laws and rules concerning financial aid.

Student Support Services. Student support services encompasses a lot of programs, the most important of which are those that seek to aid students from traditionally marginalized or under-resourced groups. These programs offer scholarships, grants, and other forms of financial aid based on need and group membership.

Student Support/Services Programs

Educational Opportunity Centers. The Educational Opportunity Centers (EOC) program provides counseling and information on college admissions to qualified adults who want to enter or continue a program of postsecondary education. The program also provides services to improve the financial and economic literacy of participants. An important objective of the program is to counsel participants on financial aid options, including basic financial planning skills, and to assist in the application process. The goal of the EOC program is to increase the number of adult participants who enroll in postsecondary education institutions.

Ronald E. McNair Postbaccalaureate Achievement. Through a grant competition, funds are awarded to institutions of higher education to prepare eligible participants for doctoral studies through involvement in research and other scholarly activities. Participants are from disadvantaged backgrounds and have demonstrated strong academic potential. Institutions work closely with participants as they complete their undergraduate requirements. Institutions encourage participants to enroll in graduate programs and then track their progress through to the successful completion of advanced degrees. The goal is to increase the attainment of PhD degrees by students from underrepresented segments of society.

Student Support Services. Through a grant competition, funds are awarded to institutions of higher education to provide opportunities for academic development, assist students with basic college requirements, and to motivate students toward the successful completion of their postsecondary education. Student Support Services (SSS) projects also may provide grant aid to current SSS participants who are receiving Federal Pell Grants (#84.063). The goal of SSS is to increase the college retention and graduation rates of its participants.

Talent Search. The Talent Search program identifies and assists individuals from disadvantaged backgrounds who have the potential to succeed in higher education. The program provides academic, career, and financial counseling to its participants and encourages them to graduate from high school and continue on to and complete their postsecondary education. The program publicizes the availability of financial aid and assist participant with the postsecondary application process. Talent Search also

continues

encourages persons who have not completed education programs at the secondary or postsecondary level to enter or reenter and complete postsecondary education. The goal of Talent Search is to increase the number of youths from disadvantaged backgrounds who complete high school and enroll in and complete their postsecondary education.

Training Program for Federal TRIO Programs Staff. Through a grant competition, funds are awarded to institutions of higher education and other public and private nonprofit institutions and organizations to support training to enhance the skills and expertise of project directors and staff employed in the Federal TRIO Programs. Funds may be used for conferences, seminars, internships, workshops, or the publication of manuals. Training topics are based on priorities established by the Secretary of Education and announced in Federal Register notices inviting applications.

Upward Bound. Upward Bound provides fundamental support to participants in their preparation for college entrance. The program provides opportunities for participants to succeed in their precollege performance and ultimately in their higher education pursuits. Upward Bound serves high school students from low-income families and high school students from families in which neither parent holds a bachelor's degree. The goal of Upward Bound is to increase the rate at which participants complete secondary education and enroll in and graduate from institutions of postsecondary education.

Upward Bound Math and Science. The Upward Bound Math and Science program is designed to strengthen the math and science skills of participating students. The goal of the program is to help students recognize and develop their potential to excel in math and science and to encourage them to pursue postsecondary degrees in math and science, and ultimately careers in the math and science profession.

Veterans Upward Bound. Veterans Upward Bound is designed to motivate and assist veterans in the development of academic and other requisite skills necessary for acceptance and success in a program of postsecondary education. The program provides assessment and enhancement of basic skills through counseling, mentoring, tutoring and academic instruction in the core subject areas. The primary goal of the program is to increase the rate at which participants enroll in and complete postsecondary education programs.

Source: U.S. Department of Education. (2020). "Federal trio programs."
https://www2.ed.gov/about/offices/list/ope/trio/index.html

Disability Support Services. While you were in high school, you may have had an Individual Educational Program (IEP) or a 504 plan to accommodate a documented disability. These plans are based on the Individuals with Disability in Education Act (IDEA) and are a common part of the K–12 landscape. However, IDEA laws do not apply to higher education in the same way as in K–12 settings. Instead, in higher education disability laws are based primarily on the Americans with Disabilities Act, which provides less specific guidance on how higher education should accommodate disabilities. As a result, some universities are proactive and helpful, whereas others frame students with disabilities as a burden. If you feel you need an accommodation, you should always try to work something out between you and your instructor; however, they are not obliged (legally) to make the course more accessible unless you have a documented disability that is recognized by the disability support service office. This office may also be the place where you can take tests, complete homework, or obtain free technological assistance (e.g., text reading programs for those with visual disabilities).

Campus Therapist. Many campuses, in addition to a disability support office, also have resources devoted to confidential mental health counseling and therapy. Most campus therapy offices offer both long-term appointments and immediate call-ins for crises. Unfortunately, many students, due to cultural stigma, do not utilize these services nearly as much as they should. If you feel like you need to work with someone to address your depression, anxiety, recent breakup, or any other issue, please contact your campus therapy professionals.

Campus Police. An increasingly common practice for institutions of higher education is to have their own police force, rather than rely on city or country police. The total enrollment of many colleges and universities dwarfs that of many U.S. towns, and even small cities, so it makes sense that a college would need a police force. Additionally, there are many laws and rules that are specific to higher education, and it is in the university's best interest to have someone trained in working in that specific type of location. You should know that most campus police departments have jurisdictional authority beyond the confines of the campus, some extending to the entire state. As a result, you should interact with campus police officers in the same way that you would any other police officer.

Administrative Roles

Administrative/Secretarial Staff. These office workers provide most of the day-to-day decision making and file most of the paperwork of the university. Depending which office they work in and who they work with (e.g., department chair or president), the office staff can have a lot of influence over what tasks get accomplished and how they are pursued. If you wish to speak with any of the following administrators, you will most likely interact with an office worker first.

Who to Talk to if You Receive an Unjust Grade

As much as we hate to say it, sometimes there are instructors who give students grades for unfair or unjust reasons. They could do so because of discrimination or bias, or out of ignorance or neglect. Whether intentional or not, instructors have a responsibility to grade fairly and diligently, and if you feel that your grade doesn't reflect the appropriate level of care, then you should follow these steps.

1. **Talk to the instructor.** Upon receiving the grade, you should wait 24 hours before emailing the professor. Think about the grade. Are you just disappointed in it, or is it really unfair? If you think it's unfair, your first step should be to wait to talk with the instructor, privately, during their office hours or during an appointment. Be prepared. Bring in the textbook or other supporting materials that show your side. If you do not feel the instructor is correct, and they refuse to change the grade, then you need to take the next step.

2. **Talk to the department chair/head.** Email the department chair/head, outlining your grievance in unemotive language. Stick to the facts and describe (as simply as possible) your issue. Do not attack the instructor, bash the course, or do anything that will make it appear as if your issue is larger than the assignment or course grade you think is unfair. Once you start attacking the instructor or other students, you undermine your own credibility. Again, bring your materials, and be ready to provide a description of your issue. If this doesn't work, then you may need to take the next step.

3. **Talk with the dean of the college or student affairs.** Follow the same steps as with the department chair. Be descriptive. Be professional.

You may be tempted to go straight to the top of the chart. Why mess will all these other people when the dean has the power? The problem is that the bureaucracy is set up specifically so that you (or others) don't come to the dean with every problem. They'd never get any work done if they were always fielding questions from everyone on campus. If you try to do this, you'll most likely be told to start with the instructor or department chair and come back if they can't fix the problem (which means all you have done is wasted your time).

The only exception to this is if you have documented evidence that an instructor has been biased against you over the course of the semester or years (if you had to take multiple courses with the instructor). If an instructor insults you, has given you unfair grades even after being talked to by the department chair in the past, or has physically touched you, then you skip talking with the instructor and email both the department chair/head and the dean at the same time, and set up an appointment with the dean.

Department Chairs/Heads. These administrators are often faculty members who, in addition to teaching, oversee the department's long-term planning and course rotation and lead departmental initiatives. If you have an issue with an instructor that cannot be resolved (e.g., an unfair grade or contentious interaction), then you will most likely want to make an appointment to talk with the department chair or head. You will want to email the office staff to set up the appointment.

Associate Deans and Deans. Deans and associate deans (who are their assistants) are the next level up in the campus hierarchy. Deans are often in charge of multiple departments, called colleges (e.g., College of Arts and Humanities) or schools (e.g., School of Science and Technology). They oversee budgetary responsibilities, make hiring decisions, raise money for their area, and lead long-term planning initiatives. Deans rarely, if ever, teach, and are typically considered full-time management (rather than faculty). Some deans are former faculty members, whereas others are private-sector employees who have decided to work in higher education.

Vice Presidents and Provosts. Above the deans are the vice presidents or provosts of the university. Vice presidents oversee specific functions, such as vice president of finance, vice president of academic affairs, or vice president of student affairs, and their jobs are split between raising money for the university and directing their areas. Some vice presidents are former faculty members, whereas others are private-sector employees who have decided to work in higher education.

President. The highest-ranking member of an institution is the president. Some presidents are very involved in the day-to-day decisions of the institutions, whereas others devote almost all of their time to fundraising and marketing. Most presidents do a bit of both. Some presidents are former faculty members, whereas others are private-sector employees who have decided to work in higher education.

Board of Regents/Trustees. Many public universities are a part of a state university system and have a board of regents or board of trustees that oversees the decision making of all the state campuses under its jurisdiction. The board of regents/trustees appoints the university presidents, sets tuition rates, and advocates for universities to the legislature.

Legislature/governor. Ultimately, universities are controlled by the state legislature and governor. The legislature sets the budget and can raise/reduce funding for higher education, which can (in turn) affect tuition rats, hiring decisions, and building maintenance/construction. The governor often appoints people to the board of regents/trustees, which means that those people can vary widely in talent, political affiliation, and dedication to higher education.

As you can see, the university bureaucracy comprises of many, many people working in a variety of settings, contexts, and levels. Higher education, from coaches to deans and beyond, fulfill a variety of tasks and navigate a wide range of federal, state, and city codes, laws, and rules. Although people within the institution inhabit a range of positions, the sad reality is that some of these people will be hostile (overtly or covertly) to some types of students. Position, intelligence, or rank are not guarantees that a person won't discriminate based on race, class, sex/gender, or able-bodiedness. In fact, those forms of discrimination are magnified as their personal prejudice is bolstered by the institutional resources they can bring to bear (e.g., expelling a student, sabotaging a grade, or engaging in police brutality). Knowing the bureaucratic culture, and who to talk to in times of need, is thus more important than just rote memorization of an organizational chart. Rather, it is the knowledge that you may need to have when confronted by discrimination, prejudice, or bias.

Although the central purpose of the institution is to educate the public, and instructors are the ones who are primarily responsible for this goal, they are just one group among many that steers the direction of the university. It's important, then, to know who you need to talk to if you want to see changes happen on your campus. In the next section, we'll talk about how student associations provide an important vehicle for practicing democracy and influencing the decision-making process on campuses.

Activism for Shared Governance

As we stated in Chapter 2, there are many reasons that a society invests in higher education, and the most important reason in our view is how education can help people practice democracy. To us, democracy is more than just voting in elections or working on a political campaign (although, those things are certainly important). Rather, democracy is an ethic that you can practice by becoming active in the decision-making processes of the institutions you are a part of— whether companies you work for; organizations you have joined; or city, state, or federal governments that oversee where you live. In higher education, there are formal and informal ways that shared governance can be practiced. Most explicitly, this is the student government association (SGA) of your campus. You may think that your SGA doesn't have a lot of power, and traditionally that might even be the case. Increasingly, student governments have emerged as a powerful part of campus decision making and your involvement in that group can have real influence on securing an educational environment that supports students' potential to pursue their capabilities.

The first responsibility that most SGAs have is financial oversight over allocating money the university administration sets aside for student groups and activities. This money is often collecting through student activities fees, which

Figure 3.3

are mandatory parts of the cost of going to college each semester. In most universities, SGA funds can be used by student groups to fund trips, on-campus speakers, and other types of organizational needs. These funds can also be allocated to individuals or classes who wish to present their research papers, art projects, theatre performances, or other types of academic activities. Important to this process is the deliberation among the student senators and other members of the SGA about creating criteria for vetting what requests are funded and which are not. If, for example, a student wants funding to present an essay they wrote about the inferiority of people of color to White people at a White nationalist conference, should student activity fees support that? What if the student wants the SGA to match funds their organization raised to invite an openly anti-LGBTQ speaker? Making sure your SGA has the moral imagination and political will to create fair, rigorous, and ethical guidelines is a daunting task, and one that can ensure that your campus's culture promotes inclusiveness, equity, and social justice.

The second responsibility that SGAs often oversee is negotiation between students and administrators/board members/legislators about issues such as meal plans, building renovations, and tuition and fees. If an SGA doesn't advocate for students' interests, other parties (e.g., administrators) will make decisions with incomplete or erroneous knowledge. These are issues that are extremely important to students' everyday lives and can make or break some students' financial capabilities to access college. For example, Texas State University's SGA worked to increase student representation in parking fines (Texas State University, n.d.), Fresno State's SGA ran multiple campaigns to pay for a new

Who Gets to Speak?

One of the biggest questions facing higher education right now is who gets to speak in public venues on campus. On one side, some people argue that free speech should mean that anyone can say anything without fear of censure. On the other side, some people argue that some forms of talk are so harmful or erroneous that they should not have access to public resources to spread their message. Take these examples:

1. Alt-right leader Milo Yiannopoulos referring to a faculty member as a "fat faggot" during a presentation on campus.

2. Conspiracy theorist Alex Jones stating that the Sandy Hook Elementary School massacre was faked, that no children were killed, that the parents were actors, and that the whole thing was staged so the government would have a reason to confiscate legally obtained guns.

3. White supremacist Richard Spencer leading a group of people in chants of "Jews will not replace us" and "blood and soil."

Each of these examples are currently permitted under the U.S. Supreme Court's interpretation of the First Amendment. How would a responsible SGA handle a speaker who they knew would say these things on their campus?

student union (Ramirez, 2018), and UC–Berkeley runs the campus's bookstore (ensuring profits go back to support student organizations) (Associated Students of the University of California, n.d.). These instances show that SGAs don't have to limit themselves to the stereotypical planning of dances and ice cream socials. Rather, SGAs work to oversee important aspects of campus life and, in turn, dramatically affect how decisions are made. Students (through their SGAs) should always be in talks with campus officials (tenure-track and tenured faculty are a great place to start) about how to best support student life. Faculty can help you frame issues and provide invaluable context. In the end, no one knows student needs better than students.

The final responsibility that SGAs have is to be vocal about student rights. SGAs have as much power as students invest in it—very active and outspoken SGAs can greatly influence conversations and decision making in ways that benefit student life. SGA power is especially true if the campus has a student newspaper or if the SGA has connections to local media outlets to get their message out. In these cases, SGAs can work to raise consciousness, advocate on how best address issues that affect student life, the campus body, and thus the surrounding community. Even absent these outlets, SGAs can still effect change through marches, protests, and other forms of coordinated activism for change. And, SGAs, as an organized political body, are well positioned to lead these types of activities. Students at the University of Wisconsin, led by the SGA, held a sit-in at a UW Board of Regents meeting, calling for more funding to the university and pushing back against cuts to programs (Williams, 2018); SGA members organized a rally in response to CU–Boulder's president cutting nearly 90% of the student activity budget (Burness, 2018); University of Michigan SGA members voted unanimously to oust the university president for what they believed was the poor handling of Larry Nassar's sexual misconduct with U.S. Olympic Team female gymnasts (Jesse, 2018); and SGA members at the University of Georgia demanded their university join the other 250 universities and colleges in supporting high school students' right to protest the lack of meaningful gun reform in the face of continued school shootings (Webb, 2018). Perhaps the largest, and most well-organized, SGA campaign has been led by students at Howard University, who have issued a series of demands in response to the revelation that the university had misappropriated student financial aid funds (Alim, 2018). Students mobilized a sit-in, stating that they would not leave the university president's office until their calls for reform and transparency were met. To date, Howard University and the student protestors have agreed to one of the nine proposed changes (Vera, 2018). In short, SGAs have a responsibility to ensure that student interests are protected and often have a lot of the resources necessary to pursue student-centered goals.

List of Howard University Student Demands

Throughout its history, Howard University has failed to prioritize the interests of its student body, and we refuse to suffer the impact of administrative negligence in silence. In order to transform our institution into a democratic, Black University that acts as a safe-haven for all Black students, we must have student power and administrator accountability. In the words of Fredrick Douglas, "power concedes nothing without a demand." Therefore, these are our demands:

- We demand that Howard University provide adequate housing for all students under the age of 21 and extend the Fall 2018 housing deposit deadline to May 1.
- We demand an immediate end to unsubstantiated tuition hikes and complete access to administrative salaries.
- We demand that Howard University actively fight rape culture on campus in an effort to prevent sexual assault.
- We demand that Howard University implement a grievance system to hold faculty and administrators accountable in their language and action toward students with marginalized identities.

continues

- We demand that Howard University hire more counselors and implement an inclusive attendance policy that accounts for mental and emotional health issues.
- We demand the immediate disarming of campus police officers and the formation of a Police Oversight Committee controlled by students, faculty, staff and off-campus community representatives.
- We demand that Howard University allocate more resources toward combating food insecurity and gentrification within the LeDroit-Shaw community.
- We demand the immediate resignation of President Wayne A.I. Frederick and the Executive Committee of the Board of Trustees.
- We demand that students have the power to democratically influence the decision of the administration and the Board of Trustees by way of popular vote.

As we have said before, SGAs are only as powerful as students invest into them. And, unfortunately, some administrators, regents, and legislators do not know, or care, enough about the students they are supposed to serve to listen to their grievances or great ideas. Many times, it is easier for people in positions of authority to simply wait until those students they have identified as the "troublemakers" graduate, so they can implement whatever plan they wanted to in the beginning. In those cases, it is important to ensure you have the willpower and determination to see your advocacy through to the end. Make sure your SGA leadership is as united as possible about your topic of advocacy, and that you have members at all levels of their educational journey (first years, sophomores, juniors, seniors) in your group. All-too-often we see student movements led by seniors that end up fizzling out because the leadership changes over the summer and the topic gets put on the back burner for the next SGA administration. Your energies, channeled through the SGA, can help secure a better campus for yourself, your peers, and for those students who will attend the institution in the years and decades to come. It's a great deal of responsibility, one that we know you can live up to!

****

As you think about the type of culture you are entering into and what type of culture you want to leave, it's important that you adopt ethics of observation, collaboration, and justice. In this chapter, we detailed some of the ways that are considered "normal" or "in" ways of interacting with your instructors and other members in positions of authority on campus. However, our list is not, and cannot be, exhaustive. You'll find that there are hundreds of things, big and small, that characterize your institutional culture. If you dedicate yourself to studying those practices, you'll be able to make informed choices about when to follow, resist, or subvert those norms to create change.

We want to reiterate, you can't do it alone. One person, no matter how right or loud, is still, in the end, only one person. You will need to communicate your ideas to others in ways that will invite them to see the same problems you do, pursue the solutions you want, and how to make compromises to ensure equity for as many people as possible. There are dozens of groups and organizations on campus that can help you do this work. The SGA is a particularly powerful group because it oversees so many aspects of campus culture and student life. If you want to see your campus become a place that supports students' potential to realize their capabilities, you will need to have the voice of many of students with you. If you stay true to the process and goals of social justice, you'll find that working through these channels can help your college or university realize its obligation to equity and fairness.

Discussion Questions

- How do you tell the status of one faculty member from another?

- As you entered college, what did you think was appropriate communication when speaking to faculty? Staff? Members of administration?

- After reading this chapter, have these ideas changed?

Student Challenge
Find out the following information about your student government:

- Who are members of student government on your campus?

- What do they do?

- How do you join? Get elected?

- What important decisions has your student government body voted on in the past year?

CHAPTER 4

Study Habits and Self-Care

Cultivating Skills, Challenging Busywork

CHAPTER OBJECTIVES

By the end of the chapter, you should be able to:

- Develop an array of study habits that are successful for you
- Recognize the signs of poor study and living habits
- Identify how busyness is a destructive habit
- Develop a set of time management skills
- Connect ethics of healthy living with activism about self-care

ORIENTING QUESTIONS

As you read the chapter, try to answer the following questions:

- What are some effective study habits?
- What is the connection between self-care and effective studying?
- What study habits are destructive?

Consider the stories of two students. Ross wakes up at 8:50 a.m. He rushes to his 9:00 a.m. class, still groggy and yawning. He walks into class 10 minutes late, sits in the back row as the instructor rolls her eyes (with judgment), and all the students watch him disrupt the discussion that was underway. Ross makes it on time for his next class, but finds the content boring, so he ends up drifting in and out of sleep. The jolt of backpacks being zipped up and desks moving becomes an alarm, alerting him to drag himself out of his desk and move on to the next class. He is left wondering what he learned, what he missed, and what is due. While he stays awake throughout his next class, the blank stare he offers suggests that he's not really retaining information—he's a sentient zombie at this point. He goes back to his home, takes a nap but forgets to set his alarm, and sleeps well into what should be his shift at his part-time job. He looks at his phone—three missed calls from work and one frantic message asking where he is. With nothing to be done about his work situation, he grabs some dinner, and goes back to his home, resolved to study. But, after a few minutes he realizes that he doesn't remember anything from his classes nor can he complete assignment. So, he sends an email to the instructor asking for directions on the essay, and decides to watch television. He goes to sleep sometime around 2:00 a.m., Cheeto dust covering his chest, so he can do it all again the next day.

Jodie wakes up at 6:50 a.m., takes her scheduled 10-minute shower, gets dressed in 30 minutes, and walks to the cafeteria to eat breakfast. At 8:00 a.m. she studies her notes for her upcoming classes, and gets to her 9:00 a.m. class with 10 minutes to spare. Each class she's alert and prepared, but it's hard for her to concentrate. She knows she has a big deadline for an essay coming up, she's leading her sorority's rush, and her job just increased her hours per week. As she leaves her last class, she gets a text from her girlfriend asking why they haven't hung out in almost 2 weeks—is she mad at her? She starts to text back, realizes this is going to take a long conversation to deal with, and resolves to call her later that night. As she puts her phone away, it starts to ring—it's the biology honors student society president calling, asking her why she isn't at the meeting. Jodie's their vice president, and she has to rush across campus to make it to the meeting. During the meeting, she volunteers to plan the upcoming banquet for the organization. She gets to her car, which has a parking ticket because she thought she would be done earlier in the day, and makes her way through traffic to her job. She's the assistant manager at a restaurant, which means

Student Voice

When it comes to studying, you almost have to find a way to be interested in the material or else it is rote memorization. Not all schools offer science courses that relate to your major, BUT YOU SHOULD LOOK FOR THEM! Anyway, the studying is never ever fun and you never really know if you remember it until you're tested, which also brings forth a ton of anxiety. —*Kristi* that when two of her employees don't show up she has to clean and close the building by herself. She gets back to her room at midnight, exhausted, but she has to finish her essay for tomorrow. As she she's putting the finishing touches on it, she realizes she forgot to call her girlfriend. She'll have to do it tomorrow. Frustrated, she finally gets to sleep sometime around 2:00 a.m., energy drink cans stacked in a small castle around her, so she can do it all again the next day.

Does any aspect of these two students' lives seem familiar to you? Maybe you fall somewhere in the middle. At this point, you have probably heard a lot about how you are supposed to deal with the newfound freedom of college life, and have been warned about procrastination, given time management strategies, and offered all sorts of information and tools for how to be productive. And, many of these forms of admonishment and advice are certainly grounded in truth. Students who are effective time managers, can establish conducive study content, manage stress, have strong support systems, are willing to solicit help from others, and have strong coping skills perform better than those students who do not practice or possess these skills (Balduf, 2009; Heller & Cassady, 2017; Kitsantas et al., 2008; Preckel, Holling, & Vock, 2006; Tuckman, 2003). Your success in college will be influenced by your mastery of course content, but just as important will be your mastery of all of the dispositional skills (e.g., time management) that will position you to make use of your knowledge in daily life.

In our time as instructors, we have dealt with countless students just like Ross and Jodie. We believe that both students' lifestyles are dangerously unsustainable, even with the best intentions. Most obviously, Ross's choices demonstrate some of the worst aspects of procrastination, poor study skills, and bad time-management habits. Ross is quickly on his way of losing his job and failing his classes if he doesn't make some big adjustments to his habits and attitude. Jodie, though, doesn't represent an ideal situation either. She's stressed, anxious, and disconnected from her peers and relationships because she is over-committed. In her pursuit of trying to do everything perfectly, she is quickly finding out that she is accomplishing nothing well. If she's not careful, Jodie may slide into depression or become physically ill because she's overtaxing herself.

Student Voice

The best way to learn the material was to relate it to daily life. Say you're trying to remember a compounds for chemistry. My friends and I would say things like, "Hey, let's go get some EtOH (alcohol) after class!" Or, "damn it's finals week I'm dead where's the potassium chloride (what they use for lethal injections)," or "this meal is bland, pass the NaCl (salt)." It really helps to just relate what you're studying to daily life. —Vera

Student Voice

People say, "You either know it or you don't." No, you need to study. Study the way that works for you, don't feel pressure to study in a way that other people want, but doesn't help you. —Iris

The purpose of this chapter, then, is to help you try to navigate between Ross and Jodie. College will certainly be a time that challenges you—make no mistake. Up until this point, your high school, military, or professional life before college was probably largely structured for you. Now, however, you will be given a great deal of seemingly "free time" and a series of tasks to complete using your own discretion about time management. You'll need to figure out how to prioritize, make checklists, and create schedules—all tasks that are (let's be honest) the most boring part of "adulting" but are invaluable to your success within and beyond college. First, we'll discuss the rise of "busyness" as a destructive habit and its influence on college life. Then, we'll map out the study habits that you can engage in that will increase your control over your life and schedule. And, finally, we'll argue how self-care is an important component of realizing a social justice framework within higher education.

Quality vs. Quantity

Busyness as a Destructive Habit

Have you ever watched *The Jetsons*, a cartoon depicting life in the future? In it, George Jetson, the father, has a job in the Spacely's Space Sprockets factory where his only job is to push a single button for an hour or two a week. This future was predicted by a variety of people in literature and media in the mid-20th century. Many people thought that as work became more efficient (i.e., taking less effort to create the same amount of goods/services) that everyday people would be

Figure 4.1

able to work less and less until, eventually, most people didn't need to work at all. John Maynard Keynes, one of the foremost economists of his day, argued that by the end of the century people would probably work about 15 hours a week—and then, only if they really wanted to (Elliot, 2008). Society has seen wave after wave of inventions that have replaced less efficient forms of labor: computers, vacuums, dishwashers, and laundry washer/dryers. When one steps back and thinks of all ways that life is more efficient today than it was a century ago, one has to wonder—why are people so busy?

The first and probably most unfortunate reason people are busy is because they believe that busyness is a signal of virtue or good morals. Some societies, and American society is chief among them, believe that "time is money" and that to not be productive is to lose money through idleness. The smart or moral person, many believe, works hard and is rewarded for their efforts in their personal and professional lives. As *The Economist* (2014) notes, "Individualistic cultures [like the U.S.], which emphasise achievement over affiliation, help cultivate this time-is-money mindset" (para. 5). These cultural norms encourage people to be busy for the sake of busyness—as if there is no virtue or benefit from deep thinking, reading, or other "slow" activities. Students fall into the trap of believing that it is better to have a dozen organizations, clubs, and jobs on their resume than it is to have fewer, yet notable, contributions or achievements. As a result, students end up of doing a whole lot of nothing particularly well, learning very little, and potentially harming their own psychological health. This desire to appear busy manifests most tellingly in people who brag about how sleep deprived, overscheduled, or overworked they are, as if such things are badges of honor rather than as predictors of poor mental and emotional health. Eating little or nothing at all at one's desk, drinking multiple energy drinks or ingesting Adderall or other drugs to power through an essay, or relieving stress through too much gaming, partying, or other activities are all a part of a culture that normalizes hyperactivity without regard for the toll it demands.

Health Check

One of the hardest things to gauge is whether you are working too hard. Because American culture valorizes work, stigmatizes mental illness, and is unempathetic to stress or anxiety, a person can quickly become isolated and unwell without even noticing the warning signs. Here are five signs that you are working too hard and may need to reprioritize things in your life:

1. **You're always tired.** If you feel like you are always on the verge of a cold, if your body aches, or if sleep is not rejuvenating, then you may need to take a step back from your work.

continues

2. **You don't have any free time.** Some people make the mistake of thinking that the most productive people never eat, sleep, or have fun. However, you must do these things to be mentally and physically well.

3. **You don't finish tasks.** Sometimes you need to disengage from something if it is giving you stress, but if you are constantly flitting from one task to another but never finishing anything then it may be the sign of chronic stress.

4. **You stop caring about results.** When you get so overworked that you just want to finish a task, and don't care about the quality of your results, then it's time to cut down on your list of things to do.

5. **You become negative toward others.** Whether it's by intentionally trying to sabotage others, spreading rumors, or just generally being disagreeable, when you're overworked you can do a lot of things that harm others. Although it might feel good to make others feel the stress or anxiety that you are dealing with, this is not a healthy way of dealing with your problems.

Everyone has bad days, and no one is always their best self. However, if you are chronically engaging in these types of behaviors, then it may be a sign that you need to take stock of your life choices. What can be cut out? What can be managed? What is beyond your control, so you'll have to learn to deal with it? It might seems like you don't have time to address these types of questions, but believe us when we say you will accomplish less and do more harm to yourself and others by neglecting this kind of introspection.

Even now, you have likely thought about how busy you are or felt like you had to keep up with others. Perhaps you have never really thought about the connection between how busy you are and if you are adopting a healthy approach to your work and life. If so, your viewpoint is one that is quite common.

Unsurprisingly, the second reason that a culture of busyness is so pervasive is because popular culture, parents, and schools encourage it. Many parents feel a strong sense of anxiety and insecurity about their child's ability to be successful in adulthood. As a result, they overschedule, overwork, and over manage their children's lives in an effort to produce a perfectly prepared person (i.e., see Pew Center, 2015). Schools also encourage this type of

---

Mindful Self-Care

Have you done these things today? In the past few days? In the past week?

- Eaten a healthy meal?
- Slept at least 7 continuous hours?
- Engaged in at least 30 minutes of exercise?
- Drank a full glass of water?
- Taken a shower or groomed?

If you haven't and you're not feeling 100%, then you may want to work on checking these off your list. If you have, and you aren't feeling well, then maybe you're having an off day. If the feeling persists for many days or weeks though, you may be sick or emotionally/psychologically drained and need to reach out for help.

behavior, usually through mandatory volunteer hours, and well-intentioned teachers and guidance counselors who push students to become involved in many activities (e.g., get a part-time job, do community service, and keep high grades) because these things "look good to college recruiters for scholarships." In other words, for nearly 20 years, many students have had little say about the direction their life is headed, and instead have had to constantly defer to adults who push them to meet higher and higher expectations out of perceived necessity rather than any kind of actual reality.

The third, and final place that encourages this type of behavior from young people is the jobs that they hold. The Bureau of Labor Statistics (2017) reports that there were nearly 32 million hourly wage workers aged 16 to 24 years. In other words, the majority of young people work jobs where they are paid by the hour rather than on a salary. Your managers and coworkers have expected you to perform a set number of tasks within a certain number of hours per day or week, and your job is to meet those requirements. As a result, your work ethic has been shaped by a highly structured and scheduled form of managerial oversight. If you are like many students, you may take pride in working hard, accomplishing your goals, and being recognized by your peers and managers for your efforts. This ethic becomes a part of your identity, and you see yourself positively because you find value in others recognizing that you execute your jobs duties responsibly.

We wish to be clear—working hard can be an important and positive facet of your life and identity. There are few things that are more rewarding than being able to look at a task one has accomplished and feeling genuine pride in a job well done—whether it's writing an essay (or a book like this one!), mowing the lawn, or building a house. However, busyness does not accomplish these goals. *Instead, busyness provides a façade of accomplishment while harming one's emotional, psychological, and physical health.* Busyness harms your abilities to fulfill your capabilities because you're overinvested in the appearance of productivity rather than focusing your energies on being fulfilled through targeted, quality activities. This problem becomes even more common now that people can be permanently connected to the internet and check emails, find information, submit assignments, and edit reports from their phones and smart devices. It means that people are always busy, always working, even when they are supposed to be relaxing, spending time with their families, or meditating/thinking about their day.

> ### Student Voice
>
> How much you get out of a class is a situation that you can create or manage. Some classes simply will not play a role in your everyday life in comparison to others. So, you have to take on the work of figuring out how to make them fit. —*Marybeth*

Busyness is a not a badge of honor, it's an indicator of poor decisions about priorities and a sure road to mental and emotional stress. The American

Psychological Association (2010) found that the most common reason people gave for not managing their stress was the belief that they were too busy. *Introspection, and self-care, are not frivolous or unwarranted, they are the most important components of a healthy lifestyle.* There is no amount of to-do checklists, time management strategies, or life plans that will help you maintain your health if you engage in an ethic of busyness. Why? Because as soon as you use those strategies to manage your work load, you will immediately pile on more work because you don't feel like you're doing enough. Your life is worth more than your productivity and is more important than an endless series of scheduled moments. The tools presented in the next section are meant to help you manage aspects of your education and daily life toward a healthy balance, not to drown yourself in an endless tide of work.

Quality Time Management Skills and Study Habits

If you're like us, these concepts are probably not the most interesting things you will encounter in your time in college. However, they will be some of the most important. As we wrote about in Chapter 3, an important part of higher education is developing the cultural capital that will make you successful within and beyond your educational experiences. Time management skills and study habits, if practiced and perfected, will travel with you in the jobs you work at, the lives you lead, and can be important tools for living well. Here we offer ways that you can maximize your investment of time and energy so you can master your role as a student and be free to pursue other interests, hobbies, or relationships in your life.

Figure 4.2

Time Management Skills

Keep a Schedule. The first, most important, and hardest thing that you will probably need to do is keep a schedule of your semester. Scheduling is especially important the first few weeks of the semester, when you are working out how to maneuver all your responsibilities into a coherent routine. Make sure to look at the course syllabi that you get at the beginning of the semester and put their readings, assignments, and tests into your schedule. For some people, a pen and paper schedule or calendar is the most effective way to keep up with their work, whereas others use their phone's calendar/alarm function, Google Calendars, or some other app. Whatever form or forms your scheduling takes, make sure that you are checking it regularly. Keeping your work, class, clubs, activities, and organizations schedule in one place will ensure you can plan accordingly and not have to feel rushed, anxious, or behind all the time.

Student Voice

For studying, I try to always read the chapters and stay on schedule. In the beginning of the semester, I take all the syllabi and try to incorporate the schedules onto one calendar. That way, I can plan ahead and make sure I have all my regular work done a week ahead of time and I can plan my work schedule accordingly. *—JoAnna*

Block Classes. When possible, group classes together (especially if they are close to each other on campus) so it's easier to maintain a learning "flow." Often, students put large gaps of time between classes with the intention that they will study between classes, but more often than not, that time gets filled with social media or socializing. Also, make sure to leave a gap in your classes to eat. Sometimes a department doesn't offer a particular class outside of a single day/time, whereas others offer multiple sections of the same course. Check your university's course catalogue (often found online by typing "course catalogue" into the university's search box) to know when classes are offered, and block your classes to best address your needs. Many universities allow students to enroll in courses based on their year (e.g., seniors get to pick before first-year students) and major (e.g., major students get preference in enrollment over general education students). If you want classes that fit your schedule you'll want to know what day you can enroll and do it as soon as the university system allows you to do so.

Schedule Study Time. You get back from your classes, you feel a little tired, and you think, "I'll just hang out for a few minutes, and watch an episode of my favorite show." Next thing you know, you've binge-watched for 3 hours, you're hungry, and you have a low-level headache from staring at your computer screen. You're not going to get any studying done at this rate. Make sure to schedule time for you to read over your notes, the textbook, or watch a documentary that directly relates to the content you are learning in class. If you think you'll study the night before the big test consider this: If you wanted to lose weight, is it better to exercise an hour a day for 2 weeks or for 14 hours on one day?

Productive Holidays. During and between semesters, you'll have university-recognized holidays. A lot of students think they will work furiously and get caught up on all of their work over breaks and holidays. However, this rarely happens because friends, family, or obligations fill up their time and they end up feeling guilty because they didn't get as much work done as they had planned. We want to be clear, you should use breaks as a holiday and enjoy yourself. Working every weekday, weekend, and holiday will quickly lead to your emotional and psychological burnout. However, holidays can be productive if you need them to be and schedule them accordingly. Schedule yourself a small amount of time (e.g., 2 to 4 hours) on a particular day or days, and make sure to honor your commitment to work during that time. You'll find that you'll make that time more productive because you have limited it, and you'll still get to enjoy your holiday time.

Keep a Routine. Although it may seem simple on the surface, keeping a steady routine can be incredibly difficult—especially if that routine involves doing things (studying) that are not fun or interesting. However, a routine can help you manage all of your day-to-day duties and reduce your stress. After keeping a routine for many weeks or months, you'll find that those activities become second nature and, as a result, don't require a lot of cognitive effort to maintain. That's good because you'll need all your cognitive endurance for your class!

Address the Small Stuff. One thing that scheduling and keeping a routine will help with is ensuring that you complete your work in a timely and effective fashion. Many people who procrastinate do so because they face a large, daunting task and they wait until the last minute to let their panic overcome their anxiety. Student who do this claim they "always get stuff done" and "do their best work when under the deadline." Often, though, those who procrastinate do worse work then those who do not. An important step to being responsible is to take control of situations, rather than putting yourself in a context that make the situation control you (like waiting until the last minute to do homework). Take your problems (e.g., homework, projects, and activities), break them into small pieces, and then complete a small task (e.g., outline a paper, write a page on a project, or accomplish one organizational goal) every day. You'll find your work is better, you'll feel more in control of your life, and you'll be less stressed!

Enforce Sleep Time. We understand there will be time when you stay up late—perhaps you're at a late-night party, binge watching your favorite show, dominating a PUG (Pick Up Group) on your favorite FPS game, or studying for a big test. Whatever the reason, there will obviously be times when you'll want or need to stay awake to "burn the midnight oil." However, staying up too late, too many nights in a week can lead to illness, stress, and depression. Sleep isn't something you can compromise on—an engine needs oil to run and your body need sleep to function. You can go for a while without it, but eventually it'll catch up to you and you'll burn out. You'll find that you have diminishing returns on staying up late (i.e., it becomes less effective the more you do it) because your mind needs deep REM sleep. Make sure you understand how much sleep you need, identify what time you are most alert (i.e., are you a late sleep or early riser?), and count the hours back from when you need to wake up to get ready.

Study Habits

Set Time for Studying. Many students study when they have an upcoming test/quiz or (and much less frequently), when they are in a class that requires discussion/participation. This style of studying (i.e., cramming) is the least effective way to retain information. You wouldn't neglect brushing your teeth for 6 months and then try to catch up on all your dental hygiene the day before you visited the dentist, would you? Similarly, setting a time to study each day, whether you need to or not, will help train your mind to understand the content of the material and make connections across the things you are reading, watching, or listening to for your classes. You don't need to spend a great deal of time every day studying if you make the commitment to studying each day. Reread your notes, skim over the chapter, or watch a video related to your classes lesson for the day—anything that can get your mind on focused on the content of the course. If you study even 30 minutes a day, every day, you'll find

Student Voice

People often think that they can cram. Skimming the night before is fine, but I do not believe in cramming before a test, quiz, or whatever is a good idea. Cramming prior to the test and being able to recall the information from short-term memory does not necessarily mean the information is going to be stored in long-term memory. All cramming shows is that it is possible to get good grades without necessarily learning the material. But in the long run, you cheated yourself out of learning. —*Ruby* that you'll be able to make stronger connections across your material and have a great command of the facts needed for tests and quizzes.

Focus and Breaks. Another important component of studying is knowing how to focus and when to take breaks. We know—in a world of social media, easy access to entertainment apps, and chatting with friends face to face—there are many distractions that can make your study time less effective. Studying, writing, or reading may feel more enjoyable when you are multitasking, but that fun won't translate into better grades or content retention. Set a timer on your phone or computer, and devote yourself to working during that time. Then, give yourself a timed break—and no cheating! Alternate between working and breaking until you have a good understanding of how long you can concentrate before needing to break, and then use that knowledge to maximize your study time effectiveness.

Blocker Apps. One way to ensure that you are concentrating on your work when you're studying or in the classroom is to use apps that block your access to the internet or to specific sites for a period of time. Studies have shown that students who focus on their cellphones or laptops instead of the class's lecture perform worse on coursework than those who pay attention. You may think you can multitask or that the lecture is worthless because the instructor's delivery is painfully boring, but the truth is that you're best served by focusing on the course material and cutting out distractions.

Study Tips: Apps for Success

Sometimes the lure of the internet is too much, and the next thing you know you've spent 3 hours sifting through your favorite social media site. Here are some popular apps you can use to keep yourself on task:

Cold Turkey (Windows only)

Focus (Mac only)

FocusON (Android only)

FocusWriter (Mac, Windows, Linux)

Freedom (all systems)

LeechBlock (FireFox add-on)

Self Control (Mac only)

Stay Focused (Google Chrome extension)

WriteRoom (Mac)/DarkRoom (Windows)

Source: A. Renner. (2015). "10 apps that block distractions."
https://wallstreetinsanity.com/10-apps-that-block-distractions/

Writing vs. Typing Notes. As laptops and smart devices have become more common, students are increasingly using electronic devices to take notes. Studies have shown that although students who take notes electronically perform better in class than those who do not take notes at all, the highest performing group were student who took notes using pen and paper (e.g., Mueller & Oppenheimer, 2014). There are many reasons that pen-and-paper notetaking increases information recall. First, kinesthetically, your hand movement on paper requires greater physical movement and imprints on your brain at a deeper level than merely typing. Second, people type faster than they write, so they try to type everything an instructor says for their notes and end up not focusing as much on the material as the person who writes slower, and therefore uses more cognitive effort to parse out what is important and what is not. Finally, those who use electronic devices are much more likely to be distracted by web surfing, checking social media, or playing games than their pen-and-paper counterparts. So, even though you may not want to, sharpen those no. 2 pencils, make sure your pen's got ink, and get to writing!

Student Voice

Honestly, I rather learn the material more than anything else. Obtaining a good grade does not necessarily mean you learned the material. Sometimes, it means you figure out how the teacher taught and learned how to pass a test. Passing the test does not mean a student can apply what they learned from the classroom to daily life, but YOU CAN if you put in the study time. —Mir

Print vs. Digital Readings. Closely related to writing and typing is the question of reading print or digital copies of course materials. Research in this area indicates that the medium you use to read information does influence your ability to retain it (Singer & Alexander, 2017). If you need to read or skim something quickly, and remember a few key facts, then digital copies of a reading are appropriate. However, if you are reading material that is long or complex, then print mediums are better. Keep this in mind when purchasing textbooks—it will probably be better to order print copies rather than digital version. And, if your instructor has course readings posted a class repository or if you are reading journal articles, then be sure to print them out, if able.

Write on Your Texts. Have you ever read a long, difficult text, only to realize halfway down the page that your eyes have been moving, but you haven't retained any information? This problem is common among people who don't regularly read to gain new information. One way to address this issue is to write on or about your text as you are going through it. Underline, bracket, highlight, or circle information in the text that you are reading. This practice can be particularly useful if you use different colored pens or highlighters to differentiate among various important points or concepts. You can also write notes about the text. Write out important quotes from the material and then write a few sentences summarizing the quote into your own words. However you do it, make sure you are being an active reader so the time you spend studying is used well.

Know Your Body. Many students have only ever studied in one way because that is what their public schools demanded from them—be quiet, don't eat, or don't talk to your fellow students. Now, however, you have the freedom to learn how you study best. Should you eat before or during studying? Do you like big comfy chairs or hardback chairs? Music or no music? And, so on. Knowing what works for you and, when possible, making your space conducive to learning is an important part of college success. We will caution you though—just because something is comfortable or pleasurable, doesn't mean that it's the best for you when it comes to studying. Listening to music, for example, may be fun, but if at the end of 3 hours you've only got a few sentences written on your essay, then all you have accomplished is having a great background score to your inactivity.

Study Groups. For some students, having a set time to meet with other members of the class to study is an incredibly powerful learning tool. For others, it's their worst nightmare. However, studies indicate that learning in groups, and especially teaching others material, is one of the most effective ways to learn material (see Paul, 2011). Although it might seem paradoxical to teach someone as a way to learn it, the practice ensures that you know the material well enough to be able to make it accessible to another person. This process, going over material, answering questions, and reframing explanations to find the most effective way of working with another all increase the amount of cognitive effort you expend on the task and, in turn, helps you

Student Voice

Everything connects in some way or another. You may think, I am learning one subject. But as you study more, you start realizing almost all subjects connect in some way. Finding those connections will help you learn more because you can connect to information you have already stored in your memory. —*Anita*

Study Tips: Ways to Get Physical With Your Learning

Some students need a space that is devoid of stimuli to really concentrate on course material. Others need some form of physical activity to get their synapses firing. Here's a list of some physical activities that may help boost your study productivity:

- Dancing
- Reading text out loud or having a text-to-speech app read it to you
- Exercising before, during, or after studying
- Practicing yoga before studying
- Eating
- Drinking a moderate amount of caffeine
- Doodling

retain and understand the material better than just silently rereading your notes by yourself. So, if possible, work with others in your classes! If, that is, you will actually work with them and not spend the 2 hours talking or flirting!

Instructor Feedback. Every year, we grade hundreds of essays and projects for students. And, every year, many students get their papers back, flip past all of our notes and comments, look at the grade, and (if satisfied) don't give the paper a second thought. Often, the only time we work through feedback with students is when one is unhappy with their grade. If this sounds like the way you think about feedback, then let us assure you that you are robbing yourself of a rich resource for improving your work. When you receive any assignment back with feedback, you should review the feedback (and yes, the grade) after class. Don't look at it at the beginning of class because you'll be anxious about the feedback or your grade and won't pay attention to the rest of class. Or, you'll be upset with your grade and may say or do something that you'll regret later. After reviewing the feedback, make notes to yourself about what you want clarification on and any advice you might want. Then, sleep on it. Waiting until the next day is especially important if you received a low grade, because (again) you might be angry and say or do something you'll regret. The next day, email your professor for an appointment to go over the feedback, and before you go to their office, review your notes again. When you see them, you should be professional and prepared—an ethic that will not only ensure you maximize your learning in the interaction, but that will also impress your instructor and increase your cultural capital (see Chapter 3).

Study Tips: Asking for Instructor Feedback

The grades and feedback that you receive from an instructor are invaluable tools for your learning. Even if you make the grade you were hoping for, the written or verbal comments your instructor offers can show you paths for growth. Due to time constraints of grading dozens (maybe hundreds) of assignments, sometimes instructors only give enough feedback to justify the grade, and expect students to set up an appointment if they want more guidance or advice. If a class is particularly important to your life goals or interesting to you, then you should ask the instructor for more feedback on an assignment. Here's how to do it:

1. Send an email to the instructor to set up an appointment to talk with them. Make sure to mention that the purpose of the visit is not about the grade, but about learning more about the subject matter. Most instructors love it when a student is interested in their area of study. See Chapter 3 on advice for writing an email.

continues

2. An instructor who has graded hundreds of papers is unlikely they will remember every detail of your work. Therefore, you need to make a copy of the assignment or print off another copy with the instructor's feedback. When you arrive at the instructor's office, give them the copy so they can refamiliarize themselves with your work and their feedback.

3. Make sure to have two to four questions ready to ask. These could include, "How can I take this type of work to the next level?" "Is this work worth revising to put into print somewhere (e.g., a research paper or an essay)?" or "What are some obstacles you've seen other students navigate who are interested in this area of study?"

We've offered a lot of advice for how to maximize your return on time invested in studying. But, as we have said before, the biggest influence for how effective this advice is will be how willing you are to practice various study habits until you land on what is best for you. Are you the worrier, waiting until the last minute to finally overcome the stress you feel about the project, leading you to complete your task the night before? Maybe you're the dreamer who thinks of a dozen ideas and can't settle on one until the deadline finally forces you to pick one and finish the project. Or, perhaps you are the procrastinator, who puts off all work because there's always something more interesting or fun to do. Whatever your previous habits were, now is the time to focus on creating new ways of studying and learning because those will be the behaviors that you carry with you within and beyond higher education. Knowing yourself—your strengths and weaknesses—is the first step to improving yourself.

Figure 4.3

We also want to caution you though—be kind to yourself. You may not make an A in every class, and you certainly won't make an A on every assignment. There will be times when you don't do your best work or when the grade you get on (what you think) is your best work isn't as high as you wanted. You need to be able to forgive yourself. You can't be perfect all the time, and pursuing that ethic will make you a miserable person because you'll either never feel fulfilled or you'll think you have made it and become an insufferable snob. Do your best. Work to improve. But, know that your work is not a reflection of your heart, mind, or soul, it's just one facet (among many) that makes up the human experience. Your ability to find joy in your work will come (and many professors can help you toward this perspective) when you see your labor as an opportunity to expand your horizons, create meaningful art, and/or experience ideas that you never would have been able to outside of higher education.

Activism for Self-Care

Most people start preschool when they are 3 years old. From your earliest memories, you probably remember people asking you, "What do you want to be when you grow up?" Maybe you wanted to be a dragon veterinarian, firefighter, doctor, or police officer; your young mind seeking out those careers that you read in books or saw on TV or in movies. Then, you graduated to kindergarten, and then onto your school until you finished 12th grade around 18. From about eighth grade until you finished high school, the drumbeat of, "What do you want to be when you grow up" became more insistent, your friends and family wanting more and more specific answers about your chosen career. Then, you went to college. "The clock is ticking, you have to make a choice," Everyone around you says. "What do you want to be when you grow up?" At this point, almost your entire life has been preparing you for this moment—how will you sell your labor to make a living? You'll be expected to make this choice, and as you leave college you'll find that you rarely (if ever) get the opportunity to learn, love, and ruminate with the same freedom again. Your days, fleeting, ephemeral, cascade one into another—a series of scheduled moments, like a story already written: work hard to have a strong resume, get a job, work to keep the job, find a partner, work to impress your boss, buy a house, work to get promoted, maybe have a kid or three, work to get a raise … and so on until one day you retire and take the vacation you're now too old to enjoy.

As it stands, too much of American culture revolves around work. According to the Organisation for Economic Co-operation and Development (2018), U.S. employees work more hours per week than any other developed country's workforce. In fact, Saad (2014) found that approximately 40% of all U.S. employees worked more than 50 hours per week, with nearly 20% working more than 60 hours (a full-time job is 40 hours per week). Time Sheets (Emch, 2018) states that the average U.S. worker gets 16 paid leave days, as compared to Norway (25 days), the United Kingdom (28 days), or France (30 days). And, only about 50% of Americans actually use those days, and approximately 60% say they work during their vacation! All of your life up to this moment has prepared you for working long hours (e.g., going to school 5 days a week for 9 hours a day), working outside of work (i.e., homework), and offering only limited, structured avenues for play (e.g., there are few opportunities to play sports outside of school-sponsored competitive teams). It's no wonder, then, that youth report being more stress now than ever (Twenge, 2014).

This may be the script that our society offers you and other young people. But, here's the secret: it doesn't have to be this way! If you want to break this tradition, for yourself and for others, then you'll need to start mobilizing others to understand and challenge the cult of work that permeates the United States and start advocating for self-care. For many people, self-care is just an excuse they use to buy the latest gadget, spa day, or vacation. Certainly, there is nothing wrong with doing any of these things. However, although it may be appealing on the surface to play the latest video game for 8 hours a day, 7 days a week, that's probably not going to be fulfilling to most people (even those who love to play video games). We believe self-care goes beyond the very shallow, materialistic mantras that characterize many of the self-improvement, dieting, self-help, and self-esteem programs. Self-care is about as securing extended periods of time to reflect on what you are learning, to enjoy nature, or to find joy in the company of others—all important parts of people's emotional and psychological development (Lafargue, 1883).

Figure 4.4

To us, self-care is characterized by two important components. First, self-care is based on the recognition that sometimes surviving, or even thriving, in our current system can be a form of activism. For many traditionally marginalized groups—who have been denied the right to vote, segregated in schools, barred from joining certain professions, or have been targeted by police violence—living each day is an act of defiance against those forces that would see these people silenced or killed. Many in these communities may, intentionally or unintentionally, center the needs of those around them (particularly those from traditionally dominant groups) and, as a result, may never acknowledge the need to take care of their own mental, emotional, or physical health. In other words, in a world that would see your idealism and passion trounced under the weight of bureaucracy, inertia, and indifference, making sure to take the time to care for yourself is a crucial component to sustainable, effective activism.

The second important component of self-care is the recognition that "self" doesn't have to mean "alone." You'll remember in Chapter 1 that we talked about how the "personal is political" or the idea that addressing needs that directly affect you can galvanize you to see opportunities for activism for your community. Similarly, we believe that if you see your "self" as connected to others, then you should adopt an outlook that holds that to care for oneself is to care for others. Not only does this ethic of seeing "self" as a part of a "community" resist the individualist culture that characterizes U.S. workaholism, it provides you opportunities to think about how the problems that affect you might not be personal problems—they may be systemic. For example, if you struggle with depression, anxiety, or stress and staff, faculty, or administrators aren't helpful or sympathetic, you may find that others have similar experiences. And, instead of blaming yourself for being weak or needy (i.e., an individualistic mindset), you can see the lack of resources and aid as a problem that affects everyone on campus. As a result, you can start to advocate, not just for yourself and not just by yourself, but rather as a part of a community of people who are not being served adequately by the system.

Our current moment in history closely resembles the early 1900s in terms of the invasion of work into all aspects of private life. In fact, one of the most well-known acts of social protest in the United Kingdom was the Kinder Scout Mass Trespass in 1932 (Lazenby, 2012). Kinder Scout was an area of beautiful land owned by the Duke of Devonshire, and was considered off-limits to the everyday people who lived in nearby Manchester. Many young people wanted to enjoy nature rather than stay in the coal-smog–infested streets of their hometown, but were turned away by the local guards and constabulary. Despite repeated warnings and arrests, hundreds of people mobilized one weekend to enjoy the countryside, breathe the fresh air, and relax in nature. Afterward, the leaders of the movement were arrested and convicted by a jury of nobles, military offers, and bureaucrats. But the movement sparked a wider discussion about working or relaxing (or "rambling," as it was called), the private property of nobles, and the freedom of everyday people to find joy outside of their jobs, eventually prompting the government to create parks for public enjoyment.

There are many ways that you can be an activist for self-care that go beyond the imperative to "treat yo'self." One approach is to work with your college to provide opportunities for students to enjoy nature without having it constrained by competitive sports or rules. Creating opportunities to enjoy long walks or hikes with others or by oneself can offer avenues for people to become more in touch with themselves and reflect on their lives. This orientation is especially important if your college is in a city or in developed rural land (i.e., farmland), making it difficult or costly to access nature trails or parks. Another way to advocate for self-care is to work with the college to provide noncredit offerings, classes, or workshops that engage students' creative capacities. Certainly, many colleges provide opportunities to hear important speakers talk about weighty topics, and you should strive to attend those as well. But, very rarely (but, just as important) do colleges offer classes for those who wish to start playing an instrument, learn to paint or brew beer, or exercise their minds by reading non-course–related books. Finally, you can work with your college to create opportunities for childcare services to ensure that university members' ability to be excellent students, instructors, or administrators is not dictated by a lack of support (a lack that disproportionately harms females). If you are interested in proposing or expanding current university programs, a great place to start those conversations is with the student government association (see Chapter 3).

Creative Ways to Stage a Demonstration

One of the tightropes to walk as an activist is how confrontational you should be when organizing for justice. On one hand, you don't want to alienate potential allies or cast your group in a poor light by doing or saying something negative or insulting. On the other hand, you and others may be personally harmed by the issue you are addressing, and it makes little sense to be civil in the face of a direct harm. One way that organizers have tried to work through this dilemma is to engage in creative demonstrations.

First, you will have to organize a group of people to meet at a public location at a specific time and (if necessary) for a set number of days. Have a sign-up sheet or use an app (although, be forewarned, an app company might collude with those you are protesting) to ensure that there are enough people to be present for the entire demonstration. The most important part of a successful demonstration is planning. The more you have planned, the better you can mobilize.

continues

Next, think of what you want your media representation to be. Will you hold signs that undermine the "official" message at a large public speaking event? Will you glitter-bomb an anti-LGTBQ public official? Perhaps you will engage in a public filibuster, where you and others continue to speak during a legislative or university meeting despite not being "formally" recognized to contribute. Remember, you need think of how you and your organization will look on the front page tomorrow and what image you are trying to cultivate. Frustrated? Sympathetic? Passive? You won't be able to completely control your image or message, but you want to make sure that you are being intentional with what you want to get communicated to the public. Make sure to have talking points, slogans, or other short soundbites ready, and a designated person to communicate with the media.

Finally, don't let yourself be baited into negative situations. For example, when the Yale graduate students tried to unionize, the university's College Republicans group held a BBQ cookout right next to those who were on a hunger strike. The situation could have easily led to verbal or even physical altercations due to the intentional provocation. However, the graduate students held firm, continued with their protest, and gained sympathy from the public as those who weren't baited into a confrontation. Some media outlets (e.g., Breitbart or Dangerous) will be hostile to your message and group because of what you are advocating for and will write/say things about you and your group that are purposely negative, calling you angry, whiny, or entitled. You can't convince people at these outlets to report differently. You can, however, make sure that your message via social media and legitimate news sources to reflect the reality of the situation and your passion for your topic of advocacy.

One way to engage in this sort of activism is to engage in *embodied activism*. We use this term to describe those actions that require someone's body to be physically present in order to encourage change. In the Kinder Scout demonstrations, this involved walking on land traditionally marked as off-limits to most Manchester citizens. For you, it may take the form of sitting outside the office of a university official (i.e., a "sit-in"), organizing a march outside of university oversight, or standing at university entrances to talk with people about your cause (i.e., an informational picket line). However you decide to proceed, what is important is that you opt for a time and place that is the most accessible to those who wish to join. For example, holding a rally at the steps of an iconic building may be photogenic, but if people with mobility disabilities cannot join the protest, then you have alienated people in your advocacy. Sometimes, holding rallies at the same time as other large events can help amplify your message by ensuring a greater audience is exposed to your ideas. Important to all of these approaches, though, is the realization that your approach to activism may break the rules, but sometimes those rules are put in place specifically so that those in power don't have to deal with issues that are important to you. Be respectful, but know that your embodied activism can put your physical safety on the line and plan accordingly.

****

Increasingly, people within and beyond higher education will talk about work–life balance. They will tell you that you can have it all with the right scheduling habits and a can-do attitude: a successful career and happy family, plenty of fun and leisure, and a continual climb up your organization's ladder as recognition for your hard work. Certainly, these skills and dispositions can help achieve these things. But, we believe that the fundamental flaw of work–life balance books, blogs, and articles is that it makes work equal to life. Work is just a facet of life, and making it equal to the richness of other aspects of living—family, friends, romance, hobbies, and life goals—is a dangerously misleading concept. Although we don't think you should live life with a devil-may-care, I-may-die-tomorrow attitude, we do think that it is important that you find those activities in life that interest, engage, or challenge you—the ones that truly bring you joy for the sake of doing them rather than because someone else makes you—and make those things the primary indicators of your success in life.

Perhaps we make it sound too easy or you feel that our advice is out of touch with your economic realities. However, we want to encourage you to believe that you, and others with you, can make a difference by focusing on these issues. You are not alone, and you will encounter many people in your classes who are managing the same things you are. Free and unstructured time is an important component of people realizing their capabilities, and a necessary facet of emotional and psychological health. Everyone around you—your instructors, administrators, and managers—will want your time, your energy, your life. They may think they are doing it to help you (some are) or that they have your best interests at heart (some do), but the truth is that making your life revolve around work will stunt you emotionally and harm your ability to develop your full range of capabilities and reach your full potential. Your life is your own—you should get to choose how to spend the time you have.

Discussion Questions

- When was your studying, in high school, busywork? What was the result?

- What are you doing to enhance your ability to understand and remember class material?

- What time management skills in this chapter were the most helpful to you?

Student Challenge

- Look at all your obligations—work, school, and personal—for the next 2 weeks. How will you prepare to meet them? Make a daily calendar guiding you toward meeting these obligations.

- Locate two resources on campus that can aid in your self-care. What services do they offer that will be of assistance to you? When do you plan to use them?

CHAPTER 5

The Environment and You

Healthy Living, Healthy World

CHAPTER OBJECTIVES

By the end of the chapter, you should be able to:

- Identify how environmental factors can influence your health and well-being

- Describe how you are navigating emerging adulthood

- Recognize healthy eating, sleeping, and exercise routines

- Connect activism on environmentalism and sustainability to healthy living

---

ORIENTING QUESTIONS

As you read the chapter, try to answer the following questions:

- What healthy habits can increase your mental, physical, and emotional health?

- What kinds of activism can promote environmental sustainability?

In April 2014, the city government of Flint, Michigan, a majority Black town with nearly 40% of its residents living below the poverty line, decided to switch the city's water supply from the Detroit Water and Sewerage Department (DWSD) to the Karegnondi Water Authority (KWA). The Flint Emergency Manager Ed Kurtz proposed the switch under the belief that the city would save nearly $200 million over the next 25 years. The city decided to utilize water from the nearby Flint River in the interim of building the infrastructure to connect to the new water source. Local and state officials assured the city that the new water source was clean, drinkable, and posed no health risks to the population.

After the switch was made, many residents started to complain about the quality of their water—noting its color and smell. Corporations, such as General Motors, stopped getting their water from the Flint water supply, but residents couldn't make the switch. Despite numerous reports from organizations, such as the Environmental Protection Agency, Virginia Tech, and the Hurley Medical Center, state and local officials continued to deny that the water was harmful. However, all independent reports showed that the water had corroded the old pipes and leeched lead into the water supply. Lead causes severe neurological and physical harm, especially to young children and pregnant women, and is harmful at levels above 5,000 parts per billion (the Virginia Tech study showed levels as high as 13,200 ppb).

Figure 5.1

Figure 5.2

In January 2016, nearly 2 years later, the governor of Michigan, Rick Snyder, declared a state of emergency for Flint, with President Obama declaring one 2 weeks later. Both the state and federal governments worked to clean up the pipes, but were too late. Now, there is little short of completely replacing the city's water infrastructure that can fix the problem. The government offered free water filters for residents using the tap water, but they were (justifiably) wary of the government's assurances that the water could be made safe. As of this writing, criminal and civil charges/suits have been brought about nine state officials and two corporations, and the water still contains lead (Kennedy, 2016).

When you think about environmentalism, perhaps you think of a hippy-type person standing in front of a bulldozer to protect a nest of endangered birds. These types of media portrayals of environmental activists—and pejoratives such as "tree hugger"—severely misrepresent the need for and breadth of environmental activism. From activism leading up to the Clean Air Acts of 1963 and 1970 to Native Americans and their allies stopping pipelines from transporting oil at Standing Rock in 2017, the fact is that environmental activism helps people lead healthier lives and enjoy clean air, water, and land. However, as Flint and dozens of oil spills, strip mines, and pesticide runoffs show, without sustained attention, our environment can degrade to dangerous levels.

As a student, you may not think that environmental concerns are very important or that there is much you can do about them. However, we believe that living a healthy lifestyle is inextricably bound to the type of environment you live in now, and in the future. Furthermore, living in a healthy environment is a key component in securing the capabilities needed to reach your full potential. In this chapter, we'll outline the problems that many students encounter about eating, sleeping, and exercising properly. Then, we'll detail healthy habits that can boost your mental, emotional, and physical health while also making you a more effective student. We'll then connect a personal healthy lifestyle to activism for environmental sustainability, and the notion that your choices—from individual to collective—can have a profound effect on the environment.

The New Freedom

Whether you've been estranged from your parents or guardians for years or you call your mom every other day to chat, the truth is that now that you are in college your relationship with your family will change. Up until this point in your life, your parents or guardians have probably made a lot of your choices for you based primarily on the fact that many of your choices have involved them spending money on you, and that you, as an individual, probably have had little or no money. If you had a part-time job, you probably either contributed money to your household (e.g., rent or the mortgage) or used it for personal reasons (e.g., buying video games) while your parents paid for the majority household expenses. Either way, your finances really weren't your own, and the way that you scheduled your time (i.e., school, work, sleeping, and recreation) was largely structured by the adults around you. Now, however, you're going to be increasingly required to make these choices on your own.

Figure 5.3

> ### Student Voice
>
> There is no way to be good at everything you are somewhat expected to be good at (exercise every day, drink tons of water, healthy social life, rigorous academic schedule, extracurricular activities, making enough money to feed yourself, pay your car, pay your rent, see your family, have a healthy relationship, no stress, no anxiety, get the full college experience) if you are a full time or even part time depending on your living situation. If you attempt to conquer it all, you may find yourself falling slightly short at everything which is really defeating. —*Heather*

As Nelson et al. (2007) write, the relationship between children and their parents/guardians evolves over the lifespan, with children often taking a more independent role as they age. For many college students, their enrollment into higher education coincides with the stage of emerging adulthood, or that time when youth develop their independence and explore various lifestyles (Arnett, 2004). Youth become less likely to share information with their parents, even when they want to, because doing so may threaten their sense of autonomy. First-generation students feel this particularly keenly because they may feel that sharing information or airing grievances to their family won't be understood or respected because their parents don't have college experiences (McFarlane et al., 2018). These practices exacerbate the confusion that many youth feel about their role—not quite adults, but certainly not children. Some parents may even worsen the situation by being overinvolved in their children's lives by doing things like talking to instructors about grades, negotiating with managers about employment, and controlling who youth can see or hang out with. In those cases, parents' over involvement in their children's lives can seriously harm their goals and ability to actualize themselves as adults.

The reality is that from 18, and onward, you will only be given more responsibilities as you age. From voting, to drinking, to health insurance, to your retirement plan, and all the little (and not so little) day-to-day decisions that animate life, you will be increasingly expected to utilize your newfound freedom well. And, whether for good or ill, your decisions will influence many of the choices you will (or can) make in the future. If, for example, you blow off your classes, spend 7 years getting your degree, and amass $60,000 in student debt, you'll find it difficult (if not impossible) to purchase a car, save enough for a down payment on a home, or even be able to afford basic necessities. Even seemingly mundane decisions (e.g., going to class and studying) can influence your life for years to come. Unfortunately, we live in a society where you are expected to navigate college on your first try and relatively early in your life. This means that there is little room for error without (sometimes tragic) consequences. However, with the right tools, you can overcome any obstacles that come your way and find success.

Being able to make these decisions requires both knowledge and willpower. Choosing to live a healthy life is exactly that—a choice. As the late celebrity chef Anthony Bourdain once said:

> There's a guy inside me who wants to lay in bed, and smoke weed all day, and watch cartoons, and old movies. I could easily do that. My whole life is a series of stratagems to avoid, and outwit, that guy. (Sheffield, 2018, para, 4)

Let's be honest—there is so much in this world that is more pleasurable than work and school. But, we believe (and hope you agree) that there can be a deep sense of satisfaction that comes from excelling in life that cannot be matched by obtaining a rare piece of equipment in a video game or binge-watching an entire season of your favorite show. It's not that school and work are boring or hard or that they get in the way of the "fun" stuff in life; rather, in proportion, each aspect of life presents different opportunities for fulfillment and self-education. Learning how to manage the various aspects of your life is an important, if unofficial, part of your college education.

> **Student Voice**
>
> Say you are taking more than one class and you cannot focus on the one assignment. Do not force it. If you find yourself stressing about how many things you have to do, stop and focus on yourself and go for a run or exercise to calm your nerves. Now, focus on one, only one, of the things you need to do. —*Derek*

Your life can be fun, fulfilling, and meaningful without having to indulge in behaviors that will harm your chances at leading a happy life. Drinking too much alcohol, eating unhealthy food, and staying up all night are normal—almost every adult around you has done these things (maybe even in that order!). So, please don't take our advice here as admonishment or an injunction to not have fun. However, making poor decisions now will most likely involve parties of people (e.g., police officers) who, when you were younger, wouldn't have necessarily been contacted. Public intoxication, getting into a fight, or destroying property will most likely not be seen as acts of youthful exuberance or poor decision making—they'll be treated as crimes that you, as an adult, have committed. And, the repercussions of those decisions—jail time, fines, or checking the "felony" box on a resume, or denial of access to certain locations—will follow you forever. In order to live a lifestyle that is sustainable, both personally and societally, we believe you first need to know the ways to ensure that you meet the day as the best version of yourself.

Healthy Living

Eating, Sleeping, and Exercising for Success

Whether you come from a home that was very health conscious or one that let you do whatever you wanted, now that you're in college you'll have more control over your body and environment. Although you'll hear a lot of talk about the "freshman 15," the truth is that students' weight and health fluctuate in college. Stress, poor eating/sleeping habits, and lack of exercise can all negatively affect a person's health, but how the body responds to those changes can differ from person to person. To live up to your full capabilities, you'll need to ensure that you're making healthy decisions about what you consume. Here, we offer some broad advice about living a healthy lifestyle, but caution you to talk to a doctor or medical professional before making any significant changes to your diet or daily living habits.

> **Student Voice**
>
> Accept the fact that you cannot think of anything for this project at this time and keep moving forward. Switch subjects and try doing one of the other assignments that interests you. After you get one done, this often helps me feel accomplished to move forward with the other projects, including the other one I had trouble completing prior. —*Benjamin*

Figure 5.4

Eating Healthy

The Role of Carbs. Although some diet crazes may tell you to cut all the carbohydrates out of your diet, this is bad advice for younger people (Coleman, 2018). Certainly, eating pizza three meals a day and not exercising is not going to be good for your waistline or heart health. However, carbs are an important source of vitamins and minerals that are essential to your health, especially as a young adult. It's important to remember that all carbs are not the same. Simple carbs, or food that is composed of easy-to-digest sugars, can be good for you if it comes from fruit or vegetables. However, most simple carbs that Americans eat come from sources that should be min-imized or avoided, such as soda, candy, baked goods, or energy drinks. These latter types of simple carbs not only are bad for your weight, they are more likely to give you a spike/valley of energy and make it harder to concentrate for long periods of time. Complex carbs come from food that is composed of complex sugar/starch structures and take your body longer to break down. As a result, your body gets a more even amount of energy for a longer amount of time than from simple carbs. And, they make you feel fuller, which means that you can eat less of them to achieve a satisfying meal. Complex carbs come from breads and pastas that are made from whole wheat flour, brown or unbleached rice, potatoes, and legumes (e.g., black beans or chickpeas) (Rodriguez, 2017).

> **Student Voice**
>
> Do not forget to treat your body well with nutritious foods. Simple sugar are not only bad for your body to accumulate, but it does not help your brain work at its best. —*Fred*

Picking Your Protein. Protein is an important component of your diet and supplies you with essential amino acids. The U.S. Food and Drug Administration (FDA, n.d.a) states that you should get about 50 grams of protein based on a diet of 2,000 calories per day. Note that that is how much protein is in the food, not the weight of the food. An 8-ounce hamburger, for example, weighs about 225 grams and contains about 61 grams of protein. You can get protein from a variety of sources, including meats (i.e., beef, poultry, and seafood), beans and peas, dairy products, eggs, nuts/seeds, and some grains and vegetables. Meats contain all the necessary amino acids your body needs but can raise your risk for health problems: some forms of fish are high in mercury, beef can negatively affect heart health, and undercooked poultry can lead to salmonella. Nonmeat forms of protein do not have these risks, but do not contain one or more amino acids that make meat a more complete form of protein. As a result, vegetarians often have to combine different types of nonmeat proteins to enjoy the same health benefits or take supplement pills. We suggest selecting a variety of protein sources and avoiding cooking methods (e.g., frying) that rob proteins of much of their nutritional value.

Adding Fiber. Many Americans do not get enough fiber in their diet (FDA, n.d.b). Fiber, or dietary fiber, has a lot of health benefits. Soluble fiber, found in beans, peas, and some fruits and vegetables, can be broken down by your body and provides some calories. Soluble fiber has also been shown to block the absorption of fat and low-density lipoprotein (i.e., the "bad" cholesterol). Insoluble fiber isn't absorbed by the body and is used to bulk stool and reduce constipation. This form of fiber is found in whole-grain foods (e.g., whole-grain flour pasta or bread or brown rice), wheat bran, and some fruits and vege-tables. Remember, not all breads or pastas provide all of the health benefits they should. If the flour has been bleached (e.g., white bread) or processed (i.e., milled), then it may be lacking some of the minerals, vitamins, and beneficial fats that whole-grain food has. Even enriched flour (i.e., flour that has some of its nutrients added back in after processing) is not as good for your body as whole-grain wheats. Check the label. If the ingredient doesn't say "whole grain," then it is probably processed, and therefore not as good for you.

Avoid Sugary and Caffeinated Drinks. We know you're probably going to consume large amounts of soda, energy drinks, and sugary coffee beverages in order stay awake, focused, and energized for schoolwork. Research indicates that drinking low to moderate amounts of caffeine (i.e., the equivalent of two cups of coffee or less per day) can have positive (or at least no negative) health effects (Whiteman, 2015). Coffee and tea, with little or no additives (e.g., cream or sugar) are healthier choices than soda or energy drinks. Soda, energy drinks, and sugary coffee have a lot of other types of additives (e.g., sodium, sugar, and fats) that mitigate or even eliminate the health benefits of moderate caffeine consumption. Drinking too much caffeine can also harm your ability to sleep, make you irritable, and harm your digestion. Caffeine is a drug and, like all drugs, must be used responsibly and in moderation. Other-wise, you can develop a caffeine addiction, and wrestle with negative health implications (e.g., headaches, muscle cramps, and concentration difficulties) in your everyday life.

Drinking Alcohol (in Moderation). Research shows that you are highly likely to consume alcohol before you turn 21. Turning 21 for some will likely be a legal license for what they may have been doing prior to being of age. Monitoring the Future found that nearly 20% of 12th graders reported binge drinking (i.e., having five or more alcoholic beverages in a row) at least once in the 2 weeks leading up to taking the survey (Johnston et al., 2017). The National Institute on Alcohol Abuse and Alcoholism (2019) found that nearly 60% of college students aged 18 to 22 drink, and that two out of three engaged in binge drinking. It's important to know that drinking alcohol, especially binge drinking, can seriously harm your intellectual and emotional development. Your brain chemistry is still developing, and will continue to do so into your mid to late 20s. Alcohol can impede and influence this process in negative ways. You will need to be sure you are drinking responsibly. The Centers for Disease Control and Prevention (CDC, 2020) recommends no more than 1 drink per day for women and 2 drinks per day for men (and, no, you can't abstain from alcohol for 6 days, and have 7 drinks [for women] or 14 drinks [for men] on a Friday!). Check the chart in the link provided in the callout box below to get a sense of what a responsible amount of alcohol consumption is based on your weight. Remember, one drink is equivalent to 14 grams of pure alcohol, or one 12-ounce 5% alcohol by volume (ABV) beer, one 5-ounce 12% ABV glass of wine, or one 1.5-ounce 40% ABV of liquor. Once you turn 21, you may be inclined to celebrate by going to bars, going to house parties, or relaxing with a beer and watching a movie. Any and all of these things, in themselves, are not a problem, but can be if you consume too much alcohol or too frequently. These problems are often exacerbated when social drinking (e.g., fraternities, sororities, and other organizations) because there is added pressure to engage in risking drinking behaviors (e.g., binge drinking, sexual violence) when under the influence of alcohol. Alcoholism is a serious disease, and using alcohol because you are sad or depressed will only make things worse. If you feel that you cannot use alcohol without engaging in binge drinking, risky behaviors (e.g., unsafe sex), or criminal activity (e.g., fighting or vandalism), then you should abstain from drinking. Drinking can be a way to celebrate, relax, or socialize, but if your drinking habits put yourself or others in harm's way, then you are putting yourself on a road of self-destruction.

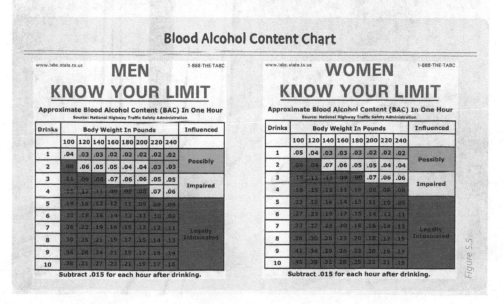

Blood Alcohol Content Chart

Figure 5.5

Veg-Out (at Least) Once a Week. If you are a meat-eater (i.e., not a vegan or vegetarian), then it is important that you monitor your meat intake. Although some meat can be an important part of your diet, too much meat, (especially processed meat) can harm your health. The World Health Organization (2015) has labeled processed meats (i.e., those which were created using some type of preservation process, such as ham, sausage, or hot dogs) as meats that have a known association to cancer, particularly colorectal cancer. Foregoing meat for just 1 day (e.g., "meatless Monday") reduces the consumption of meat and the harmful health effects associated with eating too much or processed meat. You can also make one meal a day off limits to meat (e.g., "meatless midday meal"). In addition to the health benefits, most nonmeat forms of protein (e.g., beans) are much cheaper than meat, so it'll be easier on your bank account. And, best of all, eating nonmeat forms of protein in lieu of meat is good for the global environment. Cows, for example, contribute the most methane of any animal, and are the least efficient farmland-to-protein ratio animal that can be consumed. By eating nonmeat forms of protein, you can reduce not only air pollution, but land and water pollution from large-farm fecal, pesticide, and fertilizer runoff.

Sleeping

Minimum Hours. According to the National Sleep Foundation (n.d.a), young adults aged 18 to 25 years generally need 7 to 9 hours of sleep per night. It may be permissible to get as few as 6 hours and as much as 11 hours of sleep,

Figure 5.6

depending on your level of activity, metabolism, and other factors. There's no absolutely correct amount of sleep to get for each person; however, if you dedicate yourself to getting a certain amount of sleep and you feel tired or groggy the next day, then it may be due to too little or too much sleep. Once you find your ideal amount of sleep, try to make sure that you get that much every night. You may think you can stay up all night and power through an essay with enough energy drinks, but you're probably better off getting a good night's sleep and working on the paper in the morning. Spending days without good sleep isn't a badge of honor or a marker of how dedicated you are; it's an unhealthy and unsustainable practice that can lead to depression, insomnia, and other health problems.

Set a Schedule. One of the hardest things to do in college is to set a schedule for when you are going to sleep. Some days you have very little homework or there are no parties going on, and it's easy to be in bed at the time you need to get your required amount of sleep. Other times, it seems like there are a million different things to do and getting some shut-eye is the last thing on your mind. However, it's important that you set a schedule for yourself on when you are going to go to sleep and try to stick to it. You'll find that when you stick to a schedule of sleep, you'll also have an easier time setting a schedule for getting up in the morning and being ready to face the day.

> **Student Voice**
>
> Healthy means knowing your limits, focusing on yourself, accepting things that waste your energy, and eating good nutritious meals. Working, volunteering, and going to school can be a lot, but the main thing that allows you to juggle is to know your limits. —*Maurice*

Develop a Pre-sleep Ritual. One way to promote good sleeping habits and a strong schedule is to develop a presleep ritual. Many people brush their teeth before sleeping, but there are a host of other things that can be done, such as reading, stretching, or eating a very light snack. Avoid activities that can cause wakefulness, such as looking at computer or smartphone screens, watching television, eating large meals, or drinking caffeine. And, you may think that imbibing alcohol or other depressants can help you get to sleep, but your sleep will not be as restful or effective. Getting ready for sleep means putting yourself in the mental space for it—so late-night checking your social media (or your crush's social media) is definitely a no-no.

Catching Up on the Weekends. You may think that yo-yo sleep or the practice of getting little sleep during the week and "catching up" on the weekend can get you through the semester, but there is compelling evidence that indicates that this is not the case (Webster, 2008). Most researchers agree that each night that you don't get enough sleep you are adding to your sleep deficit. The more time you shave off of your sleep—whether to work on a paper or to party—the more harm you do to your cognitive, emotional, and psychological health. If you want to do well on your exams, form good relationships with people, and feel satisfied and fulfilled, then getting good, even sleep is one of the most important components of your health.

Naps. There are few things in this world that are as glorious as an afternoon nap. But napping is not a substitute for getting a good night's sleep and, in fact, may be harming your ability to get to sleep on time. As the Sleep Foundation (n.d.b) reports, naps should only last for 20 to 30 minutes to prevent you from going into REM (i.e., rapid-eye movement), or deep, sleep. Napping for longer than this amount of time may result in you feeling tired or groggy afterward because you entered into full sleep cycle and have interrupted it. The only exception to this is if you have the time to nap for approximately 90 minutes, so you can achieve one full sleep cycle. If you feel like you need to nap for more than 90 minutes, it means you aren't getting enough sleep at night, and you need to reevaluate your sleep schedule. And, if you are constantly sleeping for long periods of time during the day but continue to feel tired or fatigued, you may wish to talk with a health professional about your physical, mental, or emotional health.

Exercising

Talk with University Employees. You should not start an exercise routine without the advice from an expert on what is best for your health. Many universities offer memberships to their recreational or gym centers as a part of your student fees. In addition to providing equipment and space, your university-trained professionals can help keep you safe and improve your health. If you are going to do an activity you have never done before (e.g., lifting weights), don't just wing it! Talk to the professionals at the center, let them give you tips for best practices. And, if necessary, let them "spot" you (i.e., ensure your safety as you lift weights). Even if you have done the activity before, it's always better to be safe than sorry. Your perfectly sculpted biceps will mean very little if you drop 300 pounds of weights on your chest while bench-pressing.

Set a Realistic Schedule and Goals. After spending all morning in classes, completing your homework, and eating lunch at the cafeteria, you probably feel like hanging out and playing a video game or binge-watching some shows for the next few hours. But, not so fast! You need to set some goals and a schedule for exercise. Physical activity isn't about getting the perfect bikini bod, swole, or other type of muscle mania. Rather, a moderate

Figure 5.7

amount of physical activity is good for your physical, emotional, and psychological well-being as well as sharpening your cognitive abilities. Many people, who haven't established an exercise routine often overdo it and plan such extraordinary tasks that they end up failing. The entire exercise industry banks on the people who sign up for a gym membership and never use it. Avoid wasting time and money by setting a simple, doable schedule. If you complete it and find enjoyment, then start to increase your workout time. The American Heart Association (2018) recommends 30 minutes of exercise per day, 5 days a week (or 150 minutes of moderate exercise per week). You don't even have to exercise all at once—take three 10-minute walks (one after each meal). You'll find your mind will be more alert and ready to learn!

> **Student Voice**
>
> I have been in college for about 10 years because I work full-time while going to school. And, I can say what I've learned is that there's no way to evade all stress, but you can minimize it. —*Irnea*

Stretching. Although you may think that you should stretch before strenuous physical activity, recent research indicates that this may not be beneficial. The Mayo Clinic (n.d.) states that stretching should not be viewed only as a form of warm-up; rather, consider mixing light stretching with a dynamic warm-up (e.g., walking, jumping jacks, or jogging) before exercise. Heavy stretching everyday minimizes the likelihood of injury due to physical activity and increased flexibility, but can harm performance if done immediately prior to exercise. Stretching should be viewed as a form of physical activity, not simply a precursor to it. Whether you are doing stretches in your home after waking up or before sleeping or going to the yoga studio, stretching can be an important part of your exercise routine.

Wear Appropriate Gear. As a college student, you probably don't have a lot of money to spend on the latest and greatest gear for whatever form of physical activity you wish to do. And, yes, you probably don't need the $300 GPS tracking watch to see how quickly you completed your cycling route, but you shouldn't skimp on getting appropriate gear for exercise if you want to stay healthy. If you plan on jogging or running, don't use your everyday shoes—buy a pair of comfortable running shoes. The benefits that exercise may have on your cardiovascular health will be quickly outweighed by the strain you put on your back, knees, and feet if you are improperly geared for running. And, not just running, but almost any type of physical activity will require you to invest some money in your health.

Bring a Friend. As with almost anything else in life, involving a friend makes it better! Gray (2011) found that college students who exercise regularly more frequently cited "bringing friends" as a top facilitator. In other words, those who exercised with friends were more likely to maintain a consistent exercise schedule. Friends can also keep you safe, whether it's spotting you on weight lifting or accompanying you as you run or cycle around town. If you don't have a friend who wants to exercise with you, then your university gym or recreation center may have a buddy system you can sign up for or you can join one of the exercise classes and meet new people. Getting healthy and finding a new friend? Sounds like a winning combination!

Student Voice

The time you spend studying is just as important as the time you spend not studying so if it fits in your schedule to see a friend, you gotta do it! If you can consolidate work and play, say by having a service industry job, I highly recommend that as well. Then you get paid to socialize. And if you get a bad grade you can't let it carry into the rest of the semester. As the great Cardi B once said, "Look myself in the mirror, I say we gon' win. Knock me down nine times but I get up ten." —*Chanelle*

Activism for Environmental Sustainability

Although it's important to establish good eating, sleeping, and exercise habits, those activities won't matter if you live in an environment that doesn't support or that actively undermines them with pollution or environmental degradation. When people think about environmentalism, they may think about increasing the amount of recycling centers on campus, planting trees, or calling for energy-efficient lightbulbs in all the buildings. There is nothing wrong with these forms of activism, and in fact we believe if there is a need on your campus for these types of resources then you should organize around these activities. For example, the Environmental Protection Agency (2009) noted that if every U.S. household switched just one lightbulb from incandescent to an energy-efficient bulb, then it would offset the pollution equivalent to 800,000 vehicles. These types of everyday ways to address the environment provide options for people to make choices that minimize their harm to the environment and promote its protection and growth. As the old saying goes, "Better take care of this planet, it's the only one we have." You wouldn't want to live in a house filled with trash, dirty air, and unclean water, so it makes sense to do things that mitigate or eliminate those harms to your community.

Figure 5.8

However, we also believe that the environment requires more attention than can be addressed through our individual consumer choices. Take, for example, the use of chlorofluorocarbons (CFCs). According to the American Chemical Society (n.d.), CFCs were once used in everyday items, such as refrigerators, aerosol sprays (e.g., hair spray), and paints. Despite evidence that CFCs were creating a hole in Earth's ozone layer (i.e., the layer of atmosphere that protects against solar damage) above the Arctic in the 1980s, people did not stop buying or using the items that used the chemical, nor did companies (which profited from their use in household items) stop producing or marketing them to consumers. After continued research, and pressure from environmental activist groups, nations around the world decided to act. The governments of 57 nations, including the United States, signed the Montreal Protocol and pledged to reduce and eventually eliminate the use of CFCs, creating real change. As Molina, one of the primary researchers into ozone loss stated, "It doesn't matter where CFCs are emitted. It is a global problem. What is important is that it led to an international agreement that solved the problem" (ACA, n.d., para. 17). And, best of all, it worked! In the 30 years that have followed, the level of CFCs has dropped significantly, and the ozone layer is starting to repair itself (Dreamer, 2016).

The activism around CFCs shows that the power of individual consumer choices is limited in addressing environmental problems that affect individuals, cities, nations, or even the entire Earth. If, for example, people stopped using CFC products in France, but consumers in the United States didn't stop, then the damage to the ozone layer would have continued. Similarly, the harm done by oil spills, fracking, improper hazardous material waste management, landfills, and traffic congestion are bigger than the sum of the individual actions of any one person or group of people. They require wider collective action that works toward change for sustainable practices.

Almost all environmental activism has to address the lack of information or active misinformation that harms the public's ability to understand and challenge bad actors. Wander and Jaehne (2000) observed that science is often called upon to advance and modify the allocation of our national resources while simultaneously being vilified for that expertise. If one thing has become clear from environmental activism, it's that the harms of pollution or environmental degradation are often subtle and long-term, making them invisible to most people. The depletion of the ozone layer, the use of harmful pesticides, or runoff from factory farms can have profound, cumulative effects on a population, but are sometimes not easily recognized until it's too late to reverse the damage. Many people may not believe there is a problem because they are not experiencing any immediate harmful effects and may be distrustful of scientists, government officials, or activists who are

Figure 5.9

working to keep the environment sustainable for living. The lack of information, and sometimes the inability or unwillingness of people to understand the harm they are at risk for, can fuel environmental degradation through inaction, indifference, and negligence.

Unfortunately, a lack of knowledge is not the only barrier. Some companies actively spread misinformation and, in their pursuit of profits, put people and other living creatures at risk. Some companies engage in *greenwashing*, or the practice of marketing their environmental-friendly stance while continuing other practices that harm or degrade the environment. For example, TransCanada assured the public that the Keystone XL

Pipeline was the safest way to transport oil from the fields to refineries near the Gulf of Mexico. However, within about a year after construction, the pipeline leaked almost 10,000 barrels worth of oil, or the equivalent of nearly 500,000 gallons (Katz, 2018). And, TransCanada is not alone. Many companies that harm the environment tout their emphasis on renewable energy (e.g., Exxon, Shell, and BP; Berke, 2017) or love of the natural world (e.g., Monsanto, n.d.) while raking in billions of dollars using practices that harm safe drinking water, clean air, viable soil, and workers. The truth is that many of these corporations' commitments to the environment are often simply marketing ploys, with little positive impact on the environment. And, they will go to extraordinary lengths to misinform the public in pursuit of their bottom line (Kahl, 2019).

Five Tips for Describing Your Issue

Describe it emotionally. Engage people's hearts through powerful imagery, a potent catchphrase, or a call to action.

Describe it factually. Make sure your assertions are based in facts, so you don't undermine your credibility.

Describe it visually. Creating performances, artistic expressions, symbols, or signs can focus people's attention.

Describe it personally. Help your audience see themselves in your cause. How does it affect or relate to them?

Describe it morally. Describe your movement and the problem you address in terms of good/bad, ethical/unethical, and safe/unsafe. Create clear lines between what is right and wrong.

Remember to combine these techniques. None of these tips are sufficient by themselves. You have to be able to articulate your issue intelligently, succinctly, and forcibly in all of these ways if you wish to create change.

Your job in environmental activism then, like with any type of activism, is to raise consciousness around issues and to help inform your community about the issues or problems. To do this, you'll need to focus on both boots-on-the-ground and digital-information activism. Before you get out into the streets, though, the first step is to articulate what issue you want to address. Remember, in all forms of activism, but especially in environmental activism, it is important that you know your audience has the same knowledge base and approach to reasoning that you do. There are people who believe that mass shootings in schools are planned or faked by the government; that millions of illegal immigrants vote in elections; or that lizard-people, Jewish people, and/or the Illuminati control the world's economies. These people are not necessarily mentally ill—many are everyday folks who live in a world divorced from evidence. In fact, the Mitchell, Gottfried, Barthal, and Sumida (2018) found that only about one in four Americans could tell the difference between a factual statement and an opinion. As they state, "When Americans call a statement factual they overwhelmingly also think it is accurate; they tend to disagree with factual statements they incorrectly label as opinions." In other words, people think their opinions are fact, and facts that they don't agree with are opinions. You have to think clearer than this while also recognizing that most people you encounter (i.e., about 75%) can't or won't. Your messaging, then, will have to be short, direct, and on target if it is to be effective. The more you say, the more opportunities you give others to misinterpret your message or, even worse, give those who oppose your activism the opportunity to reframe your message into something negative. Your ability articulate the subject in a language that your audience understands will set the stage for a common understanding of how to address the issue.

Five Tips for Identifying Your Audience

Identify those affected by the issue. There is nothing worse than an activist who has no connection or relationship with the people who actually have to navigate the issue. Make sure your activism is a way to amplify their concerns.

Identify decision makers. Who are the people who have a say in the decision-making process? Make sure to identify and (potentially) contact each person, organization, or office that has any power in the issue.

Identify opposition. These folks are not "the enemy," but they are people who are advocating for things that are counter to your activism. Who are they? What motivates them? What tactics have they used in the past in their effort to win?

Identify potential allies. Find out the people, organizations, or offices who may be willing to aid you. Sometimes this is very explicit, such as contacting an environmentalist group (e.g., the Sierra Club) for information or help on an environmental cause. Other times, allies may not be quite so explicitly connected. For example, teachers' unions (who typically only deal with workplace disputes) may be inclined to help your organization campaign against the use of pesticides that have been known to harm children's health.

Identify stakeholders. Pinpoint those parties who will be affected by the issue. These folks may not be allies or opposition, but may become one of those groups as the advocacy gains more attention.

Remember to connect these groups. Once you have identified each of these groups, you will need to map out how these groups have, may, and will interact with one another as you engage in your activism.

After you begin informing and persuading people, you'll need to work with others to identify your audience, articulate the issue, and compose a vision for change (O'Hair, Rubenstein, & Stewart, 2010). First, you need to think about who your audience is in your message. Are you trying to convince people who don't believe in your message? Or, are you informing people who don't know anything about your topic? Or, are you trying to give information and emotional energy to an already sympathetic audience? Or, perhaps you're looking to persuade a group of people who are sympathetic to your cause to engage in a specific type of action (e.g., sign a petition, march in a demonstration, or write an official). *Whatever your aim, you must be purposeful and knowledgeable about what you are trying to accomplish.* For example, if you approach a group of people who are not knowledgeable or passionate about your cause and you are very aggressive and agitated, then it may turn them off your message. Conversely, if you go to a group that's very passionate about an issue, and you are very qualified and milquetoast about the problem, then they may doubt your sincerity to the cause. Knowing who *not* to talk to is just as important as knowing who to talk to as well. If you have a message and another person seems hostile or indifferent to your message, then you may want to move on to someone else. Your time may be better spent informing a person than it is trying to convince someone who has already made up their mind (O'Hair et al., 2010).

Five Tips for Composing a Vision for Change

Keep it simple. Have a detailed document that outlines your activism and organization for internal purposes, but do not use it for engaging with the public. Instead, public communication should be short, direct, and explicit. Slogans should generally be around five words.

Keep it positive. Slogans or chants that incite violence or name-call can detract from your advocacy. Make sure your activism is animated by a positive vision for what kind of world you want through your work.

Keep it concrete. Make sure that your slogan directs attention to your cause. For example, if you are advocating for reducing pesticide runoff in a river, "Love the Planet" may be a fine sentiment, but it's not concrete. Instead, a slogan such as "Clean Rivers = Healthy Children" better describes your cause, and the connections you are trying to bring attention to through your activism.

Keep it factual. If your activism is based on faulty information, then people will be less likely to believe that your cause is worthy. Keeping your vision factual can raise your cause's credibility.

Keep it inclusive. Using chants or slogans that attack other people can very easily backfire. Not only will your opposition use your language to discredit your movement,

continues

potential allies may be turned off by what they perceive as your hateful rhetoric. For example, many people have made jokes about President Trump being in a same-sex relationship with Russia's president, Vladimir Putin. These jokes not only do not address the substance of the issue (e.g., Russian interference in U.S. elections), it does so by equating bad administrative behavior with same-sex desire.

Remember to connect visions. Once you have brainstormed a few ideas, try to make an argument for why your vision addresses each of the different tips. You may not be able to address each one, every time, but the more you can, the better your slogan will be. For example, "We are the 99%" is a slogan about income inequality and asserts that the needs of the many (the 99%) should be given precedence over the desires of the rich (the 1%). It's simple, positive, factual, and inclusive. However, it's not, on its face, concrete. What things should be done to address the needs of the 99%? What changes can be made and how would it help? Those aren't addressed in the slogan. However, "We are the 99%" continues to be one of the most powerful slogans of the 21st century.

Finally, you'll offer your vision for change. This part of your messaging is where you propose your solution and address how it will fix the problem or galvanize some form of action. Make sure that you are not asking too much or too little of your audience. If they are in the streets ready to march, signing a petition may seem underwhelming. And, conversely, asking them to march in a demonstration may be too much if they aren't sufficiently knowledgeable or passionate about the topic. After you have described the problem or issue, people who are sympathetic to your cause will want to do something about it. Your job is to articulate exactly what you want to do with others to create change, and then describe exactly how that action will produce some type of change. How will putting pressure on a senator by calling their office help your cause? How will staging a sit-in at the university president's office elicit change? Once you have articulated what you are going to do, you need to describe what your college, community, state, or nation will look like once the problem has been removed. If your college divests (i.e., stops investing) from fossil fuels, what changes can the community expect? You need to be able to address how the world that you want to see is comparatively better than the world you live in right now, and be able to communicate that vision to your audience.

Overall, working with others to raise consciousness and increase information about an issue is an important step in activism for a cause. However, your group's advocacy cannot focus solely on providing information. It is easy for many corporations who will oppose your advocacy for environmental protections to buy media coverage, lobby politicians, and hire lawyers to stop or derail you. So, although you may have a person dedicated to social media management or writing to local newspapers, you'll need to engage in direct forms of activism as well. But, you have to spend the time to articulate your message and get it out to the right people on the right platforms. The "revolution may not be televised" as the song by Gil Scott Heron goes, but, it will certainly be "snapped, tweeted, and Face-booked." Get out there and get to talking!

****

While you are in college, it will be vital that your eating, sleeping, and exercise habits support your journey to be the best possible you. There will be many distractions, sidesteps, and pitfalls along the way, but if you remain vigilant and responsible, you'll find that your physical, mental, and emotional health will be in an optimal place for your success. Although certainly there will be times when you make bad decisions, we hope that they aren't so bad or so often that you harm your potential to reach your full capabilities. Part of the human experience is to take risks and have fun, and we certainly don't want to imply that you shouldn't have any, but broken homes and hearts should never be the price of your choices.

As you navigate college, and beyond, it will become increasingly important to protect your environment so that it makes obtaining good eating, sleeping, and exercise habits possible. Securing national and state parks, decreasing the use of pesticides and herbicides in farming and landscaping, limiting and eliminating fossil fuels, and securing the right to clean air, water, and land will become increasingly difficult as competition among corporations increases over scarce resources and they pander, bribe, or bully federal, state, or local governments to sell off our world's most precious resources. Your work for environmental causes will be integral to supporting a livable world now, and a sustainable future for the generations who come after.

Discussion Questions

- At this point in your college career, what changes have you noticed in your relationship with family members?

- How successful have you been at balancing fun and responsibility?

Student Challenge

- Make a list of your strongest characteristics (e.g., punctual, athletic, kind). Then make a list of your weakest characteristics (e.g., disorganized, easily distracted). After reading Chapter 5, what steps can you take to bolster your strong characteristics and improve on the weaker ones?

- Identify environmental hazards on campus and/or in the community. What contribution can you make to improving the situation?

CHAPTER 6

Romance, Fluidity, and Consent

CHAPTER OBJECTIVES

By the end of the chapter, you should be able to:

- Identify how society normalizes sexual violence

- Define consent by distinguishing between "No means No" and "Yes means Yes"

- Define types of sexual and romantic activity and pleasure

- Develop safe-sex practices and healthy communication around sexual activity

- Connect activism on sexual activism to matters of consent and sexual health

ORIENTING QUESTIONS

As you read the chapter, try to answer the following questions:

- How prevalent is sexual violence in general? On college campuses?

- What constitutes affirmative sexual consent?

- What's the difference between honest consent and manipulated consent?

On January 18, 2015, Brock Turner walked with an intoxicated woman (at the time named Emily Doe to protect her identity, who later revealed herself as Chanel Miller) back from a party and was found in an alley sexually assaulting her later that night. Two Swedish students, Peter Lars Jonsson and Carl-Fredrik Arndt, intervened during the assault, tackled Brock, and held him until police arrived. Brock's defense at the trial was that both he and the woman were intoxicated and that the assault was a matter of miscommunication between two consenting adults. Emily Doe, who was unconscious at the time that Jonsson and Arndt had intervened, stated that her level of intoxication made it impossible to give consent.

Brock Turner's father, in a letter to the judge, argued that Brock's life goals shouldn't be affected by "20 minutes of action" (Miller, 2016). On March 30, 2015, Brock was found guilty on three charges: two for sexual assault and one for attempted rape. The outrage at Brock's actions against Emily Doe, and his attempt to place blame on her for his actions, was

A Powerful Letter

Visit https://www.buzzfeednews.com/article/katiejmbaker/heres-the-powerful-letter-the-stanford-victim-read-to-her-ra to read Emily Doe's powerful letter to Brock Turner. Caution: It is explicit, and deals with violence and rape.

only matched by the outrage at his light sentencing: a mere 6 months, of which he only served 3. Brock even tried appealing his sentence, reasserting that his actions were not rape because he only wanted "outercourse" (i.e., nonpenetrative sexual activity). His appeal has been denied, but there is still the chance that he will appeal that decision to the California State Supreme Court (Hauser, 2018).

Figure 6.1

Unfortunately, Brock Turner's story is one that is all too common in today's society. According to the Rape, Abuse & Incest National Network (RAINN), there are approximately 320,000 victims of rape each year in the United States, and less than 1% of perpetrators will be incarcerated (RAINN, n.d.b). Although anyone can be a target of sexual violence, the vast majority of cases are perpetrated against women and gender nonconforming people. And, although women make up the majority of cases, trans and gender-variant people are the most at-risk for being targeted for sexual violence (RAINN, n.d.a). Sexual assault against women on college campuses is especially prevalent, with female students three times more likely to be assaulted than women in general (RAINN, n.d.a). And, although certainly anyone can be a perpetrator or victim to sexual assault, some organizations on campus foster this abusive type of culture. Men who join fraternities are approximately three times more likely to commit rape than nonfraternity men (Foubert, Newberry, & Tatum, 2007) and women who join sororities are twice as likely to experience attempted rape and four times more likely to experience completed rape than their nonsorority counterparts (Minow & Einolf, 2009).

To make matters worse, colleges and the judicial system have demonstrated an inability and unwillingness to take sexual assault seriously on campuses. For example, after finding a male student responsible for sexual assault, the Gustavus Adolphus College response was barring the student from some campus activities and making him write a 500-word essay. They did not expel the student and, in fact, allowed him to remain in on-campus housing (New, 2016). Or, Austin James Wilkerson, a male student at the University of Colorado, who was indicted on a Class 3 felony charge for raping a female student, which has a maximum penalty of 12 years in prison. Instead, Austin served no prison time and was given parole and work or school release (Fox News, 2016). Or, David Becker, a Massachusetts high school senior, who was charged with indecent assault and battery against two women. Instead of the prosecutor's recommended 2-year prison sentence and demand that he register as a sex offender, the judge gave him only 2 years of parole and counseling. Becker was also allowed to serve his sentence in Ohio, where he planned to attend college (Hauser, 2016). These stories, as well as the statistics of sexual assault, show that U.S. universities' and society's responses to sexual violence are woefully inadequate.

When most people talk about sexual violence, they conjure up images of masked men hiding in bushes waiting for unsuspecting victims. However, as RAINN (n.d.c) reports, approximately 7 out of 10 perpetrators of sexual violence knew the victim. Some of those in this group are serial rapists or previously convicted offenders; however, some are people (primarily men) who have grown up in a society that views sexual activity as an important part of their (often masculine) identity, and, as a result, are more likely to push past consensual boundaries. Drugs and alcohol certainly exacerbate the problem by lowering inhibitions and increasing the likelihood that a rapist can take advantage of another person. However, make no mistake, unwanted sexual activity—whether while under the influence or not—is still sexual violence. If students want to live, work, and play on campuses and in safe communities, then there needs to be more conversations about how to seriously and appropriately deal with sexual violence in the context of relationships.

This chapter, then, is devoted to providing a language for consent, sex positivity, and romantic relationships while addressing sexual violence. We believe that romantic and sexual activity—when they are consensual, pleasurable, and safe—are important components in making sure that people are able to realize their capabilities. Sexual violence and unsafe sex practices are impediments to realizing one's capabilities. To this end, we first start by marking an important shift in recent thinking about what constitutes sexual consent—from "No means No" to "Yes means Yes." We then explain sexual health from a sex-positive standpoint. That is to say, we are interested in talking about romantic and sexual activity from the view that when they are done consensually and safely, then they are a pleasurable part of the human experience. Finally, we offer that activism promoting bystander intervention can be a powerful way to change conversations about sexual violence for all genders. When sexual violence is viewed as a social problem, and not an individual one, then addressing it becomes a community issue in which we all have a role in making life—within and beyond college—safer.

From "No Means No" to "Yes Means Yes"

One of the most pervasive problems that faces U.S. society in general, and higher education in particular, is how to engage in consensual sexual and romantic activity. So much of U.S. media portrays females as passive recipients of male-initiated romantic activity. And, all too often, that activity is initiated despite or over the protests of the female, who eventually succumbs to the male's charm or determination. Just as unfortunate, is the near erasure of nonheterosexual relationships or opposite-sex relationships from mainstream media, which means that many young LGBTQ youth have few role models (positive or negative) for developing romantic interests or engaging in sexual activity. Finally, many public schools, from pressure from misguided parents and religious groups, either do not offer any sex education classes or only offer them in ways that cater to opposite-sex couples, with an emphasis on abstinence and pregnancy prevention rather than consent and pleasure (Planned Parenthood, n.d.a). As a result, even though the majority of Americans want comprehensive sex education for young people, most state and federal programs are ineffective, factually incorrect, and oppressive.

Figure 6.2

How Does Your State Do on Sex Ed?

Ever wondered what kind of sexual education is promoted in your state? Want to find out if it is grounded in evidence or ideology? Take a look at the University of California's Department of Nursing information: https://nursing.usc.edu/blog/americas-sex-education/

Unfortunately, people who have a poor understanding of sexual consent also are in positions of power and create laws that harm vulnerable populations. In North Carolina, lawmakers have still not changed a 1979 statute that states that a person cannot revoke consent for sex once intercourse has taken place (Redden, 2016). In Oklahoma, the court system dismissed a rape case against a 17-year-old male who had oral sex with a 16-year-old female who was unconscious and registered a .34 blood alcohol level (Redden, 2016). Former Missouri Congressman Todd Akin stated, "If it's legitimate rape, the female body has ways to try to shut the whole thing down," implying that women who get pregnant from rape were, on some level, willing participants in their own violence (Alter, 2014). Many states still recognize the "gay panic" defense, which allows a defendant to claim that they were justified in killing a gay person who made a "pass" at them (Browning, 2018). These laws, statutes, and court rulings all have the effect of enforcing a culture that seriously misunderstands the role of consent in having healthy, pleasurable sexual contact.

Traditionally, activists and organizers for sexual justice have pushed against this culture on a variety of fronts, but with the mantra of "No means No" articulating much of their efforts. We do not wish to impugn their work—their efforts have brought attention to a great many wrongs in society and have benefited many people. However, we believe the "No means No" approach to sexual consent has some serious limitations. First, it puts victims in the role of defending themselves against sexual violence and gives rise to the mistaken belief that rape would not occur if survivors were more forcible, explicit, or sincere in their rejection. The threat or use of violence (whether physical violence, or threats against one's career, livelihood, or children) can encourage a person to "go along" with sexual violence for fear of reprisal. This means assault may not "look like" what society deems as a rape (i.e., overt violence, signs of struggle, or a masked man) and, as a result, lead people to misrecognize the depth and seriousness of sexual violence a person faces. Second, it puts pressure on one party to be the gatekeeper to the other, and assumes that one party will always "want it" while the other party should "guard it." This type of thinking creates an unhealthy dynamic between people who wish to have a sexual or romantic encounter because it assumes one is the "active" member while the other is "passive." In short, the ethic of "No means No" falls short of the type of values society must have if it wants to ensure that people are safe from sexual violence.

Many people on campuses and beyond are moving toward the ethics encapsulated in the phrase "Yes means Yes," or affirmative consent. The values of this movement assert that consent must be obtained, explicitly and enthusiastically, at every level of sexual or romantic contact. In other words, there should never be any doubt that intimate contact is fully supported by both parties—before and during the interaction. The benefits of this perspective are plain. It ensures that sexual and romantic contact is mutually pleasurable because it is done without hesitation or reservation. Without the presence of affirmative consent, people in the interaction may feel guilty, violated, uneasy, or stressed because of indecision or a sense of coercion. It ensures that there is no ambiguity or sense of

Student Voice

I work at a bar on the weekend to make ends meet while I complete my degree. This one time, this man called and was just being creepy. After about a minute of talking with him, I tell him I have to go back to work. He tells me to hold on, that I'm beautiful, and that I'm about to help him have a happy ending. I hang up as quickly as I could and ran out of the office. I told my manager about the call, but that I didn't get any information. He called back three other times that night, and many times over the course of a few months. Each time asking for me by name, and each time asking me for sexual favors. We had to get the police involved, but because he used a burner phone, they could not track him. Eventually he stopped calling, but I still have an escort when I leave at night, even though it had been a few months. —*Serena*

Student Voice

I was playing with one of my class friend's baby. She must have been 9 months old, and I was making her laugh. This guy just walked up and asked me if I had kids of my own, and when I said I did not, he looked at my boyfriend told him to "get on that." We were 19. —*Toniesha*

Common Myths About Sex

Your first time having sex will be painful.

Your first time having sex will be wonderful.

Failing to get an erection means there is something wrong with you.

Masturbation causes blindness, hairy palms, decreased penis size, mental disorders, and/or erectile dysfunction.

It is safe to wait until just prior to ejaculation to put on a condom.

entitlement intruding on what should be a fun and enjoyable part of the human experience. Finally, it ensures that sexual contact cannot occur in instances where consent cannot be given (e.g., too intoxicated or unconscious). In short, if you do not receive immediate, enthusiastic, and explicit affirmation from another person, then you should forego sexual or romantic contact.

Unfortunately, many people do not know how to give or receive consent in sexual or romantic encounters because of the lack of education about the subject. In fact, Planned Parenthood (2015a) found that the majority of respondents believed that consent cannot be revoked once given or that intimate contact at one level (e.g., fondling) guarantees consent at other levels (e.g., sexual penetration). There are different ways to obtain consent, but what is important is that you receive clear signs for consent before initiating activity. The most explicit way to obtain consent is to simply ask. Some people may balk at this idea of explicitly asking because they think it ruins the mood or is unsexy. However, we believe that its sexiness is all a matter delivery. Pulling out a clipboard and checking off boxes for consent is unsexy. Breathily asking, "Do you want me to touch you there?" to receive an eye-fluttering moan of "Yes, please!" is, in our opinion, eminently sexy. Real consent means *both* people *really* want to participate in the sexual act (even if it's just making out) and there is a clear "yes" from both partners. Also, don't forget that even if a partner previously said yes, they have a right to change their mind at any point, even in the middle of a sexual act. No matter your gender or sexual orientation, we advise you keep checking in, at each step. Try saying something like: "Is this still okay?" or "Do you like this?" If you get a "No" for an answer, don't be disappointed— it means you are in a healthy relationship where both people feel free to express their desires and needs. This process isn't difficult, nor does it have to be intrusive. Rather, it is a straightforward way to ensure that sexual and romantic activity are mutually pleasurable and free from coercion.

Student Voice

I was sitting next to an older male customer, helping him make a decision on the menu. We were talking about his wife, you know, small talk, like what she liked to eat. I was wearing my dark makeup with very dark purple lipstick. In the middle of talking about his wife, the man look at me, put his hand on my leg, and told me my lips looked so kissable, and he couldn't concentrate. I didn't respond and kept trying to redirect him to the menu. At the end of the transaction, he kept hitting on me, and when I told him I wasn't interested, he scratched out my tip and stormed off. —*Donna*

Asking for consent and demanding or manipulating consent are not the same thing. If you ask someone for consent and they do not enthusiastically give a "Yes!" then you should not continue the conversation. Giving pressure, in any way, undermines the consent process and makes it impossible to know if sexual or romantic contact was genuine. Take, for example, conversation between former Hollywood producer Harvey Weinstein and model Ambra Battilana Gutierrez:

Figure 6.3

Weinstein: Hey, come here. Listen to me.

Gutierrez: I want to go downstairs.

Weinstein: I'm not gonna do anything, you'll never see me again after this. Ok? That's it. If you embarrass me in this hotel, where I'm staying at ...

Gutierrez: I'm not embarrassing you.

Weinstein: Just walk ...

Gutierrez: It's just that I don't, I don't feel comfortable.

Weinstein: Honey, don't have a fight with me in the hallway.

Gutierrez: It's not nothing, it's ...

Weinstein: Please, I'm not gonna do anything. I swear on my children. Please come in. On everything, I'm a famous guy.

Gutierrez: I'm feeling very uncomfortable right now.

Weinstein: Please come in now. And one minute. And if you wanna leave, when the guy comes with my jacket you can go. (Ponsot, 2017)

Notice how Weinstein uses a variety of tactics to induce Gutierrez to come into his hotel room: force ("Come here, listen to me), guilt ("You're embarrassing me"), cajoling ("Honey, don't have a fight with me"), promises ("I swear on my children"), and threats ("I'm a famous guy"). Although Gutierrez never explicitly says "No," there is no indication that she is, in any way, comfortable with the situation. The lack of affirmative consent should be a clear indicator that his actions constituted sexual violence. Although you may never be in the exact same position as Weinstein (i.e., a powerful man in an industry), you still need to be reflexive of the way you initiate contact with others. Because of the way that media and cultural values shape society's understanding of consent, it is all too easy to push the boundaries and not do what's right by others. Securing affirmative consent in sexual and romantic interactions is the best way to fully and completely enjoy any and all activities you and your partner wish to explore.

Sexual Health and Pleasure

When we were undergraduate students, we were subjected to the type of sexual education that characterizes most introductory "College Living" or "Health Education" classes. That is to say, we were shown a bunch of pictures of genitalia riddled with various sexually transmitted infections (STIs), told the horror stories of getting pregnant or raising a child while trying to be a student (i.e., "You'll have to drop out of college!"), and that abstinence was the only way to be safe in sexual and romantic encounters. This type of education, from middle school to college, is, in part, the reason why many U.S. citizens are completely ignorant about sexual health. For example, Frost, Lindberg, and Finer (2012) found that nearly a 25% of women and 60% of men scored either a D or F in their knowledge about common contraceptive methods. The lack of honest conversations about sexual and romantic contact is a serious barrier to people's abilities to make informed choices and fulfill their capabilities.

Want More Information?

Planned Parenthood has some of the best information on comprehensive sexual education and health. For more information, visit: https://www.plannedparenthood.org/learn/stds-hiv-safer-sex/safer-sex

In this section, we detail sexual health from a model of pleasure. That is to say, we believe sexual and romantic contact is fun and fulfilling when it is done in a way that consensual and safe. Showing horrifying pictures or telling harmful stories to scare people away from sex is neither effective nor ethical. You are an adult, and as such, need to make informed decisions about your health, and, perhaps use that knowledge to inform those around you. You'll notice that we have tried our best to not frame advice assuming you're in a monogamous, cis-heterosexual relationship. Unfortunately, sexual health and pleasure research still has a *long* way to go in order to achieve information for the range of sexual orientations and expressions that characterize the human condition. So, make the best use of the information we have provided as it pertains to your sexuality. Although we offer a list of terms and information about each activity, the truth of the matter is that if you want to know what your partner likes or dislikes you should *ask* them. Keeping open communication with your partner not only ensures that you have affirmative consent, it increases the probably that both parties will have fun.

Want More Information?

Kissing is a go-to for almost any relationship. Learn to be a good kisser at: https://www.seventeen.com/love/dating-advice/advice/a7617/best-kissing-tips/

Types of Sexual and Romantic Activity

Kissing. Pressing lips together is a sign of affection between close friends, family members, and even as a sign of greeting among strangers in some cultures. However, kissing takes a different dimension as a romantic or sexual activity. Kissing can range from a quick, relatively dry smooch to a deep, passionate tongue wrestle. Good kissing is context appropriate (e.g., "making out" in a crowded room is most likely a no-no) and reciprocal (e.g., don't throw your tongue down someone's throat when they're not ready).

Figure 6.4

Masturbation. Masturbating is the act of stimulating one's genitals or erogenous zones (e.g., breasts) for pleasure. It is a common practice among American adults. According to studies (see Castleman, 2009), approximately 60% of men and 40% of women reported masturbating in the past year (and it is likely the number is higher than people report). Although not having a sexual partner increases one's likelihood to masturbate, those who are in sexually active relationships are more likely to masturbate than those in sexually inactive relationships. Masturbating does not signal weakness or a moral failing, it is a normal, healthy part of the human experience. Masturbation, like any other activity, is only a problem if you engage in it to the detriment of other aspects of your life.

Want More Information?

Masturbation is a normal part of your sexual health. Learn more at these sites:

For women:
https://www.healthline.com/health/womens-health/how-to-masturbate-for-women#types

For men:
https://www.healthline.com/health/mens-health/how-to-masturbate-for-men

Want More Information?

Mutual masturbation can be a fun way to express sexual desire. Learn more at: https://www.liberator.com/unzipped/sex-2/mutual-masturbation-tips/

Mutual Masturbation. Mutual masturbation is performed when two or more people engage in masturbation simultaneously. Some partners perform this act because they wish to be sexually expressive without engaging in penetrative sex, because they want to be sexually expressive without the risk of STI or pregnancy, or because one partner doesn't feel like having like having intercourse (e.g., one partner is sore or tired). Others find mutual masturbation as one pleasurable activity in their larger repertoire of sexual or romantic expressions. Regardless of your reasoning, mutual masturbation can be a way to enjoy sexual or romantic activity without worrying about STIs or pregnancy (as long as bodily fluids are not exchanged).

Want More Information?

Outercourse can be a fun way to express sexual desire. Learn more at: https://www.bustle.com/articles/100754-6-ways-to-be-sexual-without-intercourse-or-penetration

Outercourse. Also known as dry sex or dry humping, outercourse is the act of sexual climax without penetrative sex. This practice may include rubbing or stimulating genitals or erogenous zones over or through clothing, watching pornographic material together, or sexy-talk (e.g., sexting). Like masturbation, some people engage in this activity because they want to be sexually expressive without the risk of STI or pregnancy, or because one partner doesn't feel like having intercourse (e.g., one partner is sore or tired). Others find outercourse as one pleasurable activity in their larger repertoire of sexual or romantic expressions. Regardless of your reasoning, mutual masturbation can be a way to enjoy sexual or romantic activity without worrying about STIs or pregnancy (as long as bodily fluids are not exchanged).

Want More Information?

Manual can be a fun way to express sexual desire. Learn more at these sites:

For women:

https://www.sextherapyinphiladelphia.com/digital-stimulation-a-how-to-guide/

https://www.bustle.com/articles/201253-7-fingering-sex-tips-to-help-your-partner-rub-you-the-right-way

For men:

https://www.sextherapyinphiladelphia.com/handjob/

Manual Sex. These activities include those that involve using hands to stimulate sexual arousal or orgasm. Often called fingering (for women) or a hand job (for men), manual sex can be either a precursor to sexual intercourse or in lieu of it. Like masturbation, some people engage in this activity because they want to be sexually expressive without the risk of STI or pregnancy, or because one partner doesn't feel like having like having intercourse (e.g., one partner is sore or tired). Others find manual sex as one pleasurable activity in their larger repertoire of sexual or romantic expressions. Regardless of your reasoning, mutual masturbation can be a way to enjoy sexual or romantic activity without worrying about STIs or pregnancy (as long as bodily fluids are not exchanged).

Instrumental Sex. Instrumental sex, or using sex toys, is another way that couples can engage in sexual or romantic contact without penetrative sex. Sex toys can include dildos, vibrators, anal beads, and strap-ons. Sex toys can be used by yourself or with your partner. Females may wish to use a sex toy in tandem with vaginal intercourse to increase their ability to reach orgasm through clitoral stimulation. You should always make sure to wash sex toys after every use and, when needed, use a condom on them to ensure that bodily fluids don't get trapped in any nook or cranny.

> **Want More Information?**
>
> Instrumental sex can be a fun way to express sexual desire. Learn more at these sites:
>
> https://health.usnews.com/health-news/health-wellness/articles/2014/03/27/a-guide-to-sex-toy-safety
>
> http://mysecretsoiree.com/blog/2015/10/29/sex-toys-101/

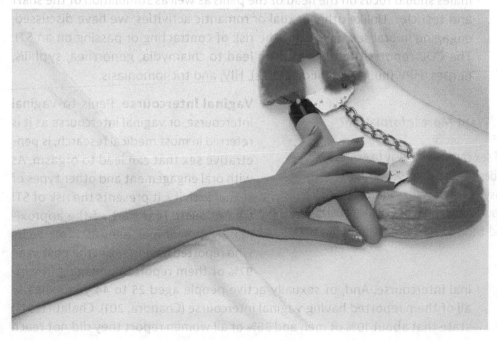

Figure 6.5

Want More Information?

Foreplay can be a fun way to express sexual desire. Learn more at: https://www.marie-claire.co.uk/life/sex-and-relationships/sex-tips-from-gay-couples-497857

Foreplay. Foreplay includes all the activities that one engages in that lead to intercourse. This act can include all of the activities mentioned thus far, plus others, such as dancing or fantasizing. Although foreplay, by definition, is the activities that lead to sex, it is important to note that anyone, at any time, can end foreplay short of sex. Foreplay does not guarantee sex! However, if sex is initiated, foreplay can often be an important part of ensuring that all parties are sexually satisfied by their partner. Foreplay is especially important for partners of women, as many females' biology make sexual arousal and orgasm slower and more difficult to achieve than males.

Want More Information?

Oral engagement/sex can be a fun way to express sexual desire. Learn more at: https://www.huffingtonpost.com/entry/what-men-need-to-know-about-vaginas_us_57608cc2e4b05e4be860231c

Oral Engagement/Sex. Oral sex is any activity where one partner uses their mouth to stimulate the erogenous zones or genitalia of their partner. Colloquially, known as "going down," "giving a blow job," or "eating out," these activities can be a precursor to intercourse or in lieu of it. Generally, oral for females should focus on the clitoris as well as using the hands for vaginal manual sex. Oral for males should focus on the head of the penis as well as stimulation of the shaft and testicles. Unlike other sexual or romantic activities, we have discussed, engaging in oral sex *does* carry the risk of contracting or passing on an STI. The CDC reports that oral sex can lead to chlamydia, gonorrhea, syphilis, herpes, HPV (human papillomavirus), HIV, and trichomoniasis.

Want More Information?

Vaginal sex can be a fun way to express sexual desire. Learn more at: https://www.psychologytoday.com/us/blog/save-your-sex-life/201108/when-sex-hurts-tips-and-tricks-overcome-discomfort

Vaginal Intercourse. Penis-to-vaginal intercourse, or vaginal intercourse as it is referred in most medical research, is penetrative sex that can lead to orgasm. As with oral engagement and other types of sexual activity, it presents the risk of STI transmission. That said, of the approximately 89% of men aged 15 to 44 years who reported having sex in the past year, 97% of them reported engaging in vaginal intercourse. And, of sexually active people aged 25 to 44 years, nearly all of them reported having vaginal intercourse (Chandra, 201). Chalabi (2015) state that about 10% of men and 36% of all women report they did not reach an orgasm in their last sexual encounter (Chalabi, 2015). 88% of men reported that their partner reached orgasm, so there is a gap in men's belief and women's reality in sexual encounters. As Chalabi (2015) notes, the more sexual acts that are performed, the higher chance there is that both parties will reach orgasm. That is, vaginal sex should be a part of a healthy repertoire of sexual acts (e.g., oral, manual, and anal sex) and foreplay. Importantly, we note that orgasms are not the sign of perfect sex, or that sex without an orgasm is bad sex. Some people cannot have orgasms, others may have difficulty depending on factors outside of their control (e.g., stress), and sometimes a person is just tired. There are a variety of reasons for not reaching an orgasm and overfocusing on reaching an orgasm can detract from the fun and intimacy of sex.

Anal Intercourse. Anal intercourse, or anal sex, is when one partner inserts their penis into another's anus, whereas anal play (e.g., anal instrumental sex, ass-to-mouth, or anal fingering) is any sexual or romantic activity involving the anus. Anal intercourse can be enjoyed by both same-sex male partners (about 90% of sexually active male couples) and opposite-sex partners (around 35% of sexually active opposite-sex couples) (WebMD, n.d.a), and anal play can be enjoyed by anyone. Although many couples find anal sex pleasurable, it is important to engage in proper preparation before engaging in it. Making sure that your partner is relaxed and comfortable, using proper lubrication, and listening to each other and your bodies can be the difference between pleasurable intercourse and disaster. Not lubricating properly or engaging in overly vigorous anal sex can tear the tissue in the anus, allowing bacteria and viruses into the bloodstream (WebMD, n.d.a). Avoid engaging in any other sexual activity after anal sex until both partners have properly washed.

> **Want More Information?**
>
> Anal intercourse can be a fun way to express sexual desire. Learn more at: https://www.refinery29.com/anal-sex-foreplay-ideas

Safer-Sex Practices

Washing. Being clean can be an important component to a healthy sex life. Just think—you were at the club dancing when you and another person decided to go back to your place for a hook up. You took a shower before you went to the club (good move!), but you've been dancing in there for a few hours—you stink of sweat, (bad) cologne, and the fruity drink that one person spilled on you. Starting off by sharing a shower can be a great way to get things going while also making sure you're clean. If you are going to engage in anal sex, it is important for you and your partner's health that you have cleaned your anal cavity, as well as anything that will go into it (e.g., penis, finger,

Common Myths About Sexual Health

- You can't get pregnant or contract an STI the first time you have sex.

- You can't get pregnant during your period.

- Anal sex is less risky than vaginal or oral sex for passing STIs.

- Condoms protect against all sexually transmitted infections.

- Only people who "sleep around" need to get checked for STIs.

- You can't get STIs from oral sex.

- You will always know if you have an STI.

- Only gay men and drug users contract HIV.

or sex toy). Finally, make sure to wash and urinate *after* engaging in sexual or romantic activity to flush out any bacteria that may have entered the urethra. Females who do not wash after sex have a higher risk of contracting a urinary tract infection (UTI; douching actually increases the likelihood of a UTI) and men who do not wash after sex can have infected, irritated skin on the penis (especially uncircumcised men) (WebMD, n.d.b).

Gloves or Finger Cot. If you are going to engage in manual sex, you may want to use a glove or finger cot. A glove can ensure that bodily fluids (e.g., semen) do not get on your hand, reducing the likelihood of passing bacteria or viruses. Gloves can also be used if you're going to engage in fisting (i.e., inserting all or a large part of your hand into another's anal cavity). A finger cot covers just one finger and ensures that your fingernails don't damage your partner's sensitive areas (e.g., clitoris or anal cavity). They also reduce the likelihood of transmitting bacteria or viruses from your fingernails to your partner.

Dental Dam. A dental dam is a small piece of latex or polyurethane used to provide a barrier between a person's mouth and their partner's genitalia (e.g., clitoris) or anus. Although you can purchase dental dams, you can also make one from a condom. Dental dams reduce the likelihood of transmitting STIs through oral sex.

Want More Information?

Want to know more about how to purchase and use a dental dam? Learn more at: https://www.cdc.gov/condomeffectiveness/Dental-dam-use.html

Want More Information?

Want to know more about how to purchase and use a condom? Learn more at: https://www.cdc.gov/condomeffectiveness/male-condom-use.html

Traditional or Male Condoms. The most commonly used form of contraceptive, condoms (i.e., prophylactics) can be acquired by purchasing them at a store or online. Many universities and local health clinics offer male condoms for free. Because the availability of male condoms is high (98% effective) and their cost is so low, there is no good reason not to wear a condom. Correct and consistent use of male condoms is a highly effective (although not perfect) way to prevent STIs and pregnancy.

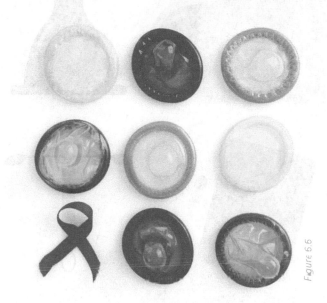

Figure 6.5

Intrauterine Implants and Contraceptives. Long-acting reversible contraceptives (LARCs) are used by females who are sexually active and who want to reduce their chances for pregnancy. Some forms are inserted into the arm, under the skin (i.e., Nexplannon), whereas others are inserted into the vaginal canal (i.e., Mirena and ParaGard) (Planned Parenthood, n.d.b). Both forms are more than 98% effective at preventing pregnancy, but they do not prevent STI transmission.

Contraceptive Pills. Contraceptive, or birth control, pills are the most used form of female contraception (CDC, 2014). Most birth control pills are hormonal supplements that, when taken as directed, prevent a woman from ovulating. This, in turn, dramatically reduces the chance of pregnancy. However, contraceptive pills do not prevent STI transmission.

Want More Information?

Want to know more about intrauterine implants and contraceptives? Learn more at: https://www.cdc.gov/reproductivehealth/contraception/index.htm

Want More Information?

Want to know more about how to purchase and use contraceptive pills? Learn more at: https://www.mayoclinic.org/drugs-supplements/ethinyl-estradiol-and-norgestimate-oral-route/description/drg-20061380

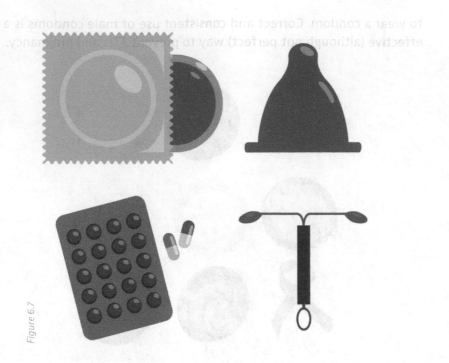

Figure 6.7

Want More Information?

Want to know more about how to purchase and use a diaphragm? Learn more at: https://www.mayoclinic.org/drugs-supplements/spermicide-vaginal-route/description/drg-20070769

Diaphragm. A diaphragm is a form of female contraceptive that is inserted in the cervix to reduce the likelihood of pregnancy. It is not used as much anymore as it needs to be fitted by a clinician. A diaphragm is 94% effective (Planned Parenthood, n.d.b), and should be used with a spermicide. Diaphragms should be inserted before sex, and are most effective when used in tandem with other forms of birth control (e.g., withdrawal or male condom). Diaphragms do not prevent STI transmission.

Withdrawal. Withdrawal, or pulling out, is used to prevent pregnancy by reducing the amount of sperm that enters the vagina by not ejaculating (aka cumming) into the vagina or vulva. This is the least effective form of contraceptive because sperm can be present in pre-ejaculate, inseminating a female even if a withdrawal is perfectly timed, every time. Withdrawal methods are most effective when used in tandem with other forms of birth control. Also, withdrawal does not prevent STI transmission.

Emergency Contraception or "Morning After Pill." There may be a time that you need to use emergency contraceptives—you forgot to take your regular birth control, a condom broke, or you used your contraceptive incorrectly. Luckily, emergency contraception can be used to prevent pregnancy. For most, emergency contraceptives take the form of a pill, using hormones much like those found in regular birth control (i.e., levo-norgestrel). If you are over 17, all forms of emergency contraception are available over the counter, although you will need to ask the pharmacist to give it to you. Taking an emergency contraception pill within 72 hours (3 days) of sexual activity is 98% effective at preventing pregnancy (WebMD, n.d.c). The emergency contraception prevents the egg's insemination by sperm (i.e., emergency contraception is not the same things as an "abortion pill").

> **Want More Information?**
>
> Want to know more about how to purchase and use emergency contraception? Learn more at: https://www.mayoclinic.org/drugs-supplements/ulipristal-oral-route/description/drg-20074458

Abortion. A woman may not know she is pregnant until after the point that emergency contraception is effective; may have taken emergency contraception, but it was ineffective; may find out that she is unable to care for a child due to a variety of circumstance; or may discover that the pregnancy may be fatal for her and/or the embryo. In these or other cases (e.g., rape or incest), a woman may opt to have an abortion, although how, when, and where a woman can obtain an abortion will vary greatly from state to state. There is the abortion pill, which is actually two types of medicine that are used to stop the progesterone hormone (mifepristone) and empty the uterus (misoprostol). You must be less than 12 weeks pregnant. This type of abortion is much like a miscarriage and is 98% effective in preventing pregnancy (Planned Parenthood, n.d.b). Another type of abortion is surgical abortion, which is an outpatient procedure that can be performed at any stage of pregnancy (depending on state law). Surgical abortions can happen in the first trimester (i.e., vacuum aspiration), second trimester (i.e., dilation and evacuation), or third trimester (i.e., dilation and extraction).

> **Want More Information?**
>
> Want to know more about how to access abortion services? Learn more at: https://www.plannedparenthood.org/learn/abortion

Common Types of STIs

Chlamydia. Chlamydia is the most frequently reported form of STI in the United States. It can be contracted by all types of people, and is transmitted through oral, anal, and vaginal sex. Chlamydia presents as vaginal discharge and a burning sensation while urinating for woman and discharge from the penis, burning sensation while urinating, and pain/swelling of one or both testicles in men. It can also present as rectal pain or discharge or bleeding from anal sex. Additionally, chlamydia can harm a woman's ability to have children. The chance of having chlamydia is reduced through condom use and being in a committed relationship with a noninfected partner. Chlamydia can be detected through medical testing, and can be cured through medication (CDC, n.d.a).

Gonorrhea. Gonorrhea can be contracted by all types of people and is transmitted through oral, anal, and vaginal sex. Gonorrhea presents as vaginal discharge, a burning sensation while urinating, and bleeding in between periods for woman and white, yellow, or green discharge from the penis, burning sensation while urinating, and pain/swelling of one or both testicles in men. It can also present as rectal discharge, anal itching; soreness; bleeding, and painful bowel movements from anal sex. The chance of having gonorrhea is reduced through condom use and being in a committed relationship with a noninfected partner. Gonorrhea can be detected through medical testing, and can be cured through medication (CDC, n.d.c).

Herpes. Herpes can be caused by the herpes simplex virus types 1 or 2. Most Americans who have the herpes virus most likely contracted it through saliva exchange with another person (e.g., kissing). Herpes presents as a blister or cold sore around the infected area. Although cold sores are a way to know if you have the virus, the unfortunate news is that a person can be infected but not present symptoms for years in between outbreaks. This means that the only way to know if a person is infected is to get tested. The chance of having herpes is reduced through condom use and being in a committed relationship with a noninfected partner. Herpes can be detected through medical testing, and can be treated, but not cured, through medication (CDC, n.d.b).

HIV. Human immunodeficiency virus, or HIV, can be contracted by all types of people and is transmitted through oral, anal, and vaginal sex. It is impossible to know if a person has HIV without medical testing. HIV leads to the destruction of the immune system (AIDS), allowing other infections (e.g., pneumonia) easier access. The chance of contracting HIV is reduced through condom use and being in a committed relationship with a noninfected partner. HIV can be detected through medical testing, and can be treated, but not cured, through medication (CDC, n.d.f).

Human Papillomavirus (HPV). HPV can be contracted by all types of people and is transmitted through oral, anal, and vaginal sex. HPV may not present any symptoms for years, making it difficult to identify without getting medically tested. HPV can cause genital warts and a variety of cancers (e.g., cervical, throat, and rectal cancers). The chance of contracting HPV is reduced through vaccination, condom use, and being in a committed relationship with a non-infected partner. HPV can be detected through medical testing but cannot be cured. However, the other medical problems it causes (i.e., warts and cancer) can be treated through medication (CDC, n.d.g).

Syphilis. Syphilis can be contracted by all types of people and is transmitted through oral, anal, and vaginal sex. There are four stages of syphilis, and the infection can be fatal. The first stage, primary syphilis, presents as a sore or sores on or around the penis, vagina, rectum, or mouth. These sores are painless and usually will disappear in 3 to 6 weeks, regardless of whether you receive treatment. In other words, it will look like your body has healed itself, but the infection has just moved to the secondary stage, which will leave non-painful mucous lesions (i.e., a rash) on your body. Without diagnosis and treatment, your body will go into latent and tertiary infection, although that could take years. The chance of contracting syphilis is reduced through condom use and being in a committed relationship with a non-infected partner. Syphilis can be detected through medical testing and can be treated through medication (CDC, n.d.e).

Last, but by no means least, partners need to be honest with each other. You don't need to give each other the third degree about each other's sexual past. However, if you think you've been exposed to an STI (i.e., had unprotected sex or contact with bodily fluids), or have exposed your partner to an STI, then you owe it to that other person to tell them before initiating sexual contact. If you were unaware of your health status before sexual contact, then you should abstain from sexual activity until the condition has been treated and tell them as soon as you find out, so they can obtain the appropriate medical treatment.

A healthy sexual life is one that is committed to mutual pleasure, safety, and responsibility. Making decisions about your body is a fundamental right for realizing your capabilities. No one—husband, girlfriend, senator, or priest—should rob your of your ability to choose what is in your best interest and health. However, there are some people who wish to do harm to others and to exploit others through violence and harm. The next section provides some ways to organize to promote sexual health and happiness.

Activism for Sexual Justice

An important step to realizing one's capabilities is to be able to feel safe from harm and to engage in romantic and sexual expression. Unfortunately, our current society does not support these ethics. Although it may seem that sexual and romantic contact is a complicated and messy affair, the truth is that it is surprisingly simple when you focus on what your partner needs or wants, and not just what you want. By obtaining affirmative consent, developing a healthy repertoire of sexual behaviors, and using safe-sex practices, you can ensure that your romantic and sexual activities are fun and pleasurable. And, even though we believe that adopting these ethics will help dramatically reduce the amount of sexual violence on and beyond college campus, we recognize that they will not be enough to eradicate sexual violence. To do that, people will need to organize and agitate for a world that emphasizes sexual justice. Although there are many ways to address sexual justice, here we focus on bystander intervention strategies. Bystander intervention is the idea that when you see a situation that could lead to sexual violence, you should intervene into the situation to ensure that it does not.

Bystander intervention models stress the importance of addressing sexual violence, or the potential for sexual violence, in the immediate moment. As Latané and Darley (1970) argue, bystander intervention is characterized by five components:

1. Noticing the event.

2. Identifying the situation as intervention-appropriate.

3. Taking responsibility to intervene into the situation.

4. Deciding how to intervene into the situation.

5. Acting to intervene into the situation.

To initiate bystander intervention, you will first need to notice the event. If a perpetrator is targeting another person, then there will often be clues that they are forcing unwanted sexual attention on their victim. For example, many victims may do things such as evade the perpetrator (e.g., go to the restroom), make angry or frustrated facial expressions, directly refuse (e.g., say "no"), aggressively refuse (e.g., push away), ask for friends' help, or leave the premises (Graham, Bernards, Abbey, Dumas, & Wells, 2017). These types of behaviors should clue you into the fact that the victim is experiencing stress, and that their interaction with the perpetrator is nonconsensual. Again, we stress that consent must be affirmative for sexual and romantic contact. If it does not appear that the interaction is enthusiastically and mutually agreed to, then it may constitute sexual violence. The next step is identifying the situation as appropriate for intervention. You may see a perpetrator initiate contact, but witness the victim as capable of dealing with the problem on their own. In that case, it is important that you continue to keep watching the perpetrator to ensure they don't escalate the situation or move on to find an easier target. If you feel that the victim cannot adequately address the situation by themselves (e.g., they are too drunk or aren't being forcible in their rejection due to isolation or fear), then you should go to step three, which is to take responsibility to intervene into the situation. Do not believe that someone else will do it for you or that others will see what you see. If you identify a situation as meriting an intervention, it is up to you to do it! That leads you to step four, which is to make the decision to intervene.

The fifth component is acting to intervene into the situation. Here is where it can get tricky because how you intervene will be directly related to the resources you have and the type of environment you are in at the time. If, for example, you're at a house party, there may not be a person of authority readily available to help. However, wherever you are, there are ways for you to intervene into the situation and prevent sexual violence. As RAINN (n.d.c) notes, the easiest way to intervene is to create a distraction, diverting the perpetrator's attention away from the target and/or providing the target time to leave the situation. For example, walk up to the situation and ask the target, "Did you still want to get some pizza? If so, we should leave now" or "Okay, I'm ready go home now, thanks for waiting." These types of lines are especially useful if you already know the targeted person. If you don't know the person, you can ask the target, "Hey, your friend over there (wave vaguely in another direction) said they needed you. You should probably go help them," or you could initiate long, pointless conversation with the perpetrator, "Don't I know you from somewhere? Weren't you in my Intro to biology class two years ago?" These types of interventions are useful because they provide a way for the target to get out of the situation and, if you are worried that you may be misreading the cues, they can stay in the situation if there isn't actually a problem.

Although low-level interventions like distractions can be useful, sometimes they are not enough and you'll have to try a different tactic. You may have to be direct and ask the target questions such as "I noticed you look frustrated. Would you mind if I sat with you?" "Do you need a ride home?" or "Who did you come with? Can I help you find them?" These questions provide a stronger avenue to get the targeted person out of the situation. If you feel that you cannot help them by yourself (e.g., there are many perpetrators targeting one victim), then you may need to enlist others to help you. You can tell the people they came with something like, "Your friend looks like they've had too much to drink. Can you take them home?" or "It looks like your friend is in trouble. Would you come over with me and help them?" You can also contact the authorities (e.g., call security or the police) when the situation warrants it. If a perpetrator is violent, threatens you or the target, or moves on to another target, you should notify a person in authority immediately (RAINN, n.d.c).

Figure 6.8

You should be prepared to face resistance, and even to "cause a scene," when you intervene into a situation. Some perpetrators may be drunk and may be more likely to yell at you because of lowered inhibitions. Other perpetrators know that if they cause a large enough scene that you may go away and allow them to continue targeting victims. Backlash from perpetrators is often swift, ranging from exclamations of innocence (e.g., "Don't cockblock me bro! We're just having a good time") to threats (e.g., "Fucking asshole! I oughta beat your ass!"). In those instance, you need to de-escalate the situation by not responding to the perpetrator, and focus your attention solely on ensuring that the target is safe. You should also notify authorities as soon as possible, not only for your own safety, but to ensure the perpetrator hasn't moved on to find an easier target. You may be the target of violence for intervening into a situation. Be sure to survey the situation! If you think you may put yourself in a violent situation, you should immediately find others to help your or notify the authorities. If neither of these is possible, make as much noise as possible, to draw attention to the situation.

Bystander intervention is especially important in settings where alcohol is present (e.g., bars, clubs, or parties). Because U.S. media portrays sexual contact as an uncontrollable, passionate, or "no-holds-bar" affair, the presence of alcohol (which lowers inhibitions) can exacerbate problems related to sexual violence. For example, Graham et al. (2017) found that although men's intoxication level did not affect their initiation of unwanted sexual activity, female's intoxication level did affect men's initiation of unwanted sexual activity. In other words, the more intoxicated a female is, the more likely that predatory men will target her. George, Cue, Lopez, Crowe, and Norris (1995) found that men, who believe that alcohol makes them less responsible for their actions and increases their sexual prowess, are more likely to pressure alcohol-drinking women for sexual and romantic contact. In addition to alcohol, structural (e.g., poor security staff) and social (e.g., expectation for aggressive behavior) dimensions can increase the likelihood that women are targeted for sexual violence (Becker & Tinkler, 2014). Although alcohol may inhibit decision making, it is not the sole cause of sexual violence. Rather, it enables a cultural system of violence (e.g., "I was drunk so I wasn't responsible for my actions") by allowing people to use it as an excuse for their behavior.

Many people may not intervene into situations for a variety of reasons. Bennett, Banyard, and Garnhart (2014) found that the most common reasons for not intervening included:

1. Failure to identify the situation as high risk (e.g., "I didn't respond because I wasn't sure if I was reading the situation correctly or not").

2. Failure to take intervention responsibility (e.g., "Someone else will take care of it. It's not my problem.").

3. Failure to intervene due to skill deficit (e.g., "I didn't know what to say or do about the situation").

4. Failure to intervene due to audience inhibition (e.g., "I didn't want to make a scene and ruin everyone's night").

Utterances like these indicates how even when people believe that sexual violence is wrong, they may not intervene into a situation. This means that you cannot count on others to intervene into situations; rather, you have to take responsibility for yourself and others, be vigilant, and be willing to make a difference.

If you already feel that you have the skills, knowledge, and disposition to intervene in situations of sexual violence, then perhaps you should work with your college on implementing bystander intervention training on your campus. Senn and Forest (2016) found that bystander intervention training in classes increased students' efficacy and willingness to intervene into situations. Students at colleges who have bystander intervention training are less likely to be victims of sexual violence than those who do not (Coker et al., 2016). Other research has found that bystander prevention training (i.e., training that addresses the social conditions that make sexual violence normal) is effective in encouraging students to take action to reduce sexual violence (Alegría-Flores, Raker, Pleasants, Weaver, & Weinberger, 2017). Finally, initiating programs beyond the college campus can help address sexual violence in communities. For example, Lundgren and Amin (2015) found that school-based dating violence training is effective for reducing sexual violence among high school students; community-based training about how to create equitable understanding of gender reduces sexual violence; and helping parents address children's maltreatment can reduce their likelihood of growing up and engaging in sexual violence. You can read these studies, and others, and start working with people within your community to create programs that address sexual violence. Overall, there is a great deal of work to do in and beyond our college campuses and every bit that you do can help secure a world free of sexual violence.

****

Our communities will stand the best chance at eliminating sexual violence when they are filled with people who privilege affirmative consent, are knowledgeable about sex, and are willing to intervene into situations of sexual violence. Important in all of these aspects is the idea that healthy, pleasurable sexual contact is only possible when we arm ourselves with facts about sex—not cave in to the fear-based appeals of those who don't understand sex or biology. Knowing your body, and your partner's, while respecting people's autonomy is a surefire way to ensure that your sexual encounters are positive.

There is never a time when sexual violence is justified or excusable. It is a violation of another person's autonomy and trust, and can do lifelong harm to their psychological and emotional health. Although most people would agree that sexual violence is wrong, there remains a lot of misconceptions about what constitutes harm. Many people, because of media portrayals, think it is their job to "wear down" the opposition through repeated contact and increased pressure. They see sexual contact as a game to be "won" or think they are "owed" sexual gratification. Both of these ideas are harmful, and we hope that you commit yourself to holding yourself and others accountable for their actions around sexual and romantic contact. Doing so will create a better world—one relationship, one community at a time.

Discussion Questions

- Have you ever intervened when you witnessed sexual violence?
  - What steps did you take?
  - How would you respond after reading Chapter 6?
- At some point, all relationships will have to make compromise and communicate those compromises in a healthy way. Think back to your own experiences in a relationship that you had in the past. Regardless of the type of relationship, what were some of the compromises that

had to made in order to either further the relationship or terminate it (if any)?

Student Challenge

- What was discussed in your high school sex education class? What wasn't covered that you needed to know?

- If you could design an ideal sex education class for high school students, what subjects would be taught and why?

CHAPTER 7

Building Cross-Cultural Relationships

CHAPTER OBJECTIVES

By the end of the chapter, you should be able to:

- Identify the role cultural differences play in building relationships
- Listen to other's cultural truths as a place to start dialogue
- Develop strategies to make deeper interpersonal relationships
- Connect activism about racism and xenophobia to creating strong intercultural relationships

ORIENTING QUESTIONS

As you read the chapter, try to answer the following questions:

- How do racism and xenophobia affect national and international relationships?
- What are the benefits of a culturally diverse classroom? Campus?
- Why is it difficult to form close cross-cultural relationships?
- What is intercultural competence?

In 2015, a group of male students in the Sigma Alpha Epsilon fraternity at the University of Oklahoma were filmed singing a racist song. To the tune of "If You're Happy and You Know It," the students sang: "You can hang him from a tree, but he'll never sign with me. There will never be a n----- at SAE" (New, 2015). In 2017, dozens of campuses were canvassed with flyers from White supremacy groups (Bauer-Wolf, 2017). And, in 2018, a student at Wayne State University brandished a knife at members of a pro-immigration group, allegedly stating, "I think all immigrants should be deported or killed" (Zaniewski, 2018). These instances, as well as countless others both large and small, make it more difficult for many racial and ethnic minority students to feel safe or included on campuses, and fulfill their academic and personal goals.

And yet, it is not just how racism or xenophobia manifests within higher education that requires attention. Those who espouse these views within colleges and universities go on to become the CEOs, lawyers, doctors, bankers, and politicians for the next generation. In other words, they are able to exercise an incredible amount of power over the capacity of people of color to access goods and services and can constrain their ability to live without fear of harm or discrimination. Take, for example, the process of redlining, which was a common bank practice for decades after World War II (Jan, 2018). City planners would mark city maps where living was undesirable or hazardous in red, and then banks would restrict loans to minorities (and particularly African Americans) so they could only live in those areas. In fact, Federal Housing Administration (FHA) guidelines stated that "incompatible racial groups should not be permitted to live in the same communities" (as cited in Gross, 2017, para. 8). As a result, racial

Figure 7.1

and ethnic minorities were relegated into housing areas that were harmful to their health and whose value stagnated or even declined. Although redlining is now explicitly against the law, the increasing gentrification of urban spaces (i.e., having largely White, wealthy people drive poor people and people of color out of urban areas through raising rent or home prices) in places such as Portland, San Francisco, and Boulder has many of the same effects. In short, White people with college degrees (primarily bankers and politicians) created systems of wealth distribution that harmed racial and ethnic minority families for generations.

> ### Student Voice
>
> It often feels like the classroom becomes this disappointing space that claims diversity but doesn't really explore equity, identity as it relates to your roles within systems or having us talk to each other. It kind of defeats the point of trying to build cross-cultural or meaningful relationships. —*Cara*

This approach to analyzing how racism and xenophobia manifests in higher education, then, offers three important insights. First, that discrimination has a harmful effect on students of color and international students within higher education. As decades of research shows, racism and xenophobia create a hostile campus climate and cause racialized stress to minority students (Gloria & Castallanos, 2003; McClain et al., 2016; Wei, Ku, & Liao, 2011). Second, White youth who learn to be racist and xenophobic go on to be discriminatory members of society who use their position in society to harm racial and ethnic minorities. And, third, that those who benefit from this system, White people, have a moral obligation to refuse the unjust rewards that they may accrue and promote equity among all races and ethnicities. Taking the example of redlining, what would have happened if White bankers had refused to practice redlining? What would have happened if White politicians hadn't barred many people of color from being politicians or bankers through Jim Crow laws? What would have happened if White homeowners had encouraged racial integration into their neighborhoods and schools? Although we may never know the answers to these questions, we know that it is not enough to merely not be racist or xenophobic. Instead, all people, and particularly White people, must be intentional and knowledgeable about building cross-cultural relationships if we are to realize a society that stands against discrimination.

This chapter is meant to help you navigate the tricky landscape of cross-cultural relationships and friendships. The ethics we explain not only apply to interactions among domestic students of differing racial and ethnic backgrounds, but also communicating between domestic and international students. We think that racial and ethnic justice can only happen in a society where people from all walks of life are deeply committed to listening and empathizing with others—particularly when the truths that are spoken are sometimes hard to imagine or hear. To achieve this goal, we first detail barriers to authentic cross-cultural relationships, particularly as those issues arise in higher education. Then, we'll highlight strategies that you can engage in that will help you make your cross-cultural relationships deeper and more meaningful. Finally, we'll argue that pursuing racial and ethnic justice is a necessary component of living in a society where all members are able to realize their full capabilities.

Barriers to Cross-Cultural Relationships

Students, both domestic and White, will have a great deal of work to do if they want to build cross-cultural relationships. One of the primary barriers to developing relationships among students from different racial or ethnic groups during college is the lack meaningful relationships before college (Bonilla-Silva, 2006).

Figure 7.2

For domestic students, this manifests primarily as a lack of opportunity to interact in any sustained or meaningful way with people who hail from another country. Although some students may have had a few international students from an educational exchange program enroll in their school, the majority of U.S. K–12 students will not be in a position to have regular, sustained contact with someone from another country. And, although there are some opportunities for U.S. students to visits other countries, these opportunities rarely encourage U.S. students to immerse themselves into the host country's culture. Rather, they are given a carefully curated sense of the country, one that panders to a tourist form of interaction (e.g., many, if not all, of their interactions will be in English, even in countries where English is not the most spoken language). Perhaps this state of affairs is the reason for the following joke: What do you call a person who can speak three languages? Trilingual. What do you call a person who can speak two languages? Bilingual. What do you call a person who can only speak one language? American!

> **Student Voice**
>
> I always find it weird when my peers make fun of or are angry with professors who have accents. I always recognize that this is a person who can likely teach, understand, and create in multiple languages. —*Thomas*

The lack of meaningful contact across different cultures is also present within the United States. The process of redlining that we wrote about in the introduction is one of the reasons why PK–12 schools remained segregated by race and ethnicity, even after the famous *Brown v. Board of Education* U.S. Supreme

Court decision ended formal segregation policies. For example, Kozol (2005) has documented dozens of school systems across the nation where Black and Latinx students were forced to enroll in schools that have less resources and opportunities while White, middle- and upper-class students were enrolled in higher-performing schools. Housing, public schooling, religious affiliation, and the workplace—no institution within the United States is exempt from segregation.

Although some may try to rationalize this issue by saying, "Some people just like being around their own kind," the fact is that when racial and ethnic minorities are segregated from White people within the United States, they are almost always provided less resources, support, and opportunities than their White counterparts. As a result, many White people do not understand the unique barriers that people of color face, which makes it difficult to truly empathize with them as they try to navigate racism and xenophobia.

> ### Student Voice
>
> My biggest fears about reaching out to someone who seems different from myself is often about wanting to learn and do so authentically. When I talk or interact, I am often left with crippling anxiety which leaves me curled up for 3 days and worrying if I said something offensive or missed an opportunity. —*Carolina*

The lack of meaningful contact between domestic and international students, and White students and racial/ethnic minority students, means that everyone will need to do a lot of work to unlearn the ignorance/prejudice that characterizes their worldview. We wish to be clear, we are not saying that all domestic students intentionally discriminate against international students or that White students intentionally discriminate against racial/ethnic minority students. Although certainly there are students who are intentionally racist or xenophobic, the majority of the problems with cross-cultural interactions comes from a lack of knowledge and an unwillingness to do the hard work of correcting our own ignorance. When we are ignorant about an issue it's impossible to address it. For example, many White people who did not grow up with Latinx friends or Latinx people in their community may have gotten most of their understanding about what Central or South American people look like from media portrayals. As a result, they may not see a problem in dressing in sombreros, serapes, or wearing large mustaches for an event like Halloween. However, wearing this type of garb makes a caricature of another person's culture, and is often accompanied by racist and xenophobic stereotypes about overindulging in tequila and tacos. When White people are called out for engaging in this type of behavior, their response is

> ### Student Voice
>
> I want to speak in a way that sensitive to people's worldviews, experiences, etc. but I'm not sure how to navigate that … I don't feel my college classes have pushed that agenda, and it feels like a hole in my learning. It's interesting we don't often think about our identity until we have it contrasted with someone else's. —*Anderson*

often "it's just a joke" or "I'm not a racist" or other defenses that do not show that they understand how their behaviors are based on cultural ignorance. These types of actions are harmful to realizing a world where people are free to live without the specter of racism.

Because cultural and ideological ignorance is so prevalent, it is often difficult to form friendships across race or ethnicity. For example, nearly 40% of international students reported having no close American friends (Gareis, 2017). Because U.S. culture tends to promote individualism, people tend to see friendships as casual and aligned primarily by face-to-face common interest, work, or online groups (e.g., video games). However, other countries, (particularly collectivist cultures such as China or Japan) tend to seek deep relationships in forming friendships. As a result, some international students view U.S. Americans as self-absorbed, superficial, and unapproachable. Similarly, Ingraham (2014) reported that the average White American's friends are almost entirely White, whereas people of color have a much more racially diverse network of friendships. White people who grow up in predominately or exclusively White communities may not know how to address race or ethnicity with their friends, and as a result, they may be viewed as uncaring or ignorant of their struggles. They may make jokes or behave in ways that were viewed as uncontroversial or even accepted within their community but are viewed differently or negatively by their peers of color.

This is not to say that students should expect integration all of the time. For example, there are clubs for ethnic minority students, organizations for international students, and fraternities and sororities for racial minority students, and combinations thereof. Students from traditionally under-resourced populations often create and maintain these types of groups to create opportunities to affirm pride in their group and to find solace against dealing with the racism and xenophobia of (primarily White and domestic) students (Villalpando, 2003). In other words, you should not mistake these groups' actions as self-segregation; rather, they may be separating themselves from the majority domestic or White-dominated culture of the institution for their own psychological and emotional health. Many racial and ethnic minority students navigate White and domestic culture every day, all-day, and so the opportunity to find solidarity with others in their group outside of that demand can be an important positive influence. Learning not just how, but when, to reach out to form a friendship is an important part of building cross-cultural relationships.

As you navigate college, remember that you have the power to create relationships, include others, and build meaningful communities across cultures. Your campus most likely has opportunities to interact with students from diverse backgrounds. You should pursue these opportunities! Join clubs that promote cross-cultural interaction (e.g., Language Partnerships) or encourage a club that you are a part of to cohost events with students from racial or ethnic minority clubs. When done correctly, building cross-cultural relationships can help address feelings of isolation and loneliness, increase empathy, and cultivate cognitive complexity for you and for those around you (Rodríguez, Nagda, Sorensen, & Gurin, 2018). Retreating into what is most comfortable for you does a disservice to you and those from other cultures—it increases the chances that you will never expand your horizons about the world and know how to address injustice. Choosing to remain apart from others may feel like the easier choice, but in the end, it is the route to intellectual stagnation and decay. Challenge yourself and your peers to do more than talk and get active—you'll find the rewards of cross-cultural relationships far outweigh your fears.

Cultivating Better Cross-Cultural Relationships

Intercultural competence, whether across international/domestic or across various races/ethnicities, is an important component of creating meaningful, lasting cross-cultural relationships (Ting-Toomey, 2005). This form of competence encompasses a deep knowledge of your own culture and a recognition that how you talk, think, and behave are culturally bound. In other words, you need to recognize that what you think of as normal, natural, or neutral may just be someone else's weird, scary, or evil. This is not to say that all actions are relativistic and there is no right or wrong. But it is to say that what we think of as universal or common sense is often just a reflection of our own perceptions, expectations, and experiences, which might very well represent prejudices and shortcomings. Rather than wallow in that ignorance, it is our task to be better than petty prejudices and imposed structures to become people who truly and meaningfully understand each other. Important to this task is the commitment to learn about ourselves, and each other, and do the hard work of challenging our taken-for-granted sense of the world.

Figure 7.3

In this section, we detail things to do and things to avoid if you wish to cultivate a strong relationship with someone from another culture. We wish to caution, though, that these actions are not a recipe for success, nor should you only limit yourself to doing these things. Relationships are complex, and each one will require you to step outside of your comfort zone to do more than talk or pay lip-service to diversity and equity. However, if you come from a background with little experience in interacting with people from other cultures (whether internationally or domestically), then these are some actions that you can take that can be helpful in cultivating thoughtful relationships.

Things to Do

Listen. One of the hardest things to do for most people is to simply listen to another person. Listening is not a passive activity; it requires you to commit your attention and empathy to the other person. As Covey (2004) notes, "Most people do not listen with the intent to understand; they listen with the intent to reply" (p. 239). To be empathetic to another person is to move beyond simply hearing others to, instead, begin to see others as if their emotional and psychological health was your own (Rogers, 1959). Truly listening to others suggests that you should be able to capture not just the words, but the emotional and psychological components, of what someone else has said. Important to good listening is the ability to support other's struggles without comparing them to your own, avoid judging other's problems as trivial, and not rushing straight to giving advice. If the other person is an English Language Learner, then be aware that you may struggle to understand them because you probably only speak one language and have heard it spoken primarily with one type of accent, most of your life. In other words, you have responsibility to put effort into listening—certainly others have had to put in a great deal of effort to acquire another language!

Figure 7.4

A Lesson in Good Listening

Ann: I feel like school's really difficult right now. I don't know if I'm going to make it to the end of the semester.

Beth: I'm sorry that school is giving you problems. What, specifically, is making it difficult?

Ann: My biology class is! I don't understand it and the professor is no help.

Beth: I had the same problems last year with the same professor. Would you like to talk about what I did to make it through?

Notice how Beth's communication acknowledges Ann's struggle, doesn't judge her, and provides an opportunity to ask for aid. Beth's communication shows support for Ann without lecturing her or attacking her agency.

Avoid Ambiguity. Miscommunication arises when people are not careful to address ambiguity in communication (Gareis, 2017). For example, in high-context cultures (e.g., China and Japan), people are more likely to communicate in indirect ways and let the contextual or situational factors clue the other person in to what they are trying to communicate. U.S. American and many European cultures tend to be low-context cultures and are much more explicit in their communication styles. As a result, international students may feel that they have adequately communicated something, and that to be explicit would be rude or demeaning. Or, because of the overt manner in which U.S. Americans and Europeans communicate they may feel intimidated by interacting in a challenging manner. Thus, the U.S. and European students may not understand that their communication style can come across as obnoxious, and they may miss important information that international students are trying to convey. When in doubt, it is better to clarify what people are saying. Don't be afraid to ask someone what they meant or to repeat.

Self-Disclose. Although you shouldn't make every conversation about you, you shouldn't be afraid to self-disclose! Revealing information about yourself often invites others to reciprocate that level of disclosure. Broach subjects such as favorite (or not-favorite) shows, sports, hobbies, classes, and music, and be ready to listen to the other person as they recount their likes and dislikes as well. Recognize that exchanging low-level or superficial information, even on a regular basis, with another person usually doesn't constitute your relationship as a friendship. Friendships arise when you have deeper self-disclosure, and a commitment to supporting another person—even when doing so means you have to put your needs aside. Self-disclosure is a way that interpersonal trust is formed. In interpersonal relationships, communication and activities create connections at social and emotional levels. Time, effort, and investment include providing emotional support and engaging in self-disclosure rather than just getting something done. Interpersonal relationships also have repeated interaction over time. When two people disclose increasingly private or nonpublic information, your ability to treat that information as sensitively and closely as your own will increase your bond with another.

Keep an Open Mind. One of the hardest things to do in cross-cultural interactions is to keep an open mind. Sometimes what people from another culture might say or do may seem foolish, wrong, or trivial to us, but may be of great importance to them (and vice-versa). From what food to eat, to how to greet one another, to proper attire, each culture has aspects that make it unique. This is particularly true for White students as they interact with racial and ethnic minority students. When students of color talk about their own lived experiences, or about the history of racism and xenophobia of the United States, it is hard for many White students to not become defensive and antagonistic. Instead of feeling personally attacked, recognize that if you want to have a true, meaningful relationships with a person of color, you may learn things about yourself or about history that you may not like to hear.

A Lesson in Bad Listening

David: I feel like school's really difficult right now. I don't know if I'm going to make it to the end of the semester.

Allan: I feel the same way! Last week, I had three essays due and a test. I stayed up all night last night writing my end-of-the-semester research project. And my group members in my humanities class never show up to meetings!

David: Right ... well, it's just, I'm not doing well in my biology class. And, I don't feel like I get any help when I go to the professor's office hours.

Allan: That happened to me, too. I had the same professor last semester and I hated that class. I didn't learn anything!

Notice how Allan has only heard David insofar as it allows him to redirect the conversation back to himself. Allan's communication shows a lack of empathy and exacerbates David's struggles.

Be Mindful of Nonverbals. Sometimes what we don't say is more important than the words we use. Many cultures have their own ways of expressing anger, distaste, fear, misunderstanding, and happiness, and in order to build strong relationships, you'll have to learn how to be mindful of your own idiosyncrasies. For example, President Bush (43) once made the "Hook 'em Horns" salute with his hands—a seemingly innocent gesture for the Texas Longhorns. Although this gesture is widely known and utilized by people within the United States, this sign is viewed as "Hail Satan" in Norwegian culture, a sign that your wife is cheating on you in Italy, and an obscene insult in many African countries (Cotton, 2013). Other typical U.S. American gestures, such as simply pointing your finger, giving a thumbs up, or showing the bottoms of your feet can be insulting in some cultures. Recognizing what nonverbal behaviors can cause miscommunication or stress is an important part of being a respectful communicator.

Figure 7.5

Learn the Language. Ideally, you try to learn another language so you can converse with people from that culture without having to force them to cater to your linguistic needs. Unfortunately, language acquisition in the United States is dismal compared to other countries. For example, in Europe, nearly 92% of all students take courses in a foreign language, whereas in the United States only about 20% do so (Devlin, 2018). This difference in instruction is likely why only about 25% of U.S. citizens report knowing a language other than English, and of those, only 43% believe they speak their second language "very well" (Devlin, 2015). If you don't have the time to enroll in language courses or immerse yourself in another language by going to another country, there are many programs (both free and for a price) that you can sign up for to enhance your language abilities. English language learning students often cite language barriers as a primary reason for difficulty in making friends, so even learning a small amount of another language can help you bond with another person. And, learning another language is a valuable skill to have in our increasingly connected, multilingual world.

Admit Ignorance. Do you know everything there is to know about another culture? Probably not. So, there's no reason to act like you do! Ask questions and don't be afraid to admit that you don't know something. This doesn't mean you shouldn't try to find out information on your own or you run around interrogating people from another culture about every aspect of their lives. Keep in mind that you may have only asked the question once to one person, but that person may have answered that question 50 times from 50 other people. As a result, they may feel frustrated, angry, or tired about having to educate people all the time. At the same time, admitting when you don't know something and seeking information to address your gap in knowledge can be a powerful way to show humility. Best of all, it will help you treat people better based on your newfound knowledge!

Get Involved. As discussed earlier, many international and racial/ethnic minority groups put on a great deal of content in your institution to raise awareness about their culture and to educate others. Plays, dances, and workshops are just a few of the programs that are offered to create better relationships across cultural identities. Domestic and White students should attend these events to increase their knowledge of others, as well as show support for their hard work. You should also see if there are ways to support them beyond just showing up though. Maybe they could use help setting up or breaking down their presentations or would like the chance to show their work in a new venue or even are taking donations for causes. Instead of expecting others to do all the work educating the campus community, you can do some of the work to show your appreciation for their labor.

Keep Your Word. It might seem obvious to say that being honest is an important component to creating or maintaining a friendship, but it bears repeating: keeping your word is vital to a healthy relationship. U.S. students put a great deal of emphasis on work and, as a result, may overcommit themselves with too many things. As a result, you may find yourself canceling your appointment to a conversational partner program or not showing up to a performance you promised you would attend. Although sometimes things come up that are beyond your control, often these decisions show a lack of planning, and therefore a lack of care, on the part of the person reneging on their promise. Demonstrate that you will show up when you say you will, that you will give help if you say tell someone "If you ever need help, give me a call," and be authentic in what you will and won't do.

Learn About Your Own Culture. It may seem odd, but self-awareness about one's culture is an important part of creating relationships with people from other cultures (Gareis, 2017). People who know a lot about their own culture tend to recognize that their culture is isn't simply "the way everybody does things" or "the way that everybody should do things." Rather, people who are sensitively engaged in their own culture are more empathetic, complex, and open-minded about other peoples' cultures. Read history books, anthropology reports, intercultural communication studies, and sociological research to get a sense of what it means to inhabit the identities that you do.

Ten Cultural Norms of Americans

1. **Tipping.** Companies in many other countries pay waitstaff a minimum wage, and so don't expect to tip.

2. **Patriotism.** People in many countries don't express patriotism because of its close ties to nationalism. It is rare to see people in other countries have flags in their front yards, on their cars, or as their underwear.

3. **Eating on the go.** In many countries, eating is a ritualized experience and should not be rushed. The idea of eating at one's desk or not eating a full meal (e.g., eating a bag of chips for lunch) is considered rude.

4. **Putting ice in supersized sodas.** Many countries drink tea, soda, and beer at room temperature. And, drink sizes are much smaller, with no free refills!

5. **Refer to ourselves as Americans.** U.S. citizens often call themselves "Americans" even though there is a North America, Central America, and South America.

6. **Personal space.** U.S. Americans, especially from rural areas, expect a great deal more personal space than people from most countries.

7. **Dry cities/counties.** The way that state, county, and municipal governments restrict access to alcohol is almost unheard of in most countries of the world.

8. **Small talk.** U.S .citizens often engage in mindless banter or "small talk" that can be off-putting for those who come from other countries.

9. **Sex-crazy prude.** U.S. citizens have strict social taboos about how people (especially women) can dress, and shame those who dress "sexy." At the same time, the United States is one of the primary creators and consumers of pornographic media.

10. **Portion sizes.** Most restaurants in the United States provide more food than an average person could or should eat, and more than their counterparts in other countries. As a result, many people ask for doggie bags—another thing that people in most countries do not do.

Hold Yourself and Others Accountable. This is perhaps the hardest thing to do because there is never a time when you have "got it." Every time you interact with someone from another culture, there is always the chance for miscommunication, offense, and hurt. You should be open and honest about your mistakes, readily and freely apologize for offense, and, if necessary, seek to redress any harm you may have caused. This ethic can be hard for people who have little interaction with people from other cultures because no one has ever, and perhaps no one ever will, force them to adjust their communication with another person or sincerely offer apologies. You will have to be vigilant about your interactions with others, and you will have to hold yourself to account for your actions. If you are willing to do so you will find that people from other cultures will respect your commitment to do the hard work of building bridges in unfamiliar circumstances, and that can be the beginning of a great, authentic, friendship.

Things to Avoid

Avoid Fetishizing. One issue that domestic and White people often struggle with is the line between building relationships and being unthinkingly infatuated (i.e., fetishizing) others. People who fetishize others may brag about the number of friends they have who are from a different racial or ethnic group (e.g., "I have a lot of Black friends") or have unhealthy sexual fantasies (e.g., "I only find Asian women attractive"). Conversely, having only same-group friends or believing that some races, ethnicities, or cultures are simply not attractive is wrong, too. People from other cultures are not baubles or trinkets to be collected or disposed—they are complex, multifaceted beings who are owed careful and sensitive respect.

Avoid Toxic Peers. You may think that you are a good person who is genuinely interested in creating cross-cultural relationships with students from other cultures, races, or ethnicities. However, you may also have friends that are less interested in these goals. If you have friends who regularly make disparaging comments, tell jokes about other groups of people, or who support causes that harm marginalized groups, then you should think about reevaluating your relationships with them. Perhaps they just don't have any good experiences with people from other cultural groups, and you can help them become a more emphatic and open person. Or, perhaps they are set on seeing people from other groups as inferior or as a threat, and they will not change their mind. If they are of the latter group, you shouldn't enable their bad behavior. Find others who are committed to living a free and open world, and work to create that society. It may be hard to walk away from a friendship, especially if you've had the relationship for many years, but you are only harming yourself and others by supporting a person who will make decisions—large or small—to harm people from other groups.

Avoid Jokes, Costumes, or Stories That Are Discriminatory. You may think you have the type of relationship where it's fine to refer to someone using a racial or ethnic slur, tell a racist joke, or wear a costume of another culture's garb, but you don't, and you shouldn't engage in these types of behaviors. This is not to say that you should never make jokes or talk about race, ethnicity, or culture, but you need to ask yourself, "Would they genuinely find this funny or are they just humoring me because they think I'm too ignorant to understand the hurt I'm causing?" For an international student, for example, you may be their only U.S. friend, and they may fear losing your relationship if they confront you about your insensitive comment. If you can't answer definitively that they find your banter funny, then it might be best for you to find other ways to joke with your friends from other cultures. And, it shouldn't have to be said in the 21st century, but don't wear any costume that mimics another culture (especially blackface). Just don't.

Avoid Being Afraid to Make Mistakes. You're going to say and do things that are cringeworthy, embarrassing to yourself and maybe for the other people. You can't use that as an excuse for never interacting with people from other racial, ethnic, or cultural groups though. If you have a lot of anxiety and fear about making mistakes, then when you inevitably do, you'll feel an immense amount of guilt and shame. You may even go so far as to avoid talking to that person again. But, to grow as a person, and to create strong relationships, you will need to recognize that you are not perfect and be comfortable with working through discomfort.

Avoid Punishing Honest Miscommunication. If you do make a mistake, and you are called out for your error, you may feel embarrassed, angry, or frustrated. Your first reaction may be to attack the other person for calling you out on your bad or ignorant behavior. You need to remember that those feelings are yours, and not the fault of the other person. Don't take your negative emotions out on other people! This doesn't mean that you should be everyone's emotional punching bag and allow others to make you feel bad on purpose. However, when people feel guilt, it provides us an impetus to do better the next time—to address those parts of ourselves that we find unwholesome or unwelcome. Embrace those opportunities, no matter how painful, and learn to be a better person for yourself and others.

Activism Against Racism and Xenophobia

Across the world, people work hard to get through school, find jobs, support their communities, and build relationships. And, yet, many—too many—people have their efforts thwarted by barriers that they had no hand in creating. People who support, whether intentionally or not, racism and xenophobia maintain those obstacles and limit racial and ethnic minorities' abilities to fulfill their capabilities. For example, researchers found that when the exact same résumé was sent to businesses but half the résumés had a traditionally White name while others had a traditionally African American name, the White résumés were 50% more likely to receive a callback than their Black counterparts (Bertrand & Mullainathan, 2003). The people making hiring decisions don't have to wear White hoods or burn crosses—although, some might—to harm racial and ethnic minorities. They simply have to act on their cultural ignorance, and they maintain racism and xenophobia.

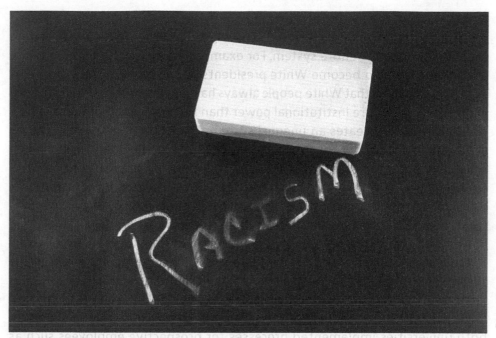

Figure 7.6

In order to address this system, we believe that institutions of higher education have to become laboratories for creating a truly inclusive culture. Often, people talk about diversity and inclusion as if they are the same thing, but they are often quite different in practice. Diversity often refers to programs that ensure a variety of perspectives are present in decision making, usually based on racial or ethnic group identity. In practice, though, this approach often results in an uneven distribution of access and resources. For example, although there are racial and ethnic minorities present at all levels of higher education, nearly 75% of full-time faculty are White, approximately nearly 75% of administrators are White, and almost 85% of college presidents are White (Espinosa, Turk, Taylor, & Chessman, 2019). The overrepresentation of White people in positions of power lends itself to the unthinking discrimination that can happen when one group of people control most of the ways that decisions are made. In other words, those who are making the decisions come primarily from one type of experience and one cultural lens, which can make it difficult to imagine an institutional culture that is truly welcoming and supportive of all types of students.

Inclusion, on the other hand, signals more than just having a variety of types of people present. Instead, it demands that institutions of higher education change to provide true power sharing among stakeholders and institutional members. As Corbet and Slee (2000) announce, "Inclusive education is an unabashed announcement, a public and political declaration and celebration of difference" (p. 134). In other words, creating an inclusive institution goes beyond merely recognizing differences, and instead adopts the ethic of celebrating and supporting it. Inclusion entails creating an institutional climate that is free from racialized stress and xenophobia. Important to pushing for inclusion in higher education is understanding the entire system. For example, White faculty become White administrators who become White presidents in universities. This pipeline of experience ensures that White people always have more opportunities to pursue higher roles and more institutional power than their racial and ethnic minority counterparts and creates an unequal system. To combat it, students, faculty, and administration will have to come together to plan how to recruit, higher, retain, support, and mentor racial and ethnic minority hires, as well as international hires, and give them real input and power sharing into institutional decision making. Empowering people from these groups can create the impetus for stronger collaboration and cross-cultural communication than if one group of people holds all the power about how to manage institutional resources.

Pursuing these goals is not easy, but you can follow the lead of other college systems that have already begun working toward these goals. For example, as Flaherty (2017) reports, Boston College and UC Riverdale were able to increase faculty diversity without having to resort to mandated quota numbers. Instead, both universities implemented processes for prospective employees such as requiring statements for how faculty support racial and ethnic minority students, removing racial/ethnic identifiers from application materials, and ensuring that hiring committees had members from various backgrounds. Implementing these programs resulted in hiring nearly four times as many racial and ethnic minority faculty as the average, putting them on the way of having a faculty whose racial and ethnic diversity mirrors the student population. If you want your college to support racial and ethnic minority students, you will need to work with your faculty and administration to ensure that those who are in power reflect the demographic makeup of the student body.

There is no downside to creating an inclusive campus. Institutions that model inclusion are better for students, faculty, and the communities they serve. Literature from dozens of scholars from a variety of disciplines demonstrates that inclusion fosters the development of student cognitive outcomes, such as problem-solving skills,

Five Things You Can Do to Increase Faculty and Administrative Diversity on Your Campus

1. Demand that search committee members represent a variety of racial, ethnic, sexual, and gender identities.

2. Promote implicit bias training for search committee members to reduce the likelihood of unconscious discrimination.

3. Request search committees ask candidates for statements on how they plan to support learning for racial and ethnic minority students.

4. Encourage the search committee to recruit candidates whose research or service directly promotes inclusion.

5. Sponsor workshops that train faculty about inclusive hiring and workplace management.

cognitive growth, cognitive complexity, and empathy (Gurin, Dey, Hurtado, & Gurin, 2002; Hurtado, 2001; Pascarella et al., 2014). Furthermore, racial and ethnic minority students perform better in environments where people of authority reflect their identity (Fairlie, Hoffman, & Oreopoulos, 2014; Gershenson Hart, Hyman, Lindsay, & Papageorge, 2018). However, that doesn't mean there won't be barriers. Everyone is not willing nor, even as try to connect, will they be willing to create a campus that supports all types of students. Don't give up! Perhaps your work will result in immediate changes, or maybe it will manifest itself with the next person who tries to address this issue. Remaining knowledgeable and engaged about your college is the only way that things will changes over the long term. Communities that are served by college service-learning projects and other types of outreach programs are enhanced when people from those communities are represented (Frey & Palmer, 2014). In short, everyone benefits from an emphasis on inclusion and true power-sharing.

In your activism for an inclusive campus, you'll encounter a great deal of resistance. Some people will say, "The best candidate should win, regardless of race." Although this is true in the ideal sense, the fact is that without concerted and intentional work to create an inclusive campus, the results of this thinking have been shown time and again throughout history—academia becomes stultified into a primarily White, primarily male institution. And, not just higher education, every job and organization faces the same problem of addressing inequality and discrimination. We do not think that there was ever a time when the "best candidate" always received a job, promotion, or pay raise—there have always been instances when unqualified and underperforming White and domestic people were hired, protected, and rewarded by racist and xenophobic managers and administrators. To assert that "only the best get a job" creates a smokescreen that continues bad-faith hiring practices and generates an institutional culture that is not only immoral, but it is woefully out of step with the increasing diversity racial and ethnic diversity of U.S. society. Others may claim, "Diversity isn't a strength," but these people often come from backgrounds (White and domestic) that fear no longer being able to control every aspect of society. Remember, when a group of people is used to being on top of everything, then equality will feel like an attack. Don't fall into the trap of believing that your racial/ethnic group or national identity somehow makes you better than other people; instead, work to realize a world where all people, from all walks of life, are offered an equal chance to fulfill their capabilities.

****

Colleges are meant to be places where people who work hard, and play by the rules, are able to reach their potential. However, this promise cannot be fulfilled as long as racism and xenophobia continue to permeate our campus cultures. A discriminatory culture can happen through the everyday communication between and among students, faculty, and administrators; keeping monuments to Confederate generals in place; retaining buildings named after people who touted eugenics; and promoting only tourist and superficial ways for domestic students to interact with international students. If you want to live in a society where students from all backgrounds have a fair playing field for pursuing their dreams and ambitions, then you will need to work to create a power structure that is representative of the students and society that colleges are meant to serve and do so equitably.

Discussion Questions

- How have your interactions with people from other cultures helped you see instances of your own cultural ignorance or stereotyping?

- Have you ever been held accountable for an act of prejudice? How did you navigate it?

- What are ways that you can work with others to build relationships across various cultures?

Student Challenge

- Make a vow to hold yourself, and others, accountable when they say or do something that is racist or xenophobic.

- Find an organization on campus that you can work with to increase faculty, staff, and administrative diversity on your campus.

CHAPTER 8

Mental and Physical Health

Navigating the Chronic and the Situational

CHAPTER OBJECTIVES

By the end of the chapter, you should be able to:

- Describe the history of stigma in mental and physical health
- Navigate higher education and its system for accommodating disabilities
- Develop a language for self-advocacy if you identify as disabled
- Develop a language for advocacy if you are an able-bodied student
- Connect activism about universal design and destigmatization with developing advocacy skills

---

ORIENTING QUESTIONS

As you read the chapter, try to answer the following questions:

- How is disability a structural, rather than individual, problem?
- What are some ways you have heard people use moral, medical, or social justice language about disability in your life?
- What are instances where you have had to advocate for others or for yourself about disability accommodations?
- How can we destigmatize disability beyond formal education?

In May 2018, Stanford University was sued by students with mental health disabilities, who alleged that the university had not provided equal access to educational resources. The students described feeling that the university pressured them to take leaves of absence rather than make accommodation for their coursework, move into off-campus housing, and write essays accepting blame for disrupting the university culture (Ingram, 2018). The student plaintiffs are seeking no monetary reward for damages, but instead want to use the lawsuit to increase access and opportunities for all students with disabilities. Although the students' bravery and commitment are commendable, their story speaks to the countless number of actions—from large to small—that can create a discriminatory culture against people with disabilities.

Currently, nearly one in four U.S. citizens identify as having a disability (Centers for Disease Control and Prevention [CDC], 2019). If you are a student with a disability, then you may have already realized that the laws and rules that governed your PK–12 experiences no longer apply in the same way in higher education. For example, the Individuals with Disability in Education Act (IDEA), which mandates that public PK–12 schools create accommodation plans for students, provide alternate facilities (e.g., classrooms) when necessary, and allow for parental notification of individualized education programs, does not apply to universities. Instead, higher education is governed by the American with Disabilities Act (ADA). Although the ADA provides many legal protections for students with disabilities, colleges are obliged to provide less service and notification than their PK–12 counterparts. Although legislative laws and judicial ruling have helped open colleges to more students with disabilities than in decades past, there are still far too many instances of poorly designed campuses and classes and inadequate support for mental health.

In regard to physical disabilities, for example, most buildings were not made with wheelchair accessible entryways until the passage of the ADA in 1990.

> **Student Voice**
>
> I feel like we need more on-campus health-related resources for blending academics and life transitions such as pregnancy, death, separation, etc. I only found out in my last semester that there were resources for these kinds of situations, but I never looked into them—I didn't know how. —Arthur

Figure 8.1

People with mobility issues had to either crawl up the stairs or wait until enough people (or a strong person) showed up to carry them up the steps. In other words, people without mobility issues may not have given stairs a second thought, or found them as a mild annoyance, whereas for many people with mobility disabilities, stairs constituted either an insurmountable barrier or a ritual in public shaming. The need to address the gap in understanding and empathy is only further supported by the fact that you will, at some point of your life, be disabled. Whether through genetics, an accident, or just growing older, you will need to live in a society that accommodates, rather than denigrates, your physical and mental health needs.

The National Survey of College Counseling Centers (Gallagher, 2014) reported that 94% of center directors reported an increase in services used over the past 5 years addressing issues such as anxiety disorders, crises requiring immediate response, psychiatric medication issues, clinical depression, learning disabilities, sexual assault on campus, self-injury issues (e.g., cutting to relieve anxiety), and problems related to earlier sexual abuse. The American College Health Association (2017a; 2017b) reported that approximately 75% of students have not received mental health services from their university, and 20% of students stated they would not seek treatment by a mental health professional for a mental health issue. The National Alliance on Mental Health (2012) found that 50% of students had not disclosed their mental health status to their university or college and that 64% of students who drop out cite mental illness as the reason for their departure. Collectively, then, the current landscape of higher education indicates that there is a large and growing number of students who identify as disabled, and that colleges are not living up to their responsibility to ensure that all students are supported. If you are a student that doesn't identify as disabled, then these issues may be largely invisible to you. Unfortunately, when people are not personally affected by something, and they remain ignorant of it, then they make decisions that may (un)intentionally harm others.

> **Student Voice**
>
> I did not go to campus resources to request a therapist because I was embarrassed and self-conscious about my issues. I didn't believe they would be suited to help me with the things I was struggling with. —*Patricia*

Our purpose in this chapter is twofold: first, to provide information for students with disabilities, and second, to offer advice for able-bodied students to be thoughtful and empathic peers. We believe that a society that sensitively and deeply understands disability is one that nurtures all members toward their fulfilling their capabilities. To do this, we first seek to destigmatize mental and physical disability, that is, to showcase it as a normal part of human variation rather than as an aberration or punishment. Then, we offer strategies for students with disabilities to utilize to navigate the new legal and institutional landscape in their quest for equal treatment and access as well as ways for able-bodied students to build relationships across disability. Finally, we argue that students should advocate for universal design within higher education and beyond as a way to create a society that supports all people who wish to fulfill their capabilities.

Stigma Within Mental and Physical Disability

As we mentioned earlier, it wasn't until 1990 that the United States passed the Americans with Disabilities Act. You might wonder, "Why did it take so long to pass a law about something that was so obviously needed?" Certainly, there were concerns about government oversight, implementation, and the costs of changing policies or buildings. But at the heart of the matter was a lack of empathy for people with disabilities, and a strong cultural connection between disability and shame. This connection, what many call the stigma, refers the situation where an individual is barred from full participation in public life due to others' cultural beliefs or prejudices, in this case about disability (Goffman, 1963). For example, a person with a history of depression may not be promoted in their job because of others' fears that they may not be able to deal with the responsibilities, even though their depression has never affected their work. In the United States, stigma about disabilities is the result of hundreds of years of erroneous thinking and has only recently been challenged. In our current society, this legacy of stigma has harmed our capacity to talk about or support disability in terms that are humane and just. Drawing on the work of various scholars, (Arneil, 2009, Livneh, 1982; Mackelprang, 2010; Smith & Applegate, 2018), we describe why disability is stigmatized within the United States and how stigma influences our relationships and communities.

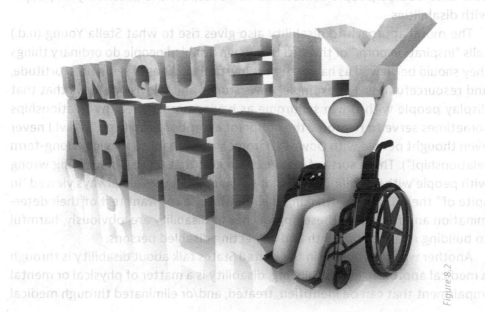

Figure 8.2

> **Student Voice**
>
> My disability does not fit the "typical" description (not even sure what that is) or government categorization, so I haven't gone through the trouble of fighting for an accommodation. It just seems like more work than it's worth. *—Bri*

> **Student Voice**
>
> In my community, going to therapy is considered an over-the-top solution for a self-sufficient problem, or not on the radar as an option at all. But seeking help through therapy should be okay for anyone! And it is more underutilized than it should be. Everyone needs help sometimes and most of us are too afraid to ask. *—Logan*

The reasons for people's attitudes toward disability and disabled people are rooted in cultural biases that have existed for hundreds of years. One approach to disability is through a moral language, and has its roots in the religious teachings of medieval Europe. In this view, disability is either a punishment from an angry deity/callous universe or a test that must be overcome to show virtue. This approach to disability invites the belief that disabled people should be treated with pity, charity, or fear. Although you might think it is a good idea to help those who need it, the problem with this approach is that it defines people with disabilities as always in need of help and never able to be fully in control of their lives. For example, one of the authors saw a man in a wheelchair struggling to get out of the chair and into his car. Another person, seeing the same thing, walked up to him and immediately started putting his hands on the person in an attempt to help—something the man let the person know he didn't want or appreciate. That a person would simply assume that their help is needed and physically touch someone else without permission reveals how able-bodied people sometimes don't respect the autonomy of people with disabilities.

The moral approach to disability also gives rise to what Stella Young (n.d.) calls "inspiration porn," or the idea that when disabled people do ordinary things they should be viewed as having almost mystical qualities of resilience, fortitude, and resourcefulness. For example, news stories and television shows that that display people with Down syndrome as having normal, healthy relationships sometimes serve to reinforce the notion or exceptionalism (e.g., "Wow! I never even thought people with Down syndrome were capable of having a long-term relationship!"). These sorts of instances suggest that there is something wrong with people with disabilities, and that their achievements are always viewed "in spite of" their disability—making their disability a constant test of their determination and fortitude. These approaches to disability are, obviously, harmful to building relationships with and respecting disabled persons.

Another way that people in the United States talk about disability is through a medical approach. In this thinking, disability is a matter of physical or mental impairment that can be identified, treated, and/or eliminated through medical intervention. This approach to disability treats people as if they are broken and need to be fixed through institutional or medical resources. In some ways, this approach has been helpful for people with disabilities. The IDEA, ADA, and other laws are built on this type of thinking; that is, that with the proper tweaks to society (e.g., building wheelchair ramps, dispensing medication to people with bipolar disorder, or providing braille textbooks for people who are blind), society can offer equal access and opportunities. Certainly, one positive aspect for this approach is that it advocates for intervention and remediation, not abandonment or fetishization, of people with disabilities. As a result, it creates a society where laws ensure a level of equality among people of various abilities by providing resources to those who need aid. However, this approach can also be harmful to building relationships across disability. One example of this is the debates in the Deaf community about whether to receive medical treatment that might address hearing impairment. People who are not Deaf may think it obvious that, when possible, Deaf people should receive medical treatment to correct or cure them of their deafness. However, many Deaf people see these treatments as a threat to the way of life and culture that they have developed as a people with a common experience and language (i.e., Sign Language). The pressure, both social and legal, that able-bodied people put on disabled people to "fit in" or "be normal" can rob people of their ability to pursue their interests freely.

Certainly, there is nothing intrinsically wrong with wanting to ensure that everyone's work, educational, or religious institution is structured in a way that is helpful for all people. However, the problem with this approach is that it is based on the notion that society should be built around what is the norm—able-bodied people—with concessions or aid given to those whose needs are not too burdensome or onerous. So, societally, we will build an elevator for a person with mobility issues—as long as it doesn't cost too much. And, we'll prescribe medicine for mental disability—as long as the person has a job that provides insurance and enough money to cover the copay. As a result, the practices that would ensure full inclusion are never realized because society includes people with disabilities at the pace of the imagination, willpower, and empathy of able-bodied people. In other words, unless and until able-bodied people change the way they think about disability and disabled people, then we will never achieve a society that is free from exclusion and oppression.

The type of cultural norms that characterize society's approach to disability also influences the way that we identify and respond to it using moral or medical language. As Livneh (1982) pointed out, our media, stories, and entertainment all have ideal role models, who are almost always portrayed as beautiful, able-bodied, and athletic. As children, we internalize these narratives, viewing ourselves and others against this measuring rod for defects or deficits. As adults, many people view their worth on the basis of their income and productivity, and disability is viewed as a threat to being independent and financially secure.

People who ascribe to these views often think people with disabilities are less than or different from so-called normal people, and just the presence of a disabled person can cause them distress or discomfort. The type of culture we inhabit is best represented by the hypothetical, and hyperbolic, claim that many people make: "I'd rather be dead than to suddenly be (insert: blind, deaf, unable to walk, or mentally disabled)." Many people ascribe to the cultural belief that people with disabilities inhabit a much different, and much less rich, form of life than able-bodied people do, and treat them with fear, contempt, and pity.

Either as a student with a disability or as an able-bodied student, you will need to learn how to navigate the culture of higher education. And, as we have described, that culture is one that is all too often based on fear and misinformation about what disability is and how to best support it. Students with disabilities are often thought of as people who get special treatment, who don't deserve to be in higher education, and who are a burden on the educational community (Golsan & Rudick, 2015). In order to overcome these challenges, you'll have to work hard to create a community that supports all students.

Negotiating Disability in Higher Education

In this section, we described ways that students with disabilities can be best supported by the institutional culture. As we mentioned earlier, higher education is governed by different rules and laws than PK–12, so we believe it is important to highlight the resources your campus may have available to you. The first list we offer shows ways that disabled students can be better advocates for themselves. We then describe the things that able-bodied students can do to make their classrooms more inclusive to, and their relationships stronger with, students with disabilities.

For Disabled Students

Connect With the Disability Resource Office. This resource is perhaps the most important place you can go to while on campus. The disability resource office (and it may be called something else, for example, disabled student services) houses the staff that oversee any accommodations that you may need and can sometimes offer testing services if you have an undiagnosed disability. They can also refer you to counseling if you are in need of therapy or psychological treatment for either long-term (e.g., bipolar disorder) or short-term (e.g., grieving the death of a loved one) disability. If able, talk with someone at the office in person, establish a connection with them, and keep their office phone number in your phone. It is incredibly important to maintain contact with your resource officer in order to ensure you are receiving the appropriate care for your disability. If you do not feel that your officer is helpful, you may wish to speak to the director of the office to see if you can be reassigned to someone else.

Figure 8.3

What Can a Disability Resource Office Do?

The disability resource office on campus should be able to provide the following to students:

- Help completing the admissions process.
- Help filling out disability documentation.
- Accessible facilities (e.g., wheelchair accessible room).
- Alternate testing (private room, extended time, or reader).
- Interpreters (for ELL and the Deaf).
- Note taking.
- Scribes.
- Reading services (including reading apps).
- Digital voice recorders or video recorders (to record lectures).
- Adaptive technology.
- Ergonomic equipment.
- Alternate format texts and audio books.

Be Firm. For better or worse, you will have to be your own advocate in many of these situations, so you will need to learn to be firm (if you are not already). Although many instructors are supportive of students with disabilities, and are happy to accommodate them in their classes, there will always be that minority who are less than helpful. Similarly, many disability staff are dedicated and knowledgeable practitioners, but some of them can say or do harmful things out of ignorance, if not malice. You will have to advocate for yourself and learn when to pick your battles and when to stand firm to argue for accommodation to your issue.

Find Supportive Instructors. An important part of learning to be firm is having a group of supportive people who can back you up in case you have an issue. You should talk with your instructors and find out which ones will be willing to listen and help you, and which may not. If you are having difficulties securing an accommodation in one class, perhaps you can ask your supportive instructor from a different class to write an email to the disability resource office on your behalf. Or, if it is a class in the same department, maybe your supportive instructor can talk with the unsupportive instructor. Your job is to find those people who are knowledgeable and supportive about disability and keep in contact with them about any issues you may face.

Student Voice

Students can express the need for more health-related resources by being designated counselors in each department because it would be more accessible and less taboo than the health center. —Alexandria

Be Persistent. Much like being firm, you will sometimes need to learn to be persistent. A lot of what goes on in disability support is legal in nature and requires tons of paperwork and bureaucracy. Sometimes you will have to fill out paperwork multiple times, remind disability resource staff or instructors about forms to fill out, or contact doctors, therapists, or counselors about setting up, canceling, or altering appointments. Having to engage in this sort of work while you are also trying to complete your classes, work a job, and/or have a love life can be incredibly draining and frustrating. However, you may have to engage in this sort of activity to ensure that you are receiving fair treatment by your college.

Be Knowledgeable. Whereas in public PK-12 your parents may have worked out the details of your accommodations with a special education instructor, in college you will have to do your own negotiation. As such, you need to be knowledgeable about the laws and rules that govern your particular issue, and how to best accommodate them, in order to maximize your ability to be successful in higher education. Although certainly the disability resource officer should know how to best support you, and should relay that information to your instructor, it may be up to you to provide specifics or corrections. Being knowledgeable means you won't be caught off-guard by bad decisions, and will know how to best advocate for yourself in case an issue arise.

Document Interactions. When you talk with disability resource staff or your instructors about how to accommodate your disability, be sure to document the interaction. You can always ask if you can audio record the interaction and check your local and state laws on the Internet on whether you can audio record without another person's permission. If you can't audio record someone, then take notes as you are talking with them. If you have a hard time taking notes, then bring someone with you to the meeting so they can provide support and take notes. By documenting interactions, you ensure that there is no miscommunication among disability resource staff, instructors and you.

Provide Documentation Early. Instructors often appreciate being notified of a need for accommodation early (rather than later) in the semester. Try to visit the disability resource office either the week before a semester starts or the first week of the semester, so you can give the proper documentation to your instructors in the first or second week of the semester. If you have a new or sudden disability (e.g., car wreck resulting in a hospital visit), then provide documentation to the student affairs office as well as your instructor as soon as you are back on campus.

Take Time for Self-Care. You may find times when you are frustrated with your instructors, disability resource staff, or fellow students about how they are handling your accommodations. Or, maybe someone said or did something in class that was hurtful to you or made you feel minimized. Make sure that you take time for self-care—however that may look to you—and decompress. Creating a space where you can feel emotionally and psychologically supported is sometimes the best antidote to the issues you may have to navigate in your interactions with faculty, staff, and students.

Find Supportive Peers. You should strive to find supportive peers in your classes. These might be other students with disabilities or able-bodied students. However, it is important that you know that you can rely on them to support you in your needs for accommodation and respect from people in the classroom. As we mentioned earlier, there is a lot of stigma about disability and knowing that you have people that you can rely on can make the difference between a good and bad day.

For Able-Bodied Students

Avoid Condescension. One of the first things for able-bodied people to avoid doing, especially if the person they are addressing has a mental disability, is being condescending to them. You may not even be aware that you are doing it, but U.S. culture so completely minimizes the experiences of and knowledge of people with disabilities that it can be an engrained, habituated way of talking with people with disabilities. Talking in a high, false, or slow voice as if the person is a child or incapable of reasoning; making promises to hang out and not following through; or ignoring or talking over people with disabilities are all common ways to minimize disabled people's lives. Be aware of your body, tone, and facial expressions when are you talking with people with disabilities.

> ### Student Voice
>
> I have an invisible disability and it is devastating when classmates speak negatively of people with my condition or when professors express that it is easy to overcome or not "serious." —Timothy

Check Space. Look around your classroom. Are the desks in rows too narrow for a person in a wheelchair to get through? Are there book bags and clutter on the ground that may trip a person who is blind? Maybe your phone's ringtone would trigger someone with PTSD? Remember, in a school classroom, everyone (not just you) owns the space. As such, everyone should have the same freedom of mobility and distraction-free environment. By identifying your own behaviors, you can begin the process of ensuring that classrooms are spaces that welcome and affirm all educational participants.

Figure 8.4

Support Disabled Students' Requests. Sometimes instructors can make course materials and classroom interactions inaccessible and, when they are notified of it, may be resistant to doing the work of making it inclusive. Unfortunately, it is sometimes easy for this type of instructor to dismiss requests if they think it is just to accommodate one student (i.e., "I have to do all this work just for one person?"). In these instances, you may need to speak up and voice support for student requests or different types of formats. For example, if the instructor provides a very poorly copied .pdf file of an article (i.e., making it impossible for those with dyslexia to read it) or only lectures without recording their talk, then you may want to talk with other students in your department about making these types of practices common across all classes. And, if you hear a student make these requests and the instructor denies or downplays them, you should talk with the disabled student to see if you can help them get in touch with the department chair or disability support services.

> **Student Voice**
>
> I have an undiagnosed and invisible illness and it is helpful when classmates share their experiences and when professors make themselves approachable by appearing nonthreatening and supportive despite the workload. —*Seong-In*

Be Sensitive. One of the hardest, yet simplest, things you can do to support people with disabilities is to not use their diagnoses as descriptors or insults. Saying something is "retarded," commenting that a person must be "blind" to not see something, that the weather is "bipolar," or that something is "crazy" or "insane" makes someone's physical or mental health and well-being a way to describe something. The problem with this type of behavior is that it continues to stigmatize people with disabilities because it connects who they are to something that is negative, distasteful, or abnormal. By avoiding these types of language habits, you can help students with disabilities feel included and affirmed—something that all people should be able to experience!

Make Mistakes and Try Again. You're not going to be perfect at interacting with or supporting students with disabilities. Don't be so afraid to make a mistake that you end up not doing anything! If you make a mistake, apologize quickly and move onto the next task or issue that needs to be addressed. If you continue to make mistakes, then you may need to take a step back and make sure that you are putting your energy in the right place.

Activism for Universal Design and Destigmatization

Higher education provides one of the few ways that people in the United States can achieve their personal and professional ambitions. At its best, colleges and universities offer a place where students can challenge their curiosity, connect

Student Voice

I want a college where there are counselors/therapists in every building, not just the Wellness or Health Center. Making students walk across campus for mental health concerns make them feel ostracized and alone. I want a reduction of the "clinical" nature of therapy because it would make it more accessible to new students and instructors alike. Also, communication between therapists and instructors to develop awareness about illnesses and disabilities and how to communicate thoughtfully in the presence of them. —*Theresa*

Student Voice

I've always appreciated the value of world mental health day and similar celebrations for raising awareness of health issues. I think days such as this should be increasingly publicized at colleges and in communities. —*Bobbie*

with others, and develop a sense of community. However, when our campuses and classrooms do not support all students to fulfill their capabilities, then society does a grave disservice to our families and communities. To create an inclusive college, students will need to come together to be activists for universal design and destigmatization of disability (Dolmage, 2015). Only when we can truthfully claim that our institutions support all learners, all the time, can we honestly claim that education is open to all students.

The first step to ensuring that colleges and universities support all students is to make sure that everything—from your classes to your departments to the entire university—supports and implements a universal design for learning approach. **Universal design** refers to the "process of making sure that all aspects of the learning environment are accessible to all participants" (Bell, Goodman, & Ouellett, 2015, p. 67). This approach to the university is much different than the traditional medical approach to disability that focuses on what concessions or accommodations the institution can make to students with disabilities while focusing primarily on how to serve able-bodied students. Instead of viewing different ways of teaching and learning as "normal vs. abnormal," or "normal vs. special education" we can, instead, seek to create a culture where all teaching and learning is inclusive from the very outset. This approach to education ensures that all students are supported from the moment they step foot on campus to the time they turn their tassel.

Make no mistake—universal design is a massive undertaking, both in terms of renovating and updating old facilities and technologies, while changing the culture of higher education to affirm all students. You will need to find out if there are buildings that are not accessible by everyone (e.g., no elevator, no automatic doors, or narrow doorways), encourage instructors to make all readings available in text-to-speak or braille, and make sure class videos shown are captioned with text. There are, of course, a lot more actions that universities can take to make their campuses more inclusive than what we have mentioned here. What is important is that these types of activities are not done only when a student with a disability requests an accommodation, but is freely available to all students, all the time. By doing so, this creates a culture where students are not shamed for asking for help or treatment; instead, it focuses attention on the variety of ways that humans learn and respects the fact that a wide range of teaching methods is the best approach to engage the variety of needs that characterize student learning. In short, universal design is a potent tool in a quest to destigmatize disability in higher education and society.

Stigma is principally a cultural phenomenon; that is, it is created and maintained through our everyday communication and encoded into our daily habits and rituals (Smith, 2007). As such, it is important that people find ways of addressing how stigma is communicated, such as challenging denigrating labels, questioning spurious or erroneous information (e.g. vaccines cause autism), and intervening when disabled people are targeted for discrimination. However, engaging in this type of work will not be easy. As Smith and Applegate (2018) point out, the stigma associated with disability is not just located in higher education; rather, it is a part of our families, schools, and religious institutions. For example, Pescosolido, Fettes, Martin, Monahan, and McLeod (2007) found that parents were twice as likely to suspect the child of potential violence and five times as likely to support forced treatment for children labeled "mentally ill" versus "physically ill." And Rose, Thornicroft, Pinfold, and Kassam (2007) found that 14-year-old students used approximately 250 terms or phrases to describe mental illness, none of which were positive. In other words, as a society, we have a lot of work to do to deprogram ourselves of all the negative stereotypes and assumptions we have about people with disabilities.

Some of the most important work being done on this issue right now is under the label *neurological* and *physiological diversity*. These terms denote a move away from the medical model that seeks to treat a disease and enforce psychological and physical conformity to instead focus on accepting a spectrum of neurological and physiological differences (see Smith & Applegate, 2017). In other words, we believe all people have rich lives, and it is everyone's responsibility to create a society where people are able to live up to their full capabilities. Some people with disabilities need medical attention and help, others are capable of feats that would dazzle our imaginations, but most lead ordinary, unremarkable lives (just like most able-bodied people). The difference is not the person, but how society is structured in a way that allows some people to thrive while others are harmed. A person with a disability is not broken, nor do they necessarily want or need to be cured; rather, they need the same society that able-bodied people have—one that doesn't fetter their ambitions with unthinking prejudice based on stigma.

****

It is important to remember that your work to advocate on this issue will be going against the grain of many hundreds of years of cultural bias and institutionalized harm. The ways that people view disability is wrapped up in how we identify and pursue what we think of as a good, full, or meaningful life. However, the stigma that surrounds disability is harmful—not just for people with a disability, but all people. In a society where we believe (whether explicitly or not) that people with disabilities lead less meaningful lives, it is just a short jump to think that they are less meaningful people. And, a society based on that type of thinking cannot realize communities where people are free to fulfill their capabilities and pursue their ambitions.

Discussion Questions

- Develop a list of all the different types of disabilities (mental and physical) that you know. Create a list of stereotypes that go with each type of disability. Share with others how you have (un)intentionally acted on or perpetuated some of these stereotypes.

- Discuss problems of access that you have noticed on campus and how you might start addressing those issues.

Student Challenge

- Create a campaign to fix an issue of accessibility on campus.
- Work with the local students with disabilities advocacy group as a member or an ally.

CHAPTER 9

Financing College
Student Debt in an Age of Rising Tuition Costs

CHAPTER OBJECTIVES

By the end of the chapter, you should be able to:

- Describe the historical context for education and its cost in the United States

- Practice financial literacy skills (e.g., banking, credit checks, and FAFSA)

- Identify financial aid opportunities within higher education

- Learn how to develop a side hustle

- Connect activism about the costs of college with your financial literacy skills

ORIENTING QUESTIONS

As you read the chapter, try to answer the following questions:

- Where should you look for financial aid resources?

- What are three student financial aid myths?

- Why are the costs of a college education rising?

In 1971–1972, the average full-time student received approximately $3,600 in financial aid, and nearly $2,400 of that money was through grants or work study. In other words, the average student took out a mere $1,200 in loans to attend college for the year. Fast forward to 2016–2017, and the average full-time student received a little over $16,000 in financial aid, and nearly $6,500 of that aid was in the form of loans (The College Board, 2019). The average student takes 5 years to complete their degree (National Student Clearinghouse, 2016), which means that the average student leaves college with over $32,500 in debt. The sharp spike in student debt over the past 40 years has resulted in a society where nearly 4 in 10 adults under 30 have student loan debt, amounting to over a trillion dollars in overall debt.

Although some may think that student loan debt is "good debt" because they received a diploma in exchange for their money, the fact is that there is no such thing as "good debt." Once you complete your degree, you'll have to pay back what you borrowed, plus interest. Depending on what types of loans you received, you could pay anywhere from 4–10% interest on your loan. If, for example, you took Direct Loans (7.9% interest) for $32,500, you would pay nearly $410 per month for the next 10 years (paying about $49,000). That's right, you're going to pay about $17,000 *more* than what you actually borrowed. Depending on what kind of job you get after college, that's money that you could have used to buy a new car, put a down payment on a house, or save for retirement—or pay rent, make essential repairs to your car, and purchase food. The burden of student debt is why young people are less optimistic about the economy, less likely to get married or have children than previous generations, and more

Figure 9.1

> ### Student Voice
>
> I never thought college was attainable for me as a senior in high school, so I never applied. Once I finally did apply I found it impossible to get financial aid, due to my parents making enough money to support me. I was never able to pay for books and honestly found it to be really intimidating. —*Barbara*

> ### Student Voice
>
> I received acceptance in to my dream college when I applied in high school. I have always wanted to go to school in Rome, Italy. However, I did the math on how expensive it would be to go to an American college in Rome for all 4 years and realized I would be coming out with almost $200k of debt for a bachelor's. I don't have $200k lying around and at that time I didn't really know what I wanted to do with my life let alone what major I was going to work towards earning a degree in. I also did not want $200k of debt just to go to my dream college. I felt like it would be a waste for me to spend so much money. —*Dani*

likely to owe money on other important purchases such as homes or cars (Deloitte, 2019; Pew, 2015).

Now, before you go running for the hills, we should remind you that a higher education degree still remains an important part of people's well-being. As Georgetown Public Policy (2014) noted, approximately 65% of all jobs will require postsecondary education and training. The Bureau of Labor Statistics (2018) estimated that in 2016, those with a BA degree had an unemployment rate of 2.7%, with weekly earnings of about $1,200. Those with some college but no degree had an unemployment rate of 4.4% and made about $800 a week. And, finally, those with just a high school diploma had a 5.2% unemployment rate and made about $700 a week. Beyond the economic benefits of a higher education degree, studies have also found that college-educated people lead happier, healthier lives. Trostel's (2015) review of the research leads him to argue that college-educated people are less prone to crime and bad health behaviors (e.g., smoking) and are more likely to donate time and money, vote and engage in community activism, and build bonds with those in their neighborhoods. His work points to a compelling conclusion—that a college education has a multitude of significant, positive influences on individuals and society.

Taken together, though, we have a pretty disturbing image of higher education. On one hand, we know that its benefits—for individuals and their families, communities, and society—are manifold. And yet, on the other hand, we know that many people are barred from attending college or drop out due to financial hardship. Even those who complete college have their success marred by the heavy burden of student debt. We find this system of education to be oppressive as it severely limits the ability of working and middle-class people to realize their capabilities. In this chapter, we first offer some reasons for the rising cost of college. We think it is important that you know that if you experience financial hardship due to student debt that you are not alone. Millions of students are, to a greater or lesser degree, going through the exact same issues as you.

As such, our overview of the reasons for student debt provide a social, rather than merely individual, diagnosis of the problem. We then detail the various costs, benefit programs, and life hacks you can use to make good financial decisions. We conclude the chapter with an examination of how to engage in activism about student debt in order to ensure that others do not have to go through the same oppressive system that you, and many others, will navigate.

Why Isn't Education Free? And, Who Should Pick Up the Tab?

People in the United States value education in three primary ways: to create a strong national workforce, to enhance one's economic prospects, and as a vehicle for democracy and social justice (Labaree, 1997). Each of these perspectives complements and contradicts the other, and reflects the complex ways that people view, navigate, and value education. For example, if a person thinks education is primarily about a national workforce, they will most likely support institutions that produce students who can contribute to national defense, cybersecurity, or engineering. This person would have very little interest in supporting art, history, or literature because they believe that these areas of study do not have an immediate connection to securing a strong nation-state. Similarly, a person who believes education is a vehicle for advancing one's economic prospects would support an education that produces students who can be business administrators, financial advisers, tax consultants, computer programmers, or other skills-based/white-collar jobs and wouldn't support education about music, culture, or community activism. Those who advocate for social justice recognize the need for a strong national economy and personal financial advancement, but also assert that people are more than their worth as consumers or competitors. Rather, drawing from the capabilities approach, they assert that education should help people realize their potential for economic, but also spiritual, psychological, and physical, well-being.

Unfortunately, decisions about how to fund education are controlled by people who stand to profit the most if their vision

Student Voice

I got into all my top schools that I applied to in high school, but I was still unsure of what I wanted to do with my life. I had some money saved up, but at the time, investing in college felt like throwing a dart in the dark. So, I took a gap year and worked a corporate job for a while only to realize I hated it. Both my parents have higher level education so I was under a lot of pressure to enroll in a 4-year university, but I didn't initially see the value in spending tens of thousands of dollars at a place where there's no real guarantee of anything. It's okay to take time to figure it out, save money in city or community college, and give yourself space to learn what you like and don't like. Sure, if you have a ton of disposable income, you can still do all that at a 4 year, but if you don't, there are a lot of other options. —*George* remains dominant. Legislators, politicians, and bureaucrats benefit when there is a strong national economy because then they can ask corporations and their lobbyists for money to run their campaigns. CEOs and other corporate sponsors benefit when there is a push to create a large labor force of talent because the more people there are that can do a job, the less a company has to pay each worker (i.e., supply and demand). As a result of governmental and corporate pressures, many institutions of higher education have increasingly moved away from their original mission to serve the public good and, instead, have narrowed their focus down to little more than just glorified job training. We strongly believe that education is more important than just its connection to employment; rather, education is an essential component of the human experience and is an integral part of their ability to realize their human capabilities.

Figure 9.2

So, if tuition continues to rise at higher than the national inflation rate, where is the money going? First, let's address the myths. The primary myth is that student financial aid is a primary driver of increasing tuition costs. The argument is that when universities have their budgets cut, they can simply raise tuition, and students will simply take out larger loans. Although it is true that as available aid increased over the past 40 years so, too, did the cost of tuition, there is little evidence to support that one causes the other. In fact, the vast majority of research finds no link between student aid and tuition (Archibald, & Feldman, 2014; The Institute for College Access & Success, 2011; Warren, 2012). The persistent myth that student aid is the driving factor, and the fact that most student aid is used by working and middle-class students, leads us to believe that this notion is propagated primarily by people who do not want to fund these projects through taxes on corporations and the wealthy—entities that have the most to lose in an economy that supports everyone's capabilities. In other words, it's a part of the neo-capitalist (see Chapter 2) imperative to slash public programs that help everyday people, thereby increasing the profits of the already super-wealthy.

The second myth is that pay for professors, particularly full-time and tenured professors, is the primary driver of costs. However, the average professor makes about the same amount of money now ($77,000) than they did in 1970 ($74,000). The professors' constant wage level over 40 years is coupled with the fact that most faculty are not full time or tenured; rather, they are part-time adjuncts who make far less than their full-time counterparts (about $30,000) (PayScale, n.d.; National Center for Educational Statistics [NCES], 2012a; 2012b). Additionally, although some may cite benefits (e.g., health insurance or retirement plan) as a reason that faculty costs contribute to the problem, the truth is that most part-time adjunct faculty don't qualify for those programs. We believe the myth that faculty wages drive up student tuition is a way to encourage students to agree to reducing faculty pay under the misguided notion that it will make college cheaper for them. In other words, it pits students against professors, encouraging them to fight each other rather than recognizing the true cause of rising tuition costs. Additionally, reducing professor pay would drive many of them into other parts of the economy, leaving those who are left to teach less equipped to support students (e.g., higher class sizes for students taught by less experienced/knowledgeable faculty), except, that is, at wealthy universities where private alumni dollars can be used to sustain fair compensation. As a result, students from wealthy families not only have the advantage of their income, but also the benefit of a better education that their wealth gives them access to. Again, we see this as a part of the neo-capitalist imperative to reduce public support for working and middle-class people, and a threat to their ability to realize their capabilities.

The final myth is that large projects (e.g., buildings) increase tuition. Certainly, some universities do not make good decisions about how to repair or construct new buildings, and that can get a university into financial trouble (Marcus, 2017). However, there is no evidence to suggest that building new residence halls or investing in fiber-optic internet is driving national tuition costs. New buildings, in particular, often do not affect tuition prices because many of them are paid for by donors, endowments, grants, or other forms of external funding (Archibald & Feldman, 2014). The idea that student living at state or community colleges is too lavish is, in our minds, a subtle form of shaming lower- and middle-class people. To wit, there is no national conversation about how "spoiled" students are at wealthy universities, only at places that serve the majority of the public (i.e., working- and middle-class students). We believe this myth has its root in the idea that society should reflect a strong stratification between the haves and the have-nots, and perpetuates the notion that everyday working people shouldn't be able to enjoy their living conditions. This type of thinking, in turn, creates a culture that severely curtails the ability of most people to realize their capabilities.

The truth of rising tuition costs, like so many problems that face our society, is complex. Part of the reason tuition has skyrocketed is rising athletics costs. Most universities subsidize their sports programs with general funds that are meant for hiring faculty and staff, making repairs, or keeping tuition stagnant. In fact, fewer than a dozen universities make a profit from their athletics programs (American Council on Education, 2014). One reason for this may be coaches' pay. For example, the top 10 highest paid football coaches earn between $5 and $11 million dollars annually (Kemenetz, 2017). Another reason is the increase in administrative and staff (not faculty) costs. For example, although the number of faculty hires largely remained stagnant, the number of administrative employees grew by 39% between 1993 and 2007 (Greene, Kisida, & Mills, 2010). University administrators' average pay is $400,000, and nearly 70 high-level administrators in public and private colleges earn more than $1 million (Jacobs, 2014; NPR, 2017). To put this in perspective, the average starting salary for professors is $60,000 (Locsin, 2014). However, the rise in administrative costs is a direct result of the federal and state governments passing more regulations on public universities, necessitating more employees to handle the higher bureaucratic load. Although both of these issues may contribute to rising tuition, neither are the main culprits in rising tuition costs.

Most research on the issue of rising tuition costs points to the continued erosion of state government financial support for higher education. From 2000 to 2010, state funding fell from about $8,300 to $6,500 per student, while the number of students rose from 13 million to over 18 million (Mitchel, Leachman, Masterson, & Waxman, 2018). As a result, students have had to increasingly make up for lost state money by paying higher tuition to attend college. Today, many students pay more than half the cost of attending college, an almost complete reversal in terms of what students and states paid 40 years ago (Bauman, 2018). In short, student debt has exploded because state governments no longer direct resources to higher education, forcing colleges to raise tuition to maintain their quality.

Why are states allocating less tax money to higher education? The primary reason for this trend is that state governments are increasingly guided by neoliberal capitalist thinking. Many legislators espouse the belief that cutting taxes for corporations or offering lucrative tax breaks to attract businesses will broaden the state's tax base by attracting new jobs to the state. For example, in Kyle's home state of Iowa, the city and state governments offered nearly $200 million dollars in tax breaks to attract an Apple Data Center (*Des Moines Register*, 2017). The center doesn't sell goods or services (e.g., groceries), so there will be little new tax money beyond the initial construction. And, it will employ only about 50 people, meaning the economic activity employees generate (e.g., income taxes, property taxes, or sales taxes) over their lives will most likely never equal the amount of tax breaks that were given. In other words, lower- and middle-class people's tax money was given away to a corporation whose annual profits reached over $53 billion in 2015 alone. Although deals like this may help legislators make friends with corporate donors and lobbyists, the truth is that the loss of tax revenue from corporations has harmed state budgets across the nation. At the same time, wages for most workers have stayed the same (Shierholz & Mishel, 2013), so tax money from income or property taxes did not close the gap from what was lost in corporate taxes. Another implication of wage stagnation is that people couldn't afford the new economic challenge of going or sending their children to college. This, in turn, meant students had to take more student loan debt because working- and middle-class families couldn't afford to pay.

The reality, then, of rising tuition costs, and the rise of student loan debt, is that a combination of internal and external factors to higher education have contributed other problems. There are certainly some things that universities can do to reduce costs, but the primary driver of higher education tuition is the retreat of state support due to cutting taxes for the wealthy and corporations coupled with stagnant wages for most workers (Archibald & Feldman, 2014). If you're going to address this problem, the first thing you need to know is how to navigate the costs and benefits of higher education to ensure that you make it through with no or minimal student debt. In the next section, we'll talk about different costs, benefit programs, and life hacks you can use to make good financial decisions.

Making the Best of Your Financial Situation

The first thing you should do is fill out your Free Application for Federal Student Aid (FAFSA) form. If you already have—great! But, you will need to fill it out every year. If your family earns less than $50,000 a year, you may qualify for federal grants and scholarships to pay for college. That's money you don't have to pay back! If your family does make more than this amount, then you still need to fill out the form. FAFSA documentation can help you obtain low-interest

Important Online Resources for Finances

https://studentaid.ed.gov

http://www.fafsa.ed.gov

http://www.myfedloan.org

http://www.studentloans.gov

https://www.wellsfargo.com/student-center/

student loans or qualify you for university or state-level grants or scholarships. Filling out the FAFSA form is free, quick, and easy, and is your best bet to get financial support. Doing so will help you mitigate the costs of college, and ensure your financial situation doesn't bar you from your educational aspirations.

Figure 9.3

College Costs

Tuition. Tuition will be the primary cost of going to college through the 4 to 6 years you are enrolled. Depending on what type of college or university you attend, you could be paying several thousand or tens of thousands of dollars in tuition. Tuition is a fixed cost. There is nothing you can do to lower it. There are only different ways to pay for it, including scholarships, grants, loans, or family/personal resources.

Fees. Almost all universities have fees in addition to tuition costs. Fees are important to know for a few reasons. First, many scholarships, grants, or other types of benefits will not pay for fees—only tuition or (in some cases) on-campus housing. Make sure to budget for fees because you may think your scholarship gives you a "full-ride" but, in actuality, you may still have to pay fees. Second, some universities allow you to opt out of some fees. Some, like healthcare fees, are often set and cannot be changed (we wouldn't advise you change it anyway, unless you have health insurance). On the other hand, some activity, gym, and athletics fees can be removed. Make sure to contact your university's bursar or financial aid personnel and inquire.

Housing. Almost all universities require that you live on campus for the first year. Although it is often a difficult process, you can fill out the paperwork necessary to live off-campus your first year. Living off-campus, especially if you live with your family, is almost always cheaper. After your first year, you're free to stay on-campus or to move off-campus. We suggest finding off-campus housing, especially if you can split rent with other trustworthy people or stay with family. Let us reemphasize "trustworthy." We have seen many students who have stayed with their friends, only to find out that their buddies don't clean up after themselves, party too much, and never pay their share of the rent. If all of you signed a single lease, for example, then you are all equally liable for damages or missed rent, even if it was your friend who got drunk and busted out a window. Housing can be a huge cost that you can manage; however, do not make finances your only part of the decision. Living in an area that has a lot of noise or partying, or with family members who are abusive, isn't worth saving the money because you're more likely to fail your classes.

Books. Almost every class you take will require you to purchase a textbook. The National Association of College Stores (2018) estimates that students will pay an average of $484 on textbooks and materials every year. Although many bookstore have moved to a book rental policy that has reduced costs, the fact remains that textbooks can be a significant financial challenge to many students. We recommend checking your textbook store to ensure you know the correct books you will need for the class. Check online—is there a previous edition of the book that is cheaper? If so, email your professor to ask if the older edition will be acceptable or if they will even use the book (sometimes a professor may be prickly about the latter question, but you have a right to know if you need to spend money or not). Price check between your on-campus bookstore, off-campus bookstore, Amazon, Half.com, AbeBooks, Chegg, and other online retailers. If your campus has a student listserv or if you feel comfortable using Facebook Marketplace, ask if

> **Student Voice**
>
> Make sure you vibe with your roommates before you live together. I lived in a dorm at another college and was randomly paired with a roommate. They were awful, and we did not get along at all. That occurrence really came to hinder my experience in some ways because I never felt comfortable in my own room. I was constantly avoiding being there and either spending the majority of my time in the library or my friends' rooms. —Carlos

> **Student Voice**
>
> If roommates are a necessity, make sure they are people that inspire you to work hard academically. Too often I have seen close friends become caught up in trivial behavior due to the influence of their peers. I fell down that rabbit hole myself. My roommates were constantly encouraging me to forego my studying and I failed enough classes to be placed on academic probation. —Jacob

Student Voice

Luckily most professors are inclined to offer alternatives to ridiculously priced textbooks. Like pdf uploads, etc. A lot of the time professors put books on the syllabus that are not actually necessary, so I always recommend waiting until the first day to buy/rent anything. No matter what the syllabus says. —*Barbara*

Student Voice

I wish I knew my first year that I didn't have to buy directly from the bookstore. I was told by my professors that I had to buy from the bookstore and I spent over $300 on books alone for three classes. My second year I figured out this wasn't true and I found the same books on Amazon for a grand total of around $100 by used sources. It is a little infuriating how expensive the books that are assigned to us are, but there are loopholes if you know where to find them. Amazon's products have used options if they exist. I bought a book that is usually $50 for $14.95 used on Amazon. There are also Facebook groups for the particular college you're going to and students sell books on these groups all the time for a lesser price. —*Dani*

anyone who took the class the previous semester is willing to sell the book. You can also check your university library or request the book through their Inter-Library Loan program (although, remember, others may use this technique, too, so you need to do this early). We recognize that textbooks can be expensive and have done our best to reduce the price of this textbook by opting for open source pictures, in-publisher typesetting/graphics, and smaller size in order to be easier on your bank account!

Tests. You probably already paid money to take the ACT or SAT to get into college. Bad news: you may have to pay for more tests. If you plan to go to graduate school in the social sciences, arts, business, or humanities, you may need to take either the GRE (Graduate Record Examination) (cost $195) or the GMAT (Graduate Management Admission Test) (cost $250). The MCAT (Medical College Admission Test) (cost $315) is for those interested in applying for medical school, while the LSAT (Law School Admissions Test) (cost $180, with a $121 necessary subscription to the Law School Data Assembly Service) is for those who wish to pursue a law degree. If you are an international student, you may need to take the Test of English as a Foreign Language (TOEFL) exam, which can cost $180 to $250. Although you should study for these tests, we do not suggest you pay for test-preparation materials. Many university libraries have these materials for free or can procure them though Inter-Library Loan. However, depending on your score, you may need to take these tests multiple times, so make sure you have budgeted correctly.

Childcare. Students who have children often struggle to find affordable, quality childcare while enrolled. We encourage you to reach out to your professors to see if they are amenable to bringing your child(ren) to class. Many professors recognize that the difficulties of finding childcare and are open to finding ways to help. Some universities offer temporary childcare services (1 to 3 hours), so a parent can attend a class. You may also ask a trusted fellow student from another class to watch over your child for a small fee, especially if the class you share with them is right before/after the time you need childcare. You can also reach out to student services to see if there are any programs or university discounts offered to childcare facilities in the community.

Benefits

Student Loans. Nearly 70% of all undergraduate students will take out student loans (The Institute for College Access & Success, 2014). However, all loans are not created equal. The most common loans are the Federal Direct Subsidized Stafford/Ford Loans and the Federal Direct Unsubsidized Stafford/Ford Loans. Loans that are subsidized means that the U.S. government will pay the interest on the loan while you are enrolled in college, full-time. Make sure to take this type of loan if you qualify for it because you will pay less on the loan after you graduate. An unsubsidized loan, however, accrues interest while you are enrolled, which means you will be paying a higher amount back once you graduate. Depending on your family's economic need, you may qualify for a Perkins Loan, which has the lowest interest rate. The good thing about any of these loans is that they are held by the U.S. Department of Education, and can't be sold to another lending company. This, in turn, ensures that the terms of your loan never change. Another benefit is that your career may qualify you for loan forgiveness programs. Once you graduate you will have a grace period (up to 6 months) that you do not have to pay back your loans. After that, you will have to start paying your loans back, unless you file for deferment based on a financial hardship (e.g., unemployment or disability). We strongly caution you against taking private loans to pay for college because private loans are often not eligible for governmental grant and forgiveness programs. Check out the Federal Student Aid website in the box to get a sense of what you will owe on your student loans.

Scholarships and Grants. Scholarships and grants are funds given by the federal or state government, nonprofit or for-profit companies, or from the university. They are often called "free money" because the funds don't have to be paid back. They can be "need-based," which means your financial situation qualifies you for the program, or "merit-based," which means your grades, application essay, community service, or other types of work qualify you for the program (sometimes, a scholarship or grant may be a mixture of the two). The most common type of grant is the Pell Grant, which is a federal

Student Loan Information

Overview of Direct Loan and FFEL Program Repayment Plans

Repayment Plan	Eligible Loans	Monthly Payment and Time Frame	Eligibility and Other Information
Standard Repayment Plan	Direct Subsidized and Unsubsidized Loans Subsidized and Unsubsidized Federal Stafford Loans all PLUS loans all _Consolidation_ Loans (Direct or FFEL)	Payments are a fixed amount that ensures your loans are paid off within 10 years (within 10 to 30 years for Consolidation Loans).	All borrowers are eligible for this plan. You'll usually pay less over time than under other plans. Standard Repayment Plan with a 10-year repayment period is not a good option for those seeking Public Service Loan Forgiveness (PSLF). Standard Repayment Plan for Consolidation Loans is not a qualifying repayment plan for PSLF.
Graduated Repayment Plan	Direct Subsidized and Unsubsidized Loans Subsidized and Unsubsidized Federal Stafford Loans all PLUS loans all Consolidation Loans (Direct or FFEL)	Payments are lower at first and then increase, usually every two years, and are for an amount that will ensure your loans are paid off within 10 years (within 10 to 30 years for Consolidation Loans).	All borrowers are eligible for this plan. You'll pay more over time than under the 10-year Standard Plan. Generally not a qualifying repayment plan for PSLF.
Extended Repayment Plan	Direct Subsidized and Unsubsidized Loans Subsidized and Unsubsidized Federal Stafford Loans all PLUS loans all Consolidation Loans (Direct or FFEL)	Payments may be fixed or graduated, and will ensure that your loans are paid off within 25 years.	If you're a Direct Loan borrower, you must have more than $30,000 in outstanding Direct Loans. If you're a FFEL borrower, you must have more than $30,000 in outstanding FFEL Program loans. Your monthly payments will be lower than under the 10-year Standard Plan or the Graduated Repayment Plan. You'll pay more over time than under the 10-year Standard Plan. Not a qualifying repayment plan for PSLF.

Figure 9.4

continues

Student Loan Information

Overview of Direct Loan and FFEL Program Repayment Plans

Repayment Plan	Eligible Loans	Monthly Payment and Time Frame	Eligibility and Other Information
Revised Pay As You Earn Repayment Plan (REPAYE)	Direct Subsidized and Unsubsidized Loans Direct PLUS loans made to students Direct Consolidation Loans that do not include PLUS loans (Direct or FFEL) made to parents	Your monthly payments will be 10 percent of *discretionary income*. Payments are recalculated each year and are based on your updated income and family size. You must update your income and family size each year, even if they haven't changed. If you're married, both your and your spouse's income or loan debt will be considered, whether taxes are filed jointly or separately (with limited exceptions). Any outstanding balance on your loan will be forgiven if you haven't repaid your loan in full after 20 years (if all loans were taken out for undergraduate study) or 25 years (if any loans were taken out for graduate or professional study).	Any Direct Loan borrower with an eligible loan type may choose this plan. You'll usually pay more over time than under the 10-year Standard Plan. You may have to pay income tax on any amount that is forgiven. Good option for those seeking PSLF.
Pay As You Earn Repayment Plan (PAYE)	Direct Subsidized and Unsubsidized Loans Direct PLUS loans made to students Direct Consolidation Loans that do not include (Direct or FFEL) PLUS loans made to parents	Your monthly payments will be 10 percent of discretionary income, but never more than you would have paid under the 10-year Standard Repayment Plan. Payments are recalculated each year and are based on your updated income and family size. You must update your income and family size each year, even if they haven't changed. If you're married, your spouse's income or loan debt will be considered only if you file a joint tax return.	You must be a *new borrower* on or after Oct. 1, 2007, and must have received a *disbursement* of a Direct Loan on or after Oct. 1, 2011. You must have a high debt relative to your income. Your monthly payment will never be more than the 10-year Standard Plan amount. You'll usually pay more over time than under the 10-year Standard Plan. You may have to pay income tax on any amount that is forgiven.

Figure 9.4 (Continued)

continues

Student Loan Information

Overview of Direct Loan and FFEL Program Repayment Plans

Repayment Plan	Eligible Loans	Monthly Payment and Time Frame	Eligibility and Other Information
		Any outstanding balance on your loan will be forgiven if you haven't repaid your loan in full after 20 years.	Good option for those seeking PSLF.
Income-Based Repayment Plan (IBR)	Direct Subsidized and Unsubsidized Loans Subsidized and Unsubsidized Federal Stafford Loans all PLUS loans made to students Consolidation Loans (Direct or FFEL) that do not include Direct or FFEL PLUS loans made to parents	Your monthly payments will be either 10 or 15 percent of discretionary income (depending on when you received your first loans), but never more than you would have paid under the 10-year Standard Repayment Plan. Payments are recalculated each year and are based on your updated income and family size. You must update your income and family size each year, even if they haven't changed. If you're married, your spouse's income or loan debt will be considered only if you file a joint tax return. Any outstanding balance on your loan will be forgiven if you haven't repaid your loan in full after 20 years or 25 years, depending on when you received your first loans. You may have to pay income tax on any amount that is forgiven.	You must have a high debt relative to your income. Your monthly payment will never be more than the 10-year Standard Plan amount. You'll usually pay more over time than under the 10-year Standard Plan. You may have to pay income tax on any amount that is forgiven. Good option for those seeking PSLF.

Figure 9.4 (Continued)

continues

Student Loan Information

Overview of Direct Loan and FFEL Program Repayment Plans

Repayment Plan	Eligible Loans	Monthly Payment and Time Frame	Eligibility and Other Information
Income-Contingent Repayment Plan (ICR)	Direct Subsidized and Unsubsidized Loans Direct PLUS Loans made to students Direct Consolidation Loans	Your monthly payment will be the lesser of 20 percent of discretionary income, or the amount you would pay on a repayment plan with a fixed payment over 12 years, adjusted according to your income. Payments are recalculated each year and are based on your updated income, family size, and the total amount of your Direct Loans. You must update your income and family size each year, even if they haven't changed. If you're married, your spouse's income or loan debt will be considered only if you file a joint tax return or you choose to repay your Direct Loans jointly with your spouse. Any outstanding balance will be forgiven if you haven't repaid your loan in full after 25 years.	Any Direct Loan borrower with an eligible loan type may choose this plan. You'll usually pay more over time than under the 10-year Standard Plan. You may have to pay income tax on any amount that is forgiven. Good option for those seeking PSLF. Parent borrowers can access this plan by consolidating their Parent PLUS Loans into a *Direct Consolidation Loan*.
Income-Sensitive Repayment Plan (ISR)	Subsidized and Unsubsidized Federal Stafford Loans FFEL PLUS Loans FFEL Consolidation Loans	Your monthly payment is based on annual income, but your loan will be paid in full within 15 years.	You'll pay more over time than under the 10-year Standard Plan. The formula for determining the monthly payment amount can vary from lender to *lender*. Available only for FFEL Program loans, which are not eligible for PSLF.

Figure 9.4 (Continued)

Student Voice

Before the end of high school, I was ready for college. My parents attended some college, but I was the only one of siblings and parents to leave to a 4-year. I did not know much as to how to go about getting financial help, so I took out student loans to pursue my educational dreams. Since no one I knew took out student loans, I did not have much help or knowledge as to what was considered good loans to take out. For example, with one student loan, the percent interest was low for someone who did not have credit. I took the student loan out realizing much later the loan interest was variable, not fixed. This experience made me realize speaking with a financial advisor would have helped. —*Kat*

Making Smart Choices, A Loan Repayment Estimator

https://studentloans.gov/myDirect-Loan/repaymentEstimator.action?_ga=2.116755521.670459497.1518977411-181024284.1513799708

program based on financial need. Pell Grants have a maximum contribution of about $6,000 a year. If you are a teacher in a high-demand field (e.g., math) and work in a low-income school, you could qualify for a TEACH grant, which can pay up to $4,000 a year. Check with your university bursar to know what scholarships or grants are available at your state or university. Those programs are not as well publicized as the national lists and can offer great opportunities.

Work Study. Work study programs are offered by most colleges, and are based on your financial need. The amount you can earn at your work study job is based on your economic need (i.e., the more you need the more hours you can work). You apply for work study jobs through your university and interview for them just like a regular job. Applying doesn't mean you automatically get hired, and you can be fired for poor performance. Being employed at a work study job has an additional benefit—the amount you make doesn't affect your reported income level for other forms of financial aid. In other words, you may make more upfront working an off-campus part-time job, but that money may reduce the amount you can receive from other grants or scholarships.

Taxes. Are you independent or are you a dependent on your family's taxes? If you are under 24 years of age, the government and university will most likely count you as a dependent. Even if your family doesn't pay for anything, you are completely self-sufficient, your parents didn't claim you on their taxes, and/or didn't fill out a FAFSA, you will still be considered a dependent. The only way to be considered independent if you are under 24 is to be married, have dependents other than a spouse, be an orphan, be a veteran or active duty member of the US Armed Forces, or fill out emancipation documents. Unfortunately, if you are considered a dependent then much of the tax and financial aid data will be based on your family's income, not just yours. However, once you have completed college or if you are independent, then you should look into the tax incentives and economic credits for higher education. For example, when you start paying back your student loans, all federal loan interest can be added as a tax deduction—meaning you may reduce your taxes or even get a tax refund!

Activity Funding. Are you a part of a recognized student organization? Or, perhaps you are going to go to a conference and present a paper for class. Your university may have funds set aside to pay for things like travel, hotel, registration, or food. The university will often want receipts for all purchases, so make sure to keep them. And, most universities will not pay for alcoholic beverages or even a restaurant bill if it has alcoholic beverages on the receipt. Make sure to know your university's policy and ask the wait staff to separate the checks if you plan on having a drink with your meal. Any time you are leaving campus for a university-recognized activity, ask your professor, student organization advisor, or department office staff if there are funds available to support travel or lodging.

Temporary Loans. Many universities recognize that some students are faced with unexpected financial hardship that their families cannot or will not pay for. In those cases, they may have a temporary loan program that offers a small amount of money (usually less than $1,000) in the form of a no-interest loan. In other words, you will have to pay the loan back, but not with the added interest (unless you miss a payment deadline).

Hacks

Cheap or Free Household/Living Items. At the end of each semester, many students leave the university as they graduate, drop out, or transfer to other campuses. And, when they do, many of them throw many of their household (e.g., furniture) or living items (e.g., clothing) in the dumpster, put them on the

Resources for Finding Scholarships and Grants

http://www.collegescholarships.org

http://www.unigo.com

http://www.scholarships.com

http://www.studentaid.ed.gov/sa/sites/default/files/federal-grant-programs.pdf

https://www.studentscholarships.org/

https://www.fastweb.com/college-scholarships

http://www.freecollegenow.org/policy-center

http://time.com/money/4830367/free-college-tuition-promise-programs/

Understanding the How and Whys of Taxes

https://apps.irs.gov/app/understandingTaxes/student/index.jsp

> ### Student Voice
>
> Hands down the best times of my life came when the school had free activities. One event they had was dodgeball and we got a lot of the freshman baseball players on one team. Some of the best experiences I have ever had came from that and we still talk about it to this day. —*Darrel*

> ### Student Voice
>
> Entertainment is everything in college. Attend everything and I mean absolutely everything that goes on in college because that's where the best memories are made. Whether it's going to sports games, improv, silly on campus things, it will be a blast if you're with the right company. College can be as fun as you want it to be or as shitty as you want it to be, it's your choice. Sidenote ... socialize with as many people as possible and your college career will be one for the books. —*Quentin*

> ### Student Voice
>
> I also always carry around my student ID whenever I go out to places for entertainment of restaurants because a lot of places offer discounts or free things for students! A few years ago Chipotle had a special rewards program for students if you bought six burritos over time you got your seventh one free. My local PetSmart gives me 10% off my purchase of $20 or more when I show my student ID. —*Darcy*

curb, or sell them in a yard sale. As the semester comes to a close, you may want to walk or drive around student-heavy neighborhoods to see if you can pick up some free or cheap items rather than pay full price for them at a retail store.

Online Trading/Buying/Selling. Similarly, Facebook Marketplace, eBay, CraigsList, and other outlets can provide places to pick up cheap or free bicycles, furniture, or electronics.

Free Activities. Want to have fun but don't want to spend money? Many universities offer free activities, such as recreational sports, theater, or parties. Bonus if the activity offers free food!

Student Status. Many businesses in college towns and cities have special deals for college students. Make sure to have your student ID card ready so you can cash in on the discounts, perks, and reward programs.

Secondhand Goods. If you're living in the dorms or with other students, it's easy to reach out to those who are taking similar classes so you can pick up their secondhand textbooks, calculators, or other important items for cheap or free.

Cooking. In the first year of college, you will probably have a combined meal/housing plan, which will mean your food needs are largely accounted for already. However, you may still need to do a little cooking and, when you move out of the resident halls you will most likely have a lot more meals that you will not get on campus. You will be faced with the choice to order out or to cook. We suggest you

Figure 9.5

learn to cook due to its health and economic benefits. Cooking, along with other creative activities, is linked to positive mental health and a reduction of stress (Conner, DeYoung, & Silvia, 2018). Because college is such a stressful time, activities such as cooking can help you cope. Cooking your own food can be healthier than eating out. No, eating an entire tray full of fried pizza bites, topped with cheddar cheese, and drenched in ranch dressing is not what we're talking about here! However, most college campuses are near grocery stores where you can access fresh fruits, vegetables, and meats instead of highly processed foods. Economically, home-cooked meals tend to be cheaper, especially if you cook a large batch of food and freeze/refrigerate the rest to eat as leftovers. For example, a box of whole-wheat noodles ($1), chicken ($5 for one pound), can of Alfredo sauce ($3), broccoli ($1), and cup of fruit ($2 for a four-pack) can make four meals for $3.00 per meal.

Student Voice

Goodwill is my best friend. I got a pair of brand new Miss Me jeans for $5 when they're usually well over $150 brand new at a Goodwill store. Thrift stores are also great for finding new clothing and hidden treasures. I always do my thrift shopping on the first few days of the month because that is when they get new clothing and things in stock. I follow a lot of Facebook groups online for trading/buying/selling used goods when I'm looking for new clothing or things I need. —*Anastasia*

Student Voice

With housing, sharing groceries helps with the food bill. When I first started living on my own, I tried to buy most things in bulk, however, this made many perishable items go to waste quickly because I could not eat it all fast enough on my own. Also, a bag of potatoes goes a long way in college. I practically survived off a 5-pound bag of potatoes for only about $3.00 a week while getting creative with recipes. —Cindy

Guides for Cheap Meal Ideas

https://www.buzzfeed.com/melissaharrison/cheap-dinner-recipes

https://www.thesimpledollar.com/20-favorite-dirt-cheap-meals/

http://www.delish.com/cooking/recipe-ideas/g3166/cheap-easy-recipes/

https://www.bonappetit.com/gallery/cheap-recipes

http://www.womansday.com/food-recipes/g2436/cheap-dinners/

Find Your Community Library

http://www.ala.org

Library Membership. In addition to your university library membership, you may want to look into obtaining a membership to your local municipal or county library. Not only do these libraries have tons of books you can read for pleasure (rather than because your professor told you to!), you can also access magazines, newspapers, movies, television shows, and (sometimes) video games.

Entertainment. If you're like most U.S. Americans, you probably consume most of your media from subscription-based services such as Netflix, Hulu, YouTube Red, Amazon Prime, Spotify, or Pandora rather than traditional network television or radio. Even though the costs of these services is relatively low (around $10 to $15 a month), this is money that can quickly add up ($100 to $180 a year per service). You may consider sharing accounts with other students in your residence hall or house. Some services, such as Amazon Prime, also provide free or reduced shipping on products you may need (e.g., textbooks), whereas others may offer discounts if you bundle services or show student ID.

Food Banks or Food Assistance. Some universities or cities offer food banks for those who do not have food security. You may also qualify for state or federal food assistance programs based on your income. These programs are available for people who need them, and you should access them if you qualify.

Internet. What kind of internet connection do you need? If you are primarily accessing the internet for email, assignments, or other work-related reasons, you may wish to opt for a cheaper internet plan. You can access better internet at cafés or on campus, and then download movies, episodes, or games there to take back home. If you want to subscribe to a higher-tier program, you may wish to limit other expenses (e.g., subscription services) to offset the higher cost. Make sure to compare available service providers' plans and prices, and read the fine print for costs after the promotional period ends. Many companies may try to lock you into a bad contract after the first 12-month sign-up bonus ends, so be careful.

Energy Saving. If you live off campus, using less electricity, water, and natural gas can have a significant impact on your wallet. Washing your clothes in cold water, using energy-efficient bulbs, opening blinds during the winter for warmth and closing them in the summer to keep cool, keeping the thermostat warmer/cooler when you are out of the house or asleep, sealing windows that leak cool/warm air, and replacing the HVAC filter regularly can all save you money. And, best of all, it reduces your environmental pollution and resource consumption.

Transportation. You may be inclined, like many U.S. Americans, to drive to and from school and work because it is quick. But, if you live close enough, walking, biking, or taking public transportation can save you big bucks. You can also commute with other students, provided they are dependable. Driving a personal vehicle means you're paying for fuel, but you may also be paying for insurance, repairs, and other incidentals. Reducing your personal driving is not only better economically, but is healthier for you and the environment.

Planned Parenthood/University Health Center. If you need contraceptives or health check-up (e.g., Pap smear or breast cancer screening), you can do so for a reduced cost or even

Student Voice

Many students aren't aware that a lot of big companies provide student discounts for their products/ services. If you aren't sure, don't be afraid to ask! For example, Apple offers a new back-to-school discount every year. When I showed my student ID they gave me a $100 gift card that I used towards my laptop. Another good one is "Spotify for Students," which offers a bundle of unlimited music streaming plus a Hulu account for half the price of their regular subscription fee. —*Martin*

Student Voice

As far as transportation goes for college I recommend finding someone you can take classes with or at the same time as and carpool. This will make the purchase of a parking pass a lot cheaper. It only works if you have someone who is very reliable to carpool with. I wouldn't pick my best friend if I know that friend skips class a lot. All in all, you need to get creative at how you manage and spend your money. —*Takahashi*

Find Your Community Health Center

https://www.plannedparenthood.org/ or call 1-800-230-PLAN

Student Voice

As far as banking goes while in college it is important to look at both banks and credit unions to see what they have to offer. Many of them will offer a student account which has less fees and no need to have a running balance in them. —*Jacqueline*

Introduction to Banking for Students

https://www.mycreditunion.gov/

https://www.wellsfargo.com/student-center/

https://www.creditkarma.com

free at Planned Parenthood or other women's health organizations. The university health center may offer many healthcare options, from diagnosis to prescriptions, at a cheaper rate than your area doctor.

Credit Union or Bank. Many banks or credit unions have rewards systems for students who open accounts. Make sure to check if they have a mandatory minimum balance clause. This will mean you always have to have at least that much money in your account, which can sometimes make it difficult if you need to access your money quickly. Also, make sure your bank or credit union has ATMs in your area. There's nothing worse than having to pay $3 to $10 in fees to access your own money! Your credit history will not be harmed if you have multiple accounts, so it may be in your best interest to open multiple accounts and maintain the minimum balance to take advantage of the promotional gifts. Some places offer as much as $100 just to keep your money there!

Figure 9.6

Credit History Explained

Your credit history is a score that ranges from 300 to 850 that evaluates your income, debt, and payment history. That score represents your credit-worthiness, with higher scores being better.

If you miss or stop making payments on your credit cards, utility bills, or loans, then it can negatively affect your credit score. Conversely, on-time payments, paying debts off before their deadline, and not "maxing out" your credit cards will help your score.

A high credit score is helpful for major purchases and loans. Home loans, car loans, and credit cards base their interest rate on your credit score. The difference between a high and low score can seriously affect how much you have to pay back on your loan or credit card.

Transunion and Equifax monitor your credit score. You can request either company to tell you your score once per year for free. You can also get free credit monitoring at websites, such as creditkarma.com.

Credit Card. Similar to the last point, many credit cards offer promotional interest rates or cash back for signing up for their product. If you know you can pay for your purchases at the end of each month, then you never accrue interest on your credit balance. This means that you are getting free money to make purchases on the things you were going to buy anyway (e.g., food). Be careful though—credit card debt can quickly overwhelm a novice and get you into a lot of financial trouble. Only apply for and use a credit card if you know you can and *will* pay the balance off at the end of each month.

Student Voice

Do not rely on your credit card for major purchases. They are best used to make small purchases that can be easily paid off. It's much easier to pay off a $50 gas charge than it is to pay of a $1,000 tuition fee. That leaves you $50, in theory, in your bank account that you would have normally spent. Instead of spending it on something, put it into a savings account. By the time you need to pay for classes or books, or an emergency comes up, you'll have money put away. This will also raise your credit score, and won't put you in a huge hole of credit card debt. —*Anna*

Credit Terms to Know

Annual fee. A yearly fee associated with the loan or credit card. A company may call it a membership or participation fee, but it is the same thing. Ideally, you'll want to avoid cards that impose an annual fee.

continues

APR. APR stands for annual percentage rate and refers to the interest rate over the course of a year. On loans or credit cards, the APR is how much interest you will pay on the loan per year.

Balance transfer. This means moving an unpaid credit card debt from one card to another. Card issuers may offer extra-low teaser rates to encourage balance transfers. If you're tempted by such an offer, be sure you know exactly when the introductory rate expires. Transfers sometimes have a "balance transfer fee," which is a one-time penalty associated with moving your debt from on loan or credit card to another.

Compound interest. This refers to the interest that accrues on unpaid interest. So, in the first year, you owed $100 at 5%, so you owed $105. Next year, if you don't pay that loan, you'll owe $105 at 5%, so now you owe $110.25. Compound interest can quickly balloon if it is calculated per day, per week, or per month, so make sure to check your credit card or loan to see when it is applied.

Default. When you do not pay a loan or credit card on time for a specified amount of time (usually two to three payments in a row), then the company will put it in default. This will have a large negative impact on your credit score. Debt collectors may begin harassing you about payments. It's not good. Avoid this.

Grace period. The grace period is the interest-free time a bank or credit card company allows between the transaction date and the billing date for cardholders who do not carry a balance. Sometimes a loan or credit card will have a special grace period for signing up, which can be as long as a year.

Late fee. If you miss your payment date, you'll be charged a late fee—sometimes as much as $50! Avoid late fees by arranging autopays on your cards to ensure you pay on time every month.

Minimum payment. This is the minimum amount you must pay to keep the account from defaulting. Usually, this amount equals 2% of the outstanding balance. To reduce debt more quickly, pay more than the minimum payment each month (and avoid adding any new charges).

Over-limit fee. If you exceed the credit limit on a card, you will be charged a fee. Over-limit fees are generally around $35 per infraction. If you go over the limit, call the credit card company and ask for it to be forgiven. Often, companies will do so for the first infraction. But if you are going over the limit, then you need to talk to someone about your debt management skills and put yourself back on a path to financial stability.

Employment. You can always apply for a part-time job to help make ends meet. Many companies in college cities and towns know students' schedules and are willing to work around their classes, organizations, and travel. Remember, though, that working a part-time job is not the reason you are at college—you are there to obtain a degree. Nor should you sacrifice your educational pursuits to make your manager happy or on the promise of being hired full time after graduation. If a manager doesn't understand your study needs, they aren't a good boss, and sacrificing yourself for a promise is a road to broken dreams. Your job is there to help you fulfill your true objective—getting a college education.

Side Hustles. Beyond formal jobs, you may be interested in side hustles. Tutoring services, driving for a rideshare service, walking pets, babysitting, cleaning houses, participating in research, shopping for someone else, washing cars, giving music lessons, writing resumes, and house sitting are just a few examples of ways that you can make money without having a dedicated part-time job.

What Can You Do About the High Cost of College?

Even though we have given you a great deal of information about navigating the financial aspects of obtaining a college degree, the nagging question remains—why do you have to do all this extra work just to get an education? If you are like us, we believe the current system unfair to working- and middle-class students and their families. If a person wants an education, whatever stage of life they are at, they should be able to access it. And, the education they receive should not just be tied to job training or professional development. Although certainly those are important aspects of college, we think people should be able to access information about how to love each other, build strong communities, appreciate art and music, and generally how to live well. In other words, we see education as an important component in securing the tenets of Nussbaum's capabilities approach, and through it, a society based in social justice.

> **Student Voice**
>
> I have had to work throughout my college career. Otherwise, I would not be able to afford to go. I live with my parents to save money. I work as a waitress in a small town. I don't make much, but I'm able to save enough during the semester to pay for the next round of classes. I've been at the same location for almost 3 years, and I've earned a lot of respect from my managers. Most managers or bosses don't care if you are in school. I've been told, by my manager, that my job is more important than school, and I would be better off dropping out. I told her that I wouldn't need a job if I didn't go to school. She didn't like that response. My other three managers realized that I had specific goals and priorities. Now, they no longer try to schedule me during my classes, or get mad at me for missing a meeting to work on school work. Working while going to school is necessary for most. It's hard, and often feels like a dead end. But as long you are able to keep your priorities straight, you'll be able to reach your goals. —Anna

> **Student Voice**
>
> I sell a lot of my designer clothing on eBay. I have even shopped at the Goodwill and found nice items only to turn around and resell them for more. —Betty

Figure 9.7

Out-of-control tuition rates need to be set in a larger discussion of economic justice. Students paying higher tuition is a direct result of a lack of state tax dollars, which is linked to handing out tax incentives to already wealthy individuals and corporations. Take, for example, the plight of Oklahoma (Carroll, 2016; *The Economist*, 2018). As of 2018, the state faced multiyear budget shortfalls totaling in the billions of dollars, prompting the legislature to make deep cuts to social services, education, and transportation. One of the main reasons for the lack of money was due to lowering the Gross Production Tax, which is a tax on companies that extract petroleum through traditional wells or fracking to 3.2% in 2014—lower than any other state in the country.

The oil industry, and the lawmakers who benefited from their sponsorship, maintained that the low tax was the primary reason that the companies drilled for oil in Oklahoma and that raising the tax would drive away businesses. As the budget deteriorated, the legislature refused to raise the tax to a level that was comparable to other states (e.g., Wyoming or Texas), which ranged from 7–13%. Instead, they continued to cut funding to essential services, driving schools to lay off teachers, reducing the school week from 5 to 4 days a week, and stopping bus services to rural students. State support for higher education declined by nearly 18%, ranking Oklahoma at the bottom in state support for students. When these measures failed to address the shortfall, they proposed raising taxes on cigarettes, gasoline at the pump, and alcohol while raising tuition at all public universities—in other words, raising costs that harm working- and middle-class people the most. Oklahoma should be a cautionary tale that reminds you how important it is to ensure that we live in an economy that works for everyone, and not just corporations and the super-wealthy. Fair taxation and responsible spending starts with a tax agenda that rewards working and middle-class families by providing a strong social safety net, well-funded schools and universities, and dependable roads and transportation services.

The problem of exploding student debt has been growing for decades, and state and federal politicians have done little to address the problem. If something bad happens once, we may call it an accident. But, when a problem persists for many years, then calling it an accident serves to cloud the issue. The only explanations for student debt include negligence, ignorance, self-interest, and lack of empathy. Some people, no matter what the facts are, will continue to support a political-economy that hurts working- and middle-class people because they are or want to curry favor with the super-wealthy, corporations, and lobbyists. You'll be better served by ignoring those people and focusing on people who mean well, but may lack your knowledge and expertise. In those cases, you may need to provide them with information that you have started to acquire in this book. But, we hope you don't stop at this book as your only source to find information about student debt and the mismanagement of taxes. Rather, we hope you find information from reputable organizations that have a strong investment in economic justice.

When you are armed with the facts, you can start to reach out to your elected officials to let them know that you want a society that works for everyday people like you.

One of the most important components of activism for economic justice is knowing who your legislators are and how to talk to them. Here are some things to keep in mind as you work with others to push legislators to listen to everyday people when they write or vote on legislation:

List of Organizations for Economic Justice

National Women's Law Center

Southern Poverty Law Center

Georgetown Center on Poverty and Inequality

Indivisible Project

Not One Cent

Tax March

National Working Families Party

AFL-CIO

Know Your Representative

Use the following links to access your state and federal representatives:

https://www.house.gov/representatives/find-your-representative

https://www.govtrack.us/congress/members

https://whoismyrepresentative.com/

https://www.usa.gov/elected-officials

1. When you call, you may get to talk to your representative. However, most of the time you will talk to their staffer. Legislative staff are vital parts of the legislative branch—they find documents, write legislation, and maintain connection to the home district. Don't be discouraged if you talk to a staffer!

Talking to Your Representative Script

Remember to be polite, concise, informative, and respectful. Also, follow up in a week to reaffirm your interest in seeing a piece of legislation passed or blocked.

Hello, my name is <name> and I live in <name of district, county, or city you reside>. I would like to speak to <name of your representative> or their legislative aide.

I am calling to request that <fill in legislator's name> pass or block <proposed piece of legislation>.

This bill as currently written would adversely affect me because <give your reason>.

Please convey my request to <fill in legislator's name>.

I will be following this legislation closely and will contact you in a week's time to follow up on this call. Thank you for your assistance.

You may be asked to repeat your name, address, and phone number. This is so that the legislator can gauge where the response is coming from (i.e., they want to make sure you are from their district).

2. The most effective mediums for contacting your representative are (in descending order): talking face-to-face at a town hall, calling on the phone, delivering a high-volume petition, writing a letter, sending an email, and contacting them through social media (e.g., tweeting at them or posting on their Facebook). Face-to-face meetings are particularly helpful if they are being recorded because poor responses can be shown on social media.

3. Face-to-face meetings and phone calls are the most effective because they cannot be ignored or "lost." When staffers are forced to talk with dozens or hundreds of people, they cannot perform the other tasks a representative wants them to do. As a result, high volumes of contact to an office are likely to elicit the desired response so the staffers can go back to work on other projects.

4. When talking or writing to a representative or staffer, it is important that you are targeted, scripted, and direct. You will most likely be angry or frustrated, but you cannot let that overwhelm you good judgment or ability to articulate your point. Stay on message!

5. Get others to show up to the meeting, call, or write as well! Schedule your student organization, friends, or community members to meet during a certain time or to call on a certain day. The more people you have the more likely they are to take notice.

It takes only a small amount of time to call and make your voice heard. Although it's important to call your representative on important issues, you need to remember that your voice is competing with the thousands, maybe even millions, of dollars the representative is receiving from various wealthy and corporate interests. Organizing with others can amplify your voice and leverage your people power into economic justice.

****

The most important thing to remember is that rising tuition costs do not happen in a bubble. They are connected to the larger political-economy of our society. When students have large amounts of student debt, it encourages them to make decisions that may make good economic sense, but are disastrous for realizing a fair society. For example, if you have a great deal of student debt, you may be so concerned with finishing college quickly, keeping your head down, and not building connections to communities that you miss the most important ways of realizing your full capabilities. And, even worse, if you leave college with a large amount of debt, you may be so fearful of losing employment that you are willing to compromise your sense of fairness or justice in order to maintain your job. We think this system is morally wrong and invite you to help create a world where people are free to realize their human capabilities—to learn and love to the fullest. Only in a such a society will we be able to identify and overcome other problems that face our friends, families, and communities.

Discussion Questions

- What is a financial aid horror story that you have heard or experienced? Is there a way to avoid experiencing the problem?
- What are ways to get out of debt or other bad financial situations?

Student Challenge

- Use a free service (e.g., Credit Karma) and check your credit score. What should you continue doing? What changes are needed to improve your score? Which changes could you realistically implement?
- Small group activity: What the best hack you recommend for college students? Make a list from easiest to most difficult to accomplish. Share your group's list with your class.

CHAPTER 10

The Value of Higher Education

Learning to Change the World

CHAPTER OBJECTIVES

By the end of the chapter, you should be able to:

- Appraise your role in higher education
- Navigate different personalities that can create conflict
- Translate higher education content into community engagement
- Safeguard the culture of higher education

ORIENTING QUESTIONS

As you read the chapter, try to answer the following questions:

- What is the foundation of public education in the United States?
- How has our historical legacy of manifesting the importance of formal education recently come under attack?
- What can you do to protect higher education as a critical site of learning?

In 1913, at the request of the United Daughters of the Confederacy, the University of North Carolina in Chapel Hill approved the creation of a monument to commemorate the men who had fought and died for the Confederacy. In his dedication of the statue, noted wealthy businessman Julian Carr (1913) declared the Confederacy tried to save the purity of the Anglo-Saxon (White) race. He reminisced:

> I trust I may be pardoned for one allusion, howbeit it is rather personal. One hundred yards from where we stand, less than ninety days perhaps after my return from Appomattox, I horse-whipped a negro wench until her skirts hung in shreds, because upon the streets of this quiet village she had publicly insulted and maligned a Southern lady ...

His speech, widely cheered by the assembled crowd, highlights the hate and racism that is imbued into every part of the statue. Originally known as the Confederate Monument or the Soldier's Monument, the statue would become a lightning rod for controversy for the next hundred years as protesters sought to remove it from campus. The statue, now known as Silent Sam, was the target of intense protests from 2011 to 2018, when, after years of inaction from the North Carolina legislature and UNC administration, students decided to remove the statue themselves. On August 20, 2018, student protestors tore the statue down. As of this writing, two students were found guilty and sentenced to 24 hours in jail and 18 months on probation. They were also sentenced to pay $500 in fines and complete 250 hours of community service. Twenty other cases against various protestors are still winding their way through the courts (Zerunyan, 2019). And, the UNC Board of Governors paid $2.5 million to the Sons of Confederate Veterans to maintain the statue off campus grounds, a major victory for neo-Confederate and White supremacist groups (Cox, 2019).

What would you have done if you were at UNC Chapel Hill? Would you have stood aside, and let the monument stand despite its roots in promoting the Confederacy (i.e., slave owners)? Would you have protested, but pushed students to go through university or legal channels to remove the statue (even though such efforts had failed for nearly a hundred years)? Or, would you have joined the protesters and sought to bring the statue down (knowing that it was against the law and you may be charged)? We cannot tell you what route you should have taken. However, we know that the world will not get better by staying silent or standing to the side. Every day that we do nothing is a day that hurt, trauma, pain, or hunger continue to affect those around us. Oppression doesn't just stop because we aren't thinking about it. It continues, inexorably, until met with the wall of our love for justice and each other. It only stops when we are united in our efforts to stop it.

In this book, we've done our best to give you some tools to be successful in college. We have offered you some vocabulary to make sense of issues that you will encounter while enrolled (and beyond); mapped out to how to navigate academic, relational, and organizational issues; and provided ways for you to become a better advocate for yourself and your community. Along the way, you've read the stories of countless students who have faced many of the same things you are going through right now. And, although everything you have read, discussed, or written about the past semester may not have been the most fun or interesting, we hope that your journey with us over the course of this book has prepared you well for the years ahead.

We strongly believe in the power of education to make the world a better place. All education, from preschool to advanced degrees, is based on the belief that the world can be better place through coming together and learning about the problems that face us as a society and a species. In this final chapter, we want to ask you to protect this sacred space that you will be a part of for the next part of your life. We want to be clear—higher education isn't perfect. There are problems with it that are unique to it, and some problems that it reflects from society at large. But the failure to be perfect—either as an institution or as people within it—isn't a reason for despair. Rather, it should call us to work harder to realize the type of world that we want to live in—a world of justice, peace, and equity. And, to not stop until we have reached that goal.

A Place to (Learn to) Change the World

Higher education in the United States is based on the messy, imperfect, but high-minded ideal that started in 15th-century Europe that knowing something—truly knowing something—was better than not knowing. It seems foolish to think this was a revolutionary idea at the time, and yet the notion that everyday people, through education, could learn to better themselves and their communities was profoundly innovative. We say it was an imperfect ideal because not every person was considered a "person"—women, people of color, and men who didn't own property were excluded from being considered people. And yet, there is a deep promise in this idea that we still pursue—that our ability to know something made us able to understand concepts such as cause and effect, systems of meaning, and human connection—and that through our efforts to understand ourselves and the world around us, humanity could raise above ignorance and violence.

The idea that people could know things, and through that knowledge, make the world a better place has produced some of humanity's greatest achievements. Vaccines, antibiotics, and microsurgery are all based on the idea that a deeper knowledge of our bodies can help us repair them when they are damaged or threatened. Questioning the divine right of rulers and the articulating political/

human rights is based on the idea that knowing ourselves as fully realized moral/ethical creatures means that no person is above the law or has been given a God-mandated right to do as they please, and that all people must respect each other's autonomy and freedom. The microwave, air conditioning, and the Internet all come from the idea that knowing how to make our world more connected, efficient, and enjoyable can help heal our loneliness and help us adapt to new environments. Dancing, music, literature, and poetry are based on the idea that our creative expressions are part of our journey to know our moral, ethical, and aesthetic potential, and that the human experience should be a life joyfully lived. And, finally, the idea that we can know things spawned the idea that knowledge should available to and be in the service of all people—creating the impetus to build public schools, public libraries, and public colleges—places where any people can go to know something.

However, recently, the very idea of public education has come under attack. Some people say we have entered the "post-fact world" or the "era of alternative facts." We are told that there is no such thing as true knowledge, that experts don't exist, and that every appeal to knowing—truly, deeply knowing something—is somehow elitist. This line of thinking is not only a grave betrayal of our historical legacy, it produces beliefs that are simply harmful to the public. Some people claim that the Sandy Hook and Stoneman Douglas shootings were staged by false flaggers and paid actors, that the earth is flat, that climate change doesn't exist, and that vaccines cause autism. We have people on websites such as Infowars, World Truth TV, and Breitbart say that there are tunnels connecting Walmarts in Texas that the federal government will use to overthrow the state government, stories that a DC pizzeria basement is really a child sex dungeon (even though the pizzeria didn't have a basement), and that former President Obama created Hurricane Matthew so the government could round everyone up in FEMA-created concentration camps. These things proliferate on the internet because, only a few decades ago, these conspiracy theorists were isolated from one another. Now, though, these ideas proliferate in the darkest parts of 4chan, 8chan, Reddit, WikiLeaks—and even in open on sites like Twitter, Facebook, Snapchat, and Instagram—because lying to people can give short-term self-gratification like upvotes, karma, money, power, and lulz. The sheer volume of beliefs and ideas shared often clouds any type of evidence-based thinking and, in a nutshell, creates the perception that having no belief or not getting involved is better than getting caught up in "drama."

You are in college and, as such, are an heir to the long historical legacy of public advocacy and engagement that has fought for the idea that knowing is better than not knowing. You can make the choice to develop knowledge; to learn how think based on evidence, reason, and logic; to create communities of practice with other people; and to push against uncomfortable myths. You get to make choices in how to understand your community's, region's, nation's or even the world's problems and create evidence-based solutions to address them. That's the legacy that those who've moved through higher education have left you. It will be difficult. Learning to think clearly, concisely, and with purpose isn't easy. Our ancestors found this out firsthand. For about 4,000 years people believed in erroneous, mystical thinking, and relied on charms against evil, leeching, and worshipping Odin, Zeus, Ra, and about 3,500 other deities to save them. And, then, when people started to challenge those systems, people sought to keep others from knowing through excommunicating, stoning, or burning at the stake those who fought against this grain.

The vast majority of human history is rife with examples of people settling for easy answers or ignoring how things affect their lives rather than pursuing true knowledge. As a result, a quest for knowledge will take practice and will be painful. Why? Unfortunately, it's easier to think like a fool—to be reactionary, without focus, and gullible, like a dog chasing the ball that hasn't even been thrown. And, worse, there are large segments of society that will turn on you for trying to better yourself or your community through learning. There are people who profit from your ignorance, fear, and pain; people who have no compunction about fanning the flames of hatred to earn another nickel. But, you need to protect the idea of higher education, and strive to learn everything you can while you are there. Because the alternative is believing foolish ideas—and in a world of nuclear weapons at hair trigger, environmental degradation across the globe, and neo-Nazis walking the streets in broad daylight—ignoring the problem or, worse, contributing to the stupidity guarantees the ruin of our nation, perhaps even our entire species.

In higher education, you will learn to think like a scholar. In a lot of ways, like scholars you'll encounter or those you'll read about, you will learn how to get comfortable with being uncomfortable. To be clear, scholars do not always have all the right answers or know everything. You will find that there are instances when scholars get things wrong, and even the most gifted scholar (as an individual) is bound to be incorrect sometime. To think like a scholar is to come together with others to produce rigorously tested knowledge that can address the problems that face us as a species—locally, regionally, nationally, and globally. Learn to find reputable evidence for your beliefs. Test your evidence through open, civil debate to make sure you are coming to reasoned, balanced conclusions. You might start with the question, "How do you/I know that?" Most important is to be as willing to be changed by others' beliefs as you want them to be changed by yours, to engage in the production of knowledge and its evaluation by using the methods of data gathering and treatment that have been proven over decades of trial and error to produce knowledge—real, true, reliable knowledge. And, if you do these things throughout your college career and beyond, you will learn to think rigorously and holistically. You might even change your views about something, gain a perspective that you didn't have before, learn something new, and even make a new friend in the things you read. But, you must do the hard work of learning. Because, frankly, there's no one else. Our society and the planet deserve—no they demand—nothing less, but the best of YOU.

Protecting Higher Education as a Place to Learn

There are many problems that face our society and species. Your responsibility in higher education is to learn how to produce, evaluate, and use knowledge that can help address these issues. However, as Lawless, Rudick, and Golsan (2019) argue, those problems are not always simply errors or the product of some people's miscalculations or misjudgments. The pollution of our water and air, wealth inequality, racism and xenophobia, and sexual violence are ingrained into society because someone enjoys or profits from such destructive actions. Often, people use their wealth, prestige, or power as a way to shield themselves from the harms their actions cause. For example, as Cohan (2015) reports, after the global economy was almost irreparably harmed due to the misconduct of Wall Street bankers and financers leading to the 2008 Great Recession, only one person was charged in the United States with criminal activity. Not only is this strikingly different from past instances when the actions of a few have harmed the global economy (e.g., the savings and loan crisis in the 1980s, which resulted in over 1,000 indictments), some of those whose actions influenced the crisis walked away richer (e.g., Jamie Dimon, CEO of JPMorgan, received a 74% raise, bringing his salary to $20 million per year). One of the great things about higher education is that through its research and teaching, it provides people with the tools for identifying, providing space for collaborating, and even possibly solving those issues. Educators and students in higher education train journalists to find and report facts, conduct research to evaluate policies and issues, and work with communities so they can advocate for themselves.

Unfortunately, those people in higher education who do this type of work have not gone unnoticed by those who wish to pursue their own agendas regardless of the (or because they want to cause) harm. Globally, there has been an increasing crackdown on academics, students, and journalists who try to expose authoritarian leaders and corporate overlords. In 2016, the authoritarian president of Turkey, Recep Tayyip Erdoğan, banned thousands of academics from their jobs, as well as hundreds of journalists, lawmakers, and judges who did not support his regime (Human Rights Watch, 2018). In 2018, the Chinese government began more aggressively surveilling Chinese scholars and China-related scholarship for antigovernment content in order to censor it (Pearson, 2019). In 2019, Brazil's strongman, President Bolsanaro, stated that the government would no longer fund universities that supported sociology or philosophy degrees because they taught material that was critical of his regime (Redden, 2019). These contemporary examples are backed by the historical instances of authoritarian leaders attacking academics, students, and journalists in Vietnam, the USSR/Russia, Iraq, and other countries around the world.

You may think that these instances are isolated to countries "over there," but the sad truth is that attacks on higher education's mission are becoming increasingly common. Academics, students, and journalists have been attacked, detained, and harassed by government officials due to antiwar protests. This was particularly true in the aftermath of 9/11 when, in a nationalistic fervor, many were targeted for speaking about against the unjust and unprovoked war with Iraq (Friedersdorf, 2013). Corporations attempt to co-opt institutions of higher education by threatening to revoke donations in exchange for changing curriculum or hiring business-friendly academics who support their corporate missions (Green & Saul, 2018). Trolls, hackers, and keyboard activists foment online mobs to harass academics who publish research on racism, sexism, or wealth inequality, sharing their private information, email bombing their offices, and threatening them with violence (American Association of University Professors, 2017). And, in 2019, the Trump administration proposed, for the third year in a row, cutting all funding for the National Endowment for the Arts and the National Endowment for the Humanities (Kreighbaum, 2019).

The problem with attacks on higher education is that they often simmer under the surface of a society until someone—usually an authoritarian leader—uses academics, students, and journalists as scapegoats for the issues they spent their lives studying for how to address. The descent comes shockingly fast, and once initiated, is almost impossible to come back from. The United States Holocaust Museum (2018) offers a timeline which shows that it took only 5 years for a full disruption of public life and civic engagement to produce the atrocities of the Holocaust. On April 7, 1933, Germany implemented the first major law (Law for the Restoration of the Professional Civil Service) to curtail the rights of Jewish citizens and the "politically unreliable" from civil service. The new law was the German authorities' first formulation of the so-called Aryan Paragraph, a regulation used to exclude Jews (and often, by extension, other "non-Aryans") from organizations, professions, and other aspects of public life. According to the BBC (2018), in the 1970s in Cambodia, over a period of less than 8 years, the Khmer Rouge killed millions of political prisoners and dissenters, including academics and those suspected of being an academic (e.g., people who wore glasses or spoke another language).

You are in a sacred place. Yes, you have come to college to obtain a degree and seek professional employment. Just as important, you have the opportunity to create a space for yourself, for those around you, and for those who will come after you to realize their talents and their life purpose. Maybe that's painting, playing an instrument, discovering a new vaccine, interrogating the status quo, building a new type of machine, writing a novel, developing a new music technique, or some other idea sparked by your interactions with peers and professors—who knows? What we do know is that for all humans to reach their potential, there must be a place that welcomes, supports, and nurtures the capabilities of every person—no matter their zip code, bank account, or appearance. Sometimes, the quest to support everyone will run against the interests of the powerful few who wish to retain their position. Sometimes, that quest will get sidetracked by your own desires for immediate gratification. But, that's exactly why we need institutions of higher education—to slow down our increasingly fast-paced world and give ourselves the time to think, grow, and learn. We must learn how to buttress democracy and transparency against the interests of those who would rob us of our chance to realize our capabilities if that means earning them a bit more profit or power. While you're in college, and once you graduate, there will be times when groups, legislators, and others try to harm higher education, and undermine its historic mission—don't let them. Protect it. Cherish it. And, learn how to make it better— for you, for those who will come after, and for those who will take our place!

****

We'd like to end this book with an appeal for you to show grace, to yourself and each other, as you navigate college and beyond. As Smucker (2017) notes, movements for social and economic justice have the unfortunate tendency to become insular and self-congratulatory—even when faced with the realization that their actions harm the cause they purport to support. We have seen people step on those around them in the effort to appear the most "woke" or sensitive to the issue at hand—people so "open-minded" they're actually "closed-minded." We have witnessed people who are incredibly similar in terms of their aims, scope, and methods in organizing and activism become bitter rivals over seemingly inconsequential differences in strategies or tactics—people fighting for scraps while blocking others from realizing their potential. And, we have seen people who make honest mistakes or slow down movement progress—not using the correct terminology, asking questions, or disagreeing with movement leaders—met with hellfire and brimstone, thus turning away potential allies. These types of issues promote a kind of competition where only the virtuous few are worthy of being a part of social justice movements while everyone else is viewed as insufficiently loyal to the cause. It creates a toxic environment and results in a movement of people who are very, very zealous about their beliefs, but too small of an organization to effect any real change to the system and too insular to recruit new people and ideas.

We are not saying that people can say or do anything they want but still claim that they are working toward social or economic justice. Being a part of a movement means you will need to do your homework—learn the terminology, history, people of the cause, how you can fit your energies into that network, and (most important) how to include new people and ideas. Instead of pouncing on people every time they fail to live up to the aspirations of our movements, we believe you should strive to show grace. Showing grace means learning how to forgive others, how to read their intentions with generosity and empathy, and not holding onto the emotional baggage that comes from not forgiving others. Rather than despair at the thought that those around you will never "get it right," we believe you should find strength in embracing grace as a way to show others that the process of activism (i.e., how we treat each other day to day) is just as important as the product (i.e., what we advocate for in our social or economic justice movements).

The ethic of grace is encapsulated in a statement attributed to Maya Angelou: "I did then what I knew how to do. Now that I know better, I do better" (Goodreads, n.d.). Being an advocate for social and economic justice is a process of becoming a better person just as much as it is a process of realizing a better world. Showing grace to yourself when you mess up or make mistakes isn't about letting yourself off the hook or not holding yourself accountable—it's about recognizing that you can do better for those around you and striving toward that goal. If we all work together to hold ourselves accountable to our movements' goals, and show grace to each other along the way, we know that there is nothing that can stop us from creating a world where everyone's economic, social, spiritual, political, and emotional needs can be met. We sincerely wish you the best on your journey through higher education and look forward to standing beside you in movements for social and economic justice in the years to come.

Discussion Questions

- Having completed reading this text and engaging in a series of discussions with classmates, what comes next?

- Where can you make a difference as an individual? As a member of a group?

Student Challenge

- Come together in groups of at least four students and establish a plan for addressing an issue in your community using a social justice approach.

Glossary

Ally A person who believes that they support marginalized or oppressed people, even if their actions harm those they are trying to help.

Bi-hatred The hatred of people who are is attracted to two or more genders.

Binary thinking Traditional thinking on sex and gender (e.g., male vs. female; masculine vs. feminine).

Biological perspective on race Argument that there are physical and/or genetic markers that make some races better than others.

Biphobia The fear of people who are is attracted to two or more genders.

Cissexism The belief that those people who identify with their designated gender/sex are normal, natural, or desirable, whereas those who do not are aberrant or abnormal.

Equality The notion that all people within a group have the same status.

Equity The notion that fairness should be brought to social policy.

Gender Refers to the cultural, rather than biological, values, beliefs, and norms that guide peoples' communication about, and performances of, sex.

Gender discrimination Beliefs, norms, attitudes, and behaviors, operating at all levels of society and with(out) conscious intent, that reinforce the subjugation of gender nonconforming people and perpetuate cissexism.

Gender/sex Term used to highlight the reality that how we think about sexual identity (e.g., male, female, or intersex) is wrapped up in societal norms about gender (e.g., masculine, feminine, or androgynous), and vice versa. In short, it is impossible to know where biology ends and culture begins when trying to differentiate groups of people based on physical, social, and genetic criteria.

Heterosexism Beliefs, norms, attitudes, and behaviors, operating at all levels of society and with(out) conscious intent, that normalize monogamous, opposite-sex desire, affect, and relationships and reinforce the subjugation of nonopposite sex desire, affect, and relationships.

Homo-hatred The hatred of people who attracted to a gender the same as their own (commonly used to describe someone who is gender binary [female or male] attracted to the same binary gender).

Homophobia The fear of people who are attracted to a gender the same as their own (commonly used to describe someone who is gender binary [female or male] attracted to the same binary gender).

Human capabilities approach A human life is characterized by a profound need to realize one's potential—economically, socially, relationally, personally, and politically.

Idealistic race-evasiveness The notion that to eliminate racism we should look past race and see each other as human.

Identity The combination of one's positionalities that creates experiences (e.g., people of different social classes have different experiences about money) and also shapes how experiences are interpreted (e.g., the values that one has toward money based on social class). As a result, it is always evolving and changing.

Intersectionality The belief that people's experiences are best understood as a network or collection of positionalities (e.g., Bob is a White, heterosexual male) rather than viewing those positionalities in isolation (e.g., Bob is White. Bob is heterosexual. Bob is male).

Microaggressions Oppressive talk that lays the groundwork for, and eventually justifies, oppressive behavior.

Monogamy The belief that it is normal or desirable to only have one partner at a time.

Neoliberal capitalism The belief that corporations and the wealthy, through marketplace competition, offer the best route to creating security, prosperity, and equity.

Normative race-evasiveness The idea that racism is no longer a problem and that most people don't see or act upon race.

Oppression Systems that bar humans from realizing their capabilities based on social group memberships and political-economy.

Pan-hatred The hatred of people who are attracted to all genders and/or do not concern gender when they are attracted toward someone.

Panphobia The fear of people who are attracted to all genders and/or do not concern gender when they are attracted toward someone.

Patriarchy The systems that privilege people viewed as male and supports toxic masculinity.

Person who allies with others A person who recognizes that their actions toward marginalized or oppressed people in each situation are the most important way to understand if they are supporting others or not.

Positionality The different parts of one's identity. Race, class, gender/sex, educational attainment, military status, and immigration status are all different positions that combine to make up one's identity.

Privilege Systems that provide unearned access (whether social or material) to goods, services, or resources.

Race-evasive perspective The notion that to eliminate racism people should stop talking about race.

Racism The beliefs, norms, attitudes, and behaviors, operating at all levels of society and with(out) conscious intent, that reinforce the subjugation of people color and perpetuate White supremacy.

Sex The biological designations that society gives to categories of people, typically based on physical features such as genitalia, and (in most Western countries) is a binary of either male or female.

Sexism The beliefs, norms, attitudes, and behaviors, operating at all levels of society and with(out) conscious intent, that reinforce the subjugation of people not viewed as male and perpetuate patriarchy.

Social democracy The belief that people, through government participation, voting, and service, offer the best route to creating security, prosperity, and equity.

Social justice The concept of fair and just relations between the individual and society. It is measured by the explicit and tacit terms for the distribution of wealth, opportunities for personal activity, and social privileges.

Sociocultural perspective A framework that there are cultural markers that make some races better than others.

Toxic masculinity The traits assigned to males that encompass dominance, devaluation of other, self-reliance, and emotional suppression.

Transgender A person who does not identify with their assigned sex. Also an umbrella term for a host of other labels for a person who rejects sex/gender binaries may adopt, such as *gender fluid*, *genderqueer*, *genderfucked*, and *trans*.

White supremacy The beliefs and (un)conscious actions that support the idea that White people are normal, cleaner, or superior to people of color.

References

Alegria-Flores, K., Raker, K., Pleasants, R. K., Weaver, M. A., & Weinberger, M. (2015). Preventing interpersonal violence on college campuses: The effect of one act training on bystander intervention. *Journal of Interpersonal Violence, 32*, 1103–1126. doi:10.1177/0886260515587666

Alim, T. (2018, March 30). Howard University students protest after financial aid scandal exposed. *WTOP*. https://wtop.com/dc/2018/03/howard-university-students-protest-after-financial-aid-scandal-exposed/slide/1/

Alter, C. (2014, July 17). Todd Akin still doesn't get what's wrong with saying "legitimate rape." *Time*. https://time.com/3001785/todd-akin-legitimate-rape-msnbc-child-of-rape/

American Association of University Professors. (2017). Targeted online harassment of faculty. https://www.aaup.org/news/targeted-online-harassment-faculty#.XMYJoKR7IPY

American Chemistry Society. (n.d.). Chlorofluorocarbons and ozone depletion. https://www.acs.org/content/acs/en/education/whatischemistry/landmarks/cfcs-ozone.html

American Civil Liberties Union. (2014). Racial disparities in sentencing. https://www.aclu.org/sites/default/files/assets/141027_iachr_racial_disparities_aclu_submission_0.pdf

American Civil Liberties Union. (n.d.). Race and the death penalty. https://www.aclu.org/other/race-and-death-penalty

American College Health Association. (2017a). Fall 2017 reference group data: Executive summary. http://www.acha-ncha.org/docs/NCHA-II_FALL_2017_REFERENCE_GROUP_EXECUTIVE_SUMMARY.pdf

American College Health Association. (2017b). Spring 2017 reference group data: Executive summary. http://www.acha-ncha.org/docs/NCHA-II_SPRING_2017_REFERENCE_GROUP_DATA_REPORT.pdf

American Council on Education. (2014). Myth: College sports are a cash cow. http://www.acenet.edu/news-room/Pages/Myth-College-Sports-Are-a-Cash-Cow2.aspx

American Council on Education. (n.d.). State funding a race to the bottom. http://www.acenet.edu/the-presidency/columns-and-features/Pages/state-funding-a-race-to-the-bottom.aspx

American Heart Association. (2018). American Heart Association recommendations for physical activity in adults and kids. http://www.heart.org/HEARTORG/HealthyLiving/PhysicalActivity/FitnessBasics/American-Heart-Association-Recommendations-for-Physical-Activity-in-Adults_UCM_307976_Article.jsp#.Wya6_yAnZPY

American Psychological Association. (2010). Stress in America findings. https://www.apa.org/news/press/releases/stress/2010/national-report.pdf

Archibald, R. B., & Feldman, D. H. (2014). *Why does college cost so much?* Oxford University Press.

Arneil, B. (2009). Disability, self-image, and modern political theory. *Political Theory, 37*, 218–242.

Arnett, J. J. (2014). *Emerging adulthood: The winding road from the late teens through the twenties* (2nd ed.). Oxford University Press.

Associated Press. (2016, May 10). Here's why your parents stayed in the same job for 20 years. http://fortune.com/2016/05/10/baby-boomers-millennials-jobs/

Associated Students of the University of California. (n.d.). History. https://asuc.org/history/

Balduf, M. (2009). Underachievement among college students. *Journal of Advanced Academics, 20*(2), 274–293.

Bauer-Worlf, J. (2017, September 22). A September of racist events. *Inside Higher Ed.* https://www.insidehighered.com/news/2017/09/22/racist-incidents-colleges-abound-academic-year-begins

Bauman, D. (2018, March 29). Who foots most of the bill for public college? In 28 states, it's students. *The Chronicle of Higher Education.* https://www.chronicle.com/article/Who-Foots-Most-of-the-Bill-for/242959

Becker, S., & Tinkler, J. (2014). "Me getting plastered and her provoking my eyes": Young people's attribution of blame for sexual aggression in public drinking spaces. *Feminist Criminology, 10,* 235–258. doi:10.1177/1557085114541142

Bell, L. A., Goodman, D. J., & Ouellett, M. L. (2016). Design and facilitation. In M. Adams, L. A. Bell, D. J. Goodman, & K. Y. Joshi (Eds.), *Teaching for diversity and social justice* (3rd ed.; pp. 55–93). Routledge.

Bennett, S., Banyard, V. L., & Garnhart, L. (2013). To act or not to act, that is the question? Barriers and facilitators of bystander intervention. *Journal of Interpersonal Violence, 29,* 476–496. doi:10.1177/0886260513505210

Berke, J. (2017, December 17). The world's largest oil and gas companies are getting greener after fighting with shareholders for months. http://www.businessinsider.com/exxon-shell-bp-announce-renewable-energy-and-climate-initiatives-2017-12

Bertrand, M., & Mullainathan, S. (2003). Are Emily and Greg more employable than Lakeisha and Jamal? A field experiment on labor market discrimination. NBER Working Papers. https://www.nber.org/papers/w9873.pdf

Bonilla-Silva, E. (2006). *Racism without racists: Color-blind racism and the persistence of racial inequality in the United States.* Rowman & Littlefield.

Bourdieu, P. (1984). *Distinction: A social critique of the judgement of taste* (R. Nice, Trans.). Harvard University Press.

Bourdieu, P. (1999). Cultural reproduction and social reproduction. In M. Waters (Ed.), *Modernity: Cultural modernity* (pp. 351–369). Routledge.

Bourdieu, P., & Passeron, J. (2000). *Reproduction in education, society, and culture* (2nd ed.). SAGE.

Browning, B. (2018, April 27). Texas man gets probation after using "gay panic" defense to explain killing his neighbor. *LGBTQ Nation.* https://www.lgbtqnation.com/2018/04/texas-man-gets-probation-using-gay-panic-defense-explain-killing-neighbor/

Bureau of Labor Statistics. (2017). Characteristics of minimum wage workers, 2016. https://www.bls.gov/opub/reports/minimum-wage/2016/home.htm

Bureau of Labor Statistics. (2018a). Employment projects. https://www.bls.gov/emp/ep_chart_001.htm

Bureau of Labor Statistics. (2018b). Measuring the value of education. https://www.bls.gov/careeroutlook/2018/data-on-display/education-pays.htm

Burness, A. (2018, April 5). Hundreds of CU Boulder students demand firing of Chancellor Phil DiStefano over budget battle. *The Denver Post.* https://www.denverpost.com/2018/04/05/cu-boulder-demand-firing-chancellor-phil-destefano/

Caiazzo, F., Ashok, A., Waitz, I. A., Yim, S. H. L., & Barrett, S. R. H. (2013). Air pollution and early deaths in the United States. Part I: Quantifying the impact of major sectors in 2005. *Atmospheric Environment, 79,* 198–208. doi:10.1016/j.atmosenv.2013.05.081

Carothers, B. J., & Reis, H. T. (2012). Men and women are from Earth: Examining the latent structure of gender. *Journal of Personality and Social Psychology, 104*, 385–407. doi:10.1037/a0030437

Carr, J. S. (1913). Unveiling of Confederate Monument at University. June 2, 1913. In the Julian Shakespeare Carr Papers #141, Southern Historical Collection, The Wilson Library, University of North Carolina at Chapel Hill. https://guides.lib.unc.edu/documenting-student-activism/1

Carroll, R. (2016, December 20). Oklahoma budget shortfall nearly $900 million: Report. *Business Insider*. http://www.businessinsider.com/r-oklahoma-budget-shortfall-nearly-900-million-report-2016-12

Castleman, M. (2009, March 20). How common is masturbation, really? *Psychology Today*. https://www.psychologytoday.com/us/blog/all-about-sex/200903/how-common-is-masturbation-really

Centers for Disease Control and Prevention (CDC). (n.d.a). Chlamydial infections. https://www.cdc.gov/std/tg2015/chlamydia.htm

Centers for Disease Control and Prevention (CDC). (n.d.b). Genital herpes. CDC fact sheet. https://www.cdc.gov/std/herpes/stdfact-herpes.htm

Centers for Disease Control and Prevention (CDC). (n.d.c). Gonorrhea. CDC fact sheet. https://www.cdc.gov/std/gonorrhea/stdfact-gonorrhea.htm

Centers for Disease Control and Prevention (CDC). (n.d.d). STD risk and oral sex. CDC fact sheet. https://www.cdc.gov/std/healthcomm/stdfact-std/riskandoralsex.htm

Centers for Disease Control and Prevention (CDC). (n.d.e). Syphillis. CDC fact sheet. https://www.cdc.gov/std/herpes/stdfact-herpes.htm

Centers for Disease Control and Prevention (CDC). (n.d.f). HIV. https://www.cdc.gov/hiv/default.html

Centers for Disease Control and Prevention (CDC). (n.d.g). HPV. https://www.cdc.gov/hpv/index.html

Centers for Disease Control and Prevention. (2019). Disability impacts all of us. https://www.cdc.gov/ncbddd/disabilityandhealth/infographic-disability-impacts-all.html

Centers for Disease Control and Prevention. (2020). Alcohol and public health. https://www.cdc.gov/alcohol/faqs.htm

Center for Popular Economics. (2012). Economics for the 99%. https://www.populareconomics.org/wp-content/uploads/2012/06/Economics_99_Percent_for_web1.pdf

Chalabi, M. (2015, August 20). The gender orgasm gap. https://fivethirtyeight.com/features/the-gender-orgasm-gap/

Chandra, A., Mosher, W. D., & Copen, C. (2011). Sexual behavior, sexual attraction, and sexual identity in the United States: Data from the 2006–2008 National Survey of Family Growth. *National Health Statistics Reports*. https://www.cdc.gov/nchs/data/nhsr/nhsr036.pdf

Cohan, W. D. (2015, September). How Wall Street's bankers stayed out of jail. *The Atlantic*. https://www.theatlantic.com/magazine/archive/2015/09/how-wall-streets-bankers-stayed-out-of-jail/399368/

Coker, A. L., Bush, H. M., Fisher, B. S., Swan, S. C., Williams, C. M., Clear, E. R., & DeGue, S. (2016). Multi-college bystander intervention evaluation for violence prevention. *American Journal of Preventative Medicine, 50*, 295–302. doi:10.1016/j.amepre.2015.08.034

Coleman, E. (2018, December 18). Are low carbs healthy for teenagers? *SF Gate*. http://healthyeating.sfgate.com/low-carbs-healthy-teenagers-11834.html

College Board. (2019). Aid per student. https://research.collegeboard.org/pdf/2019-trendsinsa-fig1.pdf

Conner, T. S., DeYoung, C. G. & Silva, P. J. (2018). Everyday creative activity as a path to flourishing. *The Journal of Positive Psychology, 13*, 181–189. doi:10.1080/17439760.2016.1257049

Corbett, J., & Slee, R. (2000) An international conversation on inclusive education. In F. Armstrong, D. Armstrong & L. Barton (Eds.), *Inclusive education; Policy, contexts and comparative perspectives* (pp. 133–146). David Fulton.

Cotton, G. (2012, June 13). Gestures to avoid in cross-cultural business: In other words, "Keep your fingers to yourself!" *Huffington Post*. https://www.huffingtonpost.com/gayle-cotton/cross-cultural-gestures_b_3437653.html

Covey, S. (2004). *7 habits of highly effective people: Power lessons in personal change*. Simon and Schuster.

Cox, K. L. (2019, December 7). With "Silent Sam" deal, UNC has betrayed its mission. CNN. https://www.cnn.com/2019/12/07/opinions/unc-sons-of-confederate-veterans-silent-sam-cox/index.html

Crenshaw, K. (1991). Mapping the margins: Intersectionality, identity politics, and violence against women of color. *Stanford Law Review, 43*, 1241–1299. doi:10.2307/1229039

Davis, G. (2015). *Contesting intersex: The dubious diagnosis*. NYU Press.

Deamer, K. (2016). Antarctic ozone hole shows 1st signs of healing. https://www.livescience.com/55250-antarctic-ozone-hole-healing.html

Deloitte. (2019). *The Deloitte global millennial survey*. https://www2.deloitte.com/global/en/pages/about-deloitte/articles/millennialsurvey.html

Des Moines Registrar. (2017, August 25). 7 things to know about the Apple data center in Waukee. https://www.desmoinesregister.com/story/news/2017/08/25/7-things-know-apple-data-center-waukee/599347001/

DeSilver, D. (2017, July 25). Most Americans unaware that as U.S. manufacturing jobs have disappeared, output has grown. Pew Research Center. http://www.pewresearch.org/fact-tank/2017/07/25/most-americans-unaware-that-as-u-s-manufacturing-jobs-have-disappeared-output-has-grown/

Devlin, K. (2015). Learning a foreign language a "must" in Europe, not so in America. Pew Research Center. http://www.pewresearch.org/fact-tank/2015/07/13/learning-a-foreign-language-a-must-in-europe-not-so-in-america

Devlin, K. (2018). Most European students are learning a foreign language in school while Americans lag. Pew Research Center. http://www.pewresearch.org/fact-tank/2018/08/06/most-european-students-are-learning-a-foreign-language-in-school-while-americans-lag/

Dewey, J. (1916). *Democracy and education: An introduction to the philosophy of education*. The Free Press.

Dimock, M. (2019). Defining generations: Where Millennials end and Generation Z begins. Pew Research Center. https://www.pewresearch.org/fact-tank/2019/01/17/where-millennials-end-and-generation-z-begins/

Doane, A. (2006). What is racism? Racial discourse and racial politics. *Critical Sociology, 32*, 255–274. doi:10.1163/156916306777835303

Dolmage, J. (2015). Universal design: Places to start. *Disability Studies Quarterly, 35*(2). http://dsq-sds.org/article/view/4632/3946

Economic Policy Institute. (2018). The productivity-pay gap. https://www.epi.org/productivity-pay-gap/

The Economist. (2014, December 20). Why is everyone so busy? https://www.economist.com/christmas-specials/2014/12/20/why-is-everyone-so-busy

The Economist. (2018, January 30). What's the matter with Oklahoma? https://www.economist.com/news/united-states/21736102-low-teacher-pay-and-severe-budget-cuts-are-driving-schools-brink-whats-matter

Elliot, L. (2008, August 31). Economics: Whatever happened to Keynes' 15-hour working week? *The Guardian*. https://www.theguardian.com/business/2008/sep/01/economics

Emch, P. (n. d.). Comparing vacation time around the world—infographic. *Timesheets*. https://www.timesheets.com/blog/2016/06/vacation-time-world-infographic/

Environmental Protection Agency. (2009, July 14). Climate for action: Save energy, greenhouse gas emissions and some cash by switching your light bulbs. https://blog.epa.gov/2009/07/14/climate-for-action-save-energy-greenhouse-gas-emissions-and-some-cash-by-switching-your-light-bulbs/

Espinosa, L. L., Turk, J. M., Taylor, M., & Chessman, H. M. (2019). *Race and ethnicity in higher education: A status report*. American Council on Education.

Fairlie, R. W., Hoffmann, F., & Oreopoulos, P. (2014). A community college instructor like me: Race and ethnicity interactions in the classroom. *American Economic Review*, 104(8), 2567-2591. doi: 10.1257/aer.104.8.2567

Flaherty, C. (2017, September 28). Making diversity happen. *Inside Higher Ed*. https://www.insidehighered.com/news/2017/09/28/how-two-institutions-diversified-their-faculties-without-spending-big-or-setting

Foubert, J. D., Newberry, J. T., & Tatum, J. (2007). Behavior differences seven months later: Effects of a rape prevention program. *NAPS Journal*, *44*(4), 728–744. doi:10.2202/1949-6605.1866

Fox News. (2016, August 11). Another college student gets light sentence for sexual assault. *New York Post*. https://nypost.com/2016/08/11/another-college-student-gets-off-easy-for-sexual-assault/

Friedersdorf, C. (2013, March 21). Behold the hatred, resentment, and mockery aimed at anti-Iraq war protestors. *The Atlantic*. https://www.theatlantic.com/politics/archive/2013/03/behold-the-hatred-resentment-and-mockery-aimed-at-anti-iraq-war-protesters/274230/

Frey, L. R., & Palmer, D. L. (Eds.). (2014). *Teaching communication activism: communication education for social justice*. Hampton Press.

Frost, J. L., Lindberg, L. D., & Finer, L. B. (2012). Young adults' contraceptive knowledge norms and attitudes: Association with risk of unintended pregnancy. *Perspectives on Sexual and Reproductive Health, 44*, 107–116. doi:10.1363/4410712

Fry, R. (2018, April 3). Millennials approach Baby Boomers as America's largest generation in the electorate. Pew Research Center. http://www.pewresearch.org/fact-tank/2016/05/16/millennials-match-baby-boomers-as-largest-generation-in-u-s-electorate-but-will-they-vote/

Gallagher, R. P. (2014). National survey of college counseling centers 2014. http://d-scholarship.pitt.edu/28178/1/survey_2014.pdf

Gareis, E. (2017). Intercultural friendships. *Oxford handbook of communication: Interpersonal communication*. http://oxfordre.com/communication/view/10.1093/acrefore/9780190228613.001.0001/acrefore-9780190228613-e-161

Gates, E. F. (2003). *Riot on Greenwood: The total destruction of Black Wall Street*. Sunbelt Eakin Press.

George, W. H., Cue, K. L., Lopez, P. A., Crowe, L. C., & Norris, J. (1995). Self-reported alcohol expectancies and postdrinking sexual inferences about women. *Journal of Applied Social Psychology, 25*, 164–186. doi: 10.1111/j.1559-1816.1995.tb01589.x

Georgetown Public Policy. (2014). Recovery: Job growth and education requirements through 2020. https://cew.georgetown.edu/wp-content/uploads/2014/11/Recovery2020.ES_.Web_.pdf

Gershenson, S., Hart, C. M. D., Hyman, J., Linsay, C., & Papageorge, N. W. (2018). The long-run impacts of same-race teachers. NBER Working Paper no. 25254. https://www.nber.org/papers/w25254

Gloria, A. M., & Castellanos, J. (2003). Latina/o and African American students at predominantly White institutions: A psychosociocultural perspective of cultural congruity, campus climate, and academic persistence. In J. Castellanos & L. Jones (Eds.), *The majority in the minority: Expanding the representation of Latina/o faculty, administrators and students in higher education* (pp. 71–92). Stylus.

Goffman, E. (1963). *Stigma: Notes on the management of spoiled identity.* Simon and Schuster.

Golsan, K. B., & Rudick, C. K. (2015). Caught in the rhetoric: How students with disabilities are framed by DSS offices in U.S. higher education. In A. Atay & M. Ashlock (Eds.), *The discourse of disability in communication education* (pp. 99–114). Peter Lang.

Graham, K., Bernards, S., Abbey, A., Dumas, T. M., & Wells, S. (2017). When women do not want it: Young female bargoers' experiences with and responses to sexual harassment in social drinking contexts. *Violence Against Women, 23*, 1419-1441. doi: 10.1177/1077801216661037

Gray, J. B. (2011). Theory guiding communication campaign praxis: A qualitative elicitation study comparing exercise beliefs of overweight and healthy weight college students, *Qualitative Research Reports in Communication, 12*(1), 34–42. doi:10.1080/17459435.2011.601523

Green, E. L., & Saul, S. (2018, May 5). What Charles Koch and other donors to George Mason University got for their money. *The New York Times.* https://www.nytimes.com/2018/05/05/us/koch-donors-george-mason.html

Greene, J. P., Kisida, B., & Mills, J. (2010). Administrative bloat at American universities: The real reason for high costs in higher education. Goldwater Institute. https://goldwaterinstitute.org/wp-content/uploads/cms_page_media/2015/3/24/Administrative%20Bloat.pdf

Greenhouse, S. (2019). *Beaten down, worked up: The past, present, and future of American Labor.* Penguin.

Gross, T. (2017, March 3). A "forgotten history" of how the U.S. government segregated America. National Public Radio. https://www.npr.org/2017/05/03/526655831/a-forgotten-history-of-how-the-u-s-government-segregated-america

Gurin, P., Dey, E., Hurtado, S., & Gurin, G. (2002). Diversity and higher education: Theory and impact on educational outcomes. *Harvard Educational Review, 72*, 330366.

Hardiman, R., & Jackson, B., & Griffin, P. (2007). Conceptual foundation for social justice education. In M. Adams, L. A. Bell, & P. Griffin, *Teaching for diversity and social justice* (2nd ed.; pp. 35–66). Routledge.

Harrington, R. (2016, December 15). Here's how much oil has spilled from US pipelines since 2010. *Business Insider.* https://www.businessinsider.com/how-much-oil-spills-from-pipelines-us-america-natural-gas-2016-12

Hart Research Associates. (2018). Fulfilling the American dream: Liberal education and the future of work. Association of American Colleges and Universities. https://www.aacu.org/sites/default/files/files/LEAP/2018EmployerResearchReport.pdf

Hathaway, I., & Muro, M. (2016, October 13). Tracking the gig economy: New numbers. Brookings Institute. https://www.brookings.edu/research/tracking-the-gig-economy-new-numbers/

Hauser, C. (2018, August 9). Brock Turner loses appeal to overturn sexual assault conviction. *New York Times*. https://www.nytimes.com/2018/08/09/us/brock-turner-appeal.html

Hauser, C. (2016, August 24). Judge's sentencing in Massachusetts sexual assault case reignites debate on privilege. *New York Times*. https://www.nytimes.com/2016/08/25/us/david-becker-massachusetts-sexual-assault.html

Heller, M. L., & Cassady, J. C. (2017). The impact of perceived barriers, academic anxiety, and resource management strategies on achievement in first-year community college students. *Journal of the First-Year Experience & Students in Transition, 29*(1), 9–32.

Henig, R. M. (2017). How science is helping us understand gender. *National Geographic*. https://www.nationalgeographic.com/magazine/2017/01/how-science-helps-us-understand-gender-identity/

Hernandez, R. (2018). The fall of employment in the manufacturing sector. Bureau of Labor Statistics. https://www.bls.gov/opub/mlr/2018/beyond-bls/the-fall-of-employment-in-the-manufacturing-sector.htm

Horovitz, B. (2012, May 4). After Gen X, Millennials, what should next generation be? *USA Today*. http://usatoday30.usatoday.com/money/advertising/story/2012-05-03/naming-the-next-generation/54737518/1

Hurtado, S. (2001). Linking diversity and educational purpose: How diversity affects the classroom environment and student development. In G. Orfield (Ed.), *Diversity challenged: Evidence on the impact of affirmative action* (pp.187203). Harvard Educational Publishing Group.

Howe, N., & Strauss, W. (1992). *Generations: The history of America's future, 1584 to 2069*. Harper Collins.

Human Rights Watch. (2017, July 25). "I want to be like nature made me": Medically unnecessary surgeries on intersex children in the US. https://www.hrw. org/report/2017/07/25/i-want-be-nature-made-me/medically-unnecessary-surgeries-intersex-children-us

Human Rights Watch. (2018, May 14). Turkey: Government targeting academics. https://www.hrw.org/news/2018/05/14/turkey-government-targeting-academics

Ingraham, C. (2014). Three quarters of whites don't have any non-white friends. *The Washington Post*. https://www.washingtonpost.com/news/wonk/wp/2014/08/25/three-quarters-of-whites-dont-have-any-non-white-friends/?utm_term=.c20e2dee35d1

Ingraham, C. (2017, December 8). Nation's top 1 percent now have greater wealth than the bottom 90 percent. *The Seattle Times*. https://www.seattletimes.com/business/economy/nations-top-1-percent-now-have-greater-wealth-than-the-bottom-90-percent/

Ingram, J. (2018, May 19). Lawsuit claims Stanford discriminated against three students with mental health disabilities. *The Stanford Daily*. https://www.stanforddaily.com/2018/05/18/lawsuit-claims-stanford-discriminated-against-three-students-with-mental-health-disabilities/

Jacobs, P. (2014, December 7). The 10-highest paid college presidents. *Business Insider*. http://www.businessinsider.com/highest-paid-college-presidents-2014-12

Jan, T. (2018, March 28). Redlining was banned 50 years ago. It's still hurting minorities today. *The Washington Post*. https://www.washingtonpost.com/news/wonk/wp/2018/03/28/redlining-was-banned-50-years-ago-its-still-hurting-minorities-today/?noredirect=on&utm_term =.50bccf87b6bc

Jesse, D. (2018, January 18). MSU student government: Change in leadership needed at "highest levels" of administration. *Detroit Free Press*. https://www.freep.com/story/news/local/michigan/2018/01/18/msu-student-government-change-leadership-needed-highest-levels-administration/1046956001/

Johnston, L. D., Miech, R. A., O'Malley, P. M., Bachman, J. G. Schulenberg, J. E., & Patrick, M. E. (2017). *2017 overview: Key findings on adolescent drug use*. Monitoring the Future. http://monitoringthefuture.org/pubs/monographs/mtf-overview2017.pdf

Kahl Jr., D. H. (2019). Challenging neoliberal justification for labor exploitation through the application of critical communication pedagogy. *Communication Teacher*. https://doi.org/10.1080/17404622.2019.1575437

Kamenetz, A. (2017, December 13). More college presidents join the millionaire's club. *National Public Radio*. https://www.npr.org/sections/ed/2017/12/13/569943593/more-college-presidents-join-the-millionaires-club

Katz, B. (2018, April 9). Keystone pipeline leak was twice as big as previously thought. *Smithsonian Magazine*. https://www.smithsonianmag.com/smart-news/keystone-pipeline-leak-was-twice-big-previously-thought-180968722/

Kelly, G. (2016, May 24). A (nearly) complete glossary of gender identities for your next census. *The Telegraph*. http://www.telegraph.co.uk/men/the-filter/a-nearly-complete-glossary-of-gender-identities-for-your-next-ce/

Kennedy, M. (2016, April 20). Lead-laced water in Flint: A step-by-step look at the makings of a crisis. National Public Radio. https://www.npr.org/sections/the two-way/2016/04/20/465545378/lead-laced-water-in-flint-a-step-by-step-look-at-the-makings-of-a-crisis

Khaleeli, H. (2014, April 16). Hijra: India's third gender claims its place in law. *The Guardian*. https://www.theguardian.com/society/2014/apr/16/india-third-gender-claims-place-in-law

Kitsantas, A., Winsler, A., & Huie, F. (2008). Self-regulation and ability predictors of academic success during college: A predictive validity study. *Journal of Advanced Academics*, *20*, 42–68. doi:10.4219/jaa-2008-867

Kochhar, R., & Cilluffo, A. (2017, November 1). How wealth inequality has changed in the U.S. since the Great Recession, by race, ethnicity and income. Pew Research Center. https://www.pewresearch.org/fact-tank/2017/11/01/how-wealth-inequality-has-changed-in-the-u-s-since-the-great-recession-by-race-ethnicity-and-income/

Kozol, J. (2005). Still separate, still unequal: America's educational apartheid. *Harper's Weekly*, *311*, 41–54.

Kreighbaum, A. (2019, March 19). Trump seeks to ax humanities endowment. *Inside Higher Ed*. https://www.insidehighered.com/news/2019/03/19/trump-proposes-axing-nea-neh/

Labaree, D. F. (1997). Public goods, private goods: The American struggle over educational goals. *American Educational Research Journal*, *34*, 39–81. doi:10.3102/00028312034001039

Lacey, M. (2008). A lifestyle distinct: The muxe of Mexico. *New York Times*. https://www.nytimes.com/2008/12/07/weekinreview/07lacey.html?scp=1&sq=muxe&st=cse

Lafargue, P. (1883). *The right to be lazy* (trans. C. Kerr). https://www.marxists.org/archive/lafargue/1883/lazy/

Latane, B., & Darley, J. M. (1970).*The unresponsive bystander: Why doesn't he help?* Appleton-Century-Crofts.

Lawless, B., Rudick, C. K., & Golsan, K. B. Distinguishing (the) right from wrong: Knowledge, curriculum, and intellectual responsibility. *Communication Education, 68*, 481–495. doi:10.1080/03634523.2019.1645871

Lazenby, P. (2012). Remember Kinder Scout—give back Britain's common land. *The Guardian.* https://www.theguardian.com/commentisfree/2012/apr/30/remember-kinder-scout-britain-common-land

Leonardo, Z. (2009). *Race, whiteness, and education.* Routledge.

Leonardo, Z. (2013). *Race frameworks: A multidimensional theory of racism and education.* Teachers College Press.

Livneh, H. (1982). On the origins of negative attitudes toward people with disabilities. *Rehabilitation Literature, 43*, 338–347.

Locsin, A. (2018, July 1). *The average pay for a entry level college professor.* https://work.chron.com/average-pay-entry-level-college-professor-5192.html

Lorde, A. (1984). *Sister outsider.* Crossing.

Lundgren, R., & Amin, A. (2015). Addressing intimate partner violence and sexual violence among adolescents: Emerging evidence and effectiveness. *Journal of Adolescent Health, 56*, S42–S50. doi:10.1016/j.jadohealth.2014.08.012

Mackelprang, R. M. (2010). Disability controversies: Past, present, and future. *Journal of Social Work in Disability & Rehabilitation, 9*, 87–98. doi:10.1080/1536710X.2010.493475

Marcus, J. (2017, October 10). Why colleges are borrowing billions. *The Atlantic.* https://www.theatlantic.com/education/archive/2017/10/why-colleges-are-borrowing-billions/542352/

Mayo Clinic. (n.d.). Stretching: Focus on flexibility. https://www.mayoclinic.org/healthy-lifestyle/fitness/in-depth/stretching/art-20047931

McClain, S., Beasley, S. T., Bianca, J., Awosogba, O., Jackson, S., & Cokley, K. (2016). An examination of the impact of racial and ethnic identity, impostor feelings, and minority status stress on the mental health of Black college students. *Journal of Multicultural Counseling and Development, 44*(2), 101–117.

McFarlane, A., Abrego, W., Eder, S., Hernandez-Sanchez, C., Koch, S., & Rudick, C. K. (2018). First-generation students' communication privacy management with parents. In A. Atay and D. Trebing (Eds.), *The discourse of special populations: Critical intercultural communication pedagogy and practice.* Routledge.

Miller, M. E. (2016, June 5). "A steep price to pay for 20 minutes of action": Dad defends Stanford sex offender. *The Washington Post.* https://www.washingtonpost.com/news/morning-mix/wp/2016/06/06/a-steep-price-to-pay-for-20-minutes-of-action-dad-defends-stanford-sex-offender/?noredirect=on&utm_term=.899a991a1f07

Minow, J. C., & Einolf, C. J. (2009). Sorority participation and sexual assault risk. *Violence Against Women, 15*, 835–851. doi:10.1177/1077801209334472

Mitchell, A., Gottfried, J., Barthel, M., & Sumida, N. (2018, June 18). Distinguishing between factual and opinion statements in the news. http://www.journalism.org/2018/06/18/distinguishing-between-factual-and-opinion-statements-in-the-news/

Mitchel, M. Leachman, M., Masterson, K., & Waxman, S. (2018). Unkept promises: States cuts to higher education threaten access and equity. *Center on Budget and Policy Priorities.* https://www.cbpp.org/research/state-budget-and-tax/unkept-promises-state-cuts-to-higher-education-threaten-access-andMonsanto. (n.d.). Commitments. https://monsanto.com/company/commitments/

National Alliance on Mental Health. (2012). College students speak: A survey report on mental health. https://www.nami.org/About-NAMI/Publications-Reports/Survey-Reports/College-Students-Speak_A-Survey-Report-on-Mental-H.pdf

National Association of College Stores. (2018). *Highlights from student watch attitudes & behaviors toward course materials 2017-18 report.* http://www.nacs.org/research/studentwatchfindings.aspx

National Center for Educational Statistics. (2012a). Table 315.10. Number of instructional faculty in degree-granting postsecondary institutions, by employment status, sex, control, and level of institution: Selected years, fall 1970 through fall 2011. https://nces.ed.gov/programs/digest/d13/tables/dt13_315.10.asp

National Center for Educational Statistics. (2012b). Table 316.10. Average salary of full-time instructional faculty on 9-month contracts in degree-granting postsecondary institutions, by academic rank, control and level of institution, and sex: Selected years, 1970–71 through 2012–13. https://nces.ed.gov/programs/digest/d13/tables/dt13_316.10.asp

National Institute on Alcohol Abuse and Alcoholism. (2019). Fall semester—A time for parents to discuss the risks of college drinking. https://www.niaaa.nih.gov/publications/brochures-and-fact-sheets/time-for-parents-discuss-risks-college-drinking

National Sleep Foundation. (n.d.a). How much sleep do we really need? https://sleepfoundation.org/how-sleep-works/how-much-sleep-do-we-really-need

National Sleep Foundation. (n.d.b). *Napping.* https://www.sleepfoundation.org/articles/napping

Navarro, Z. (2006). In search of cultural interpretation of power: The Contribution of Pierre Bourdieu. *Institute of Development Studies Bulletin, 37,* 11–22. doi:10.1111/j.1759-5436.2006.tb00319.x

Nelson, L. J., Padilla-Walker, L. M., Carroll, J. S., Madsen, S. D., McNamara Barry, C., & Badger, S. (2007). "If you want me to treat you like an adult, start acting like one!" Comparing the criteria that emerging adults and their parents have for adulthood. *Journal of Family Psychology, 21,* 665-674. doi: 10.1037/0893-3200.21.4.665

New. J. (2015, March 9). Fraternity caught on video singing racist song. *Inside Higher Ed.* https://www.insidehighered.com/quicktakes/2015/03/09/fraternity-caught-video-singing-racist-song

New, J. (2016, March 7). 500-word essay a punishment for rape? *Inside Higher Ed.* https://www.insidehighered.com/news/2016/03/07/student-goes-public-after-alleged-rapist-was-assigned-500-word-paper-punishment

NSC Blog. (2016, September 19). The new reality for college students earning a bachelors-degree takes 5 to 6 years and students attend multiple institutions. *National Student Clearinghouse.* https://nscnews.org/the-new-reality-for-college-students-earning-a-bachelors-degree-takes-5-to-6-years-and-students-attend-multiple-institutions/

Nussbaum. M. (2002). Capabilities and social justice. *International Studies Review, 4,* 123–135.

Nussbaum. M. (2011). *Creating capabilities: The human development approach.* Harvard University Press.

O'Hair, D., Rubenstein, H., & Stewart, R. (2010). *The pocket guide to public speaking* (3rd ed.). Bedford/St. Martin's.

Organisation for Economic Co-operation and Development (OECD). (2019). Hours worked. https://data.oecd.org/emp/hours-worked.htm

Palczewski, C. H., DeFrancisco, V. P., & McGeough, D. D. (2019). *Gender in communication: A critical introduction* (3rd ed.). SAGE.

Pascarella, E. T., Martin, G. L., Hanson, J. M., Trolian, T L., Gillig, B., & Blaich, C. (2014). Effects of diversity experiences on critical thinking skills over 4 years of college. *Journal of College Student Development*, 55, 86-92. doi: 10.1353/csd.2014.0009

Paul, A. M. (2011). The protégé effect. *Time*. http://ideas.time.com/2011/11/30/the-protege-effect/

PayScale. (n.d.). Average adjunct professor salary. https://www.payscale.com/research/US/Job=Adjunct_Professor/Salary

Pearson, E. (2019, April 7). More must be done to protect academic freedoms under threat from China. Human Rights Watch. https://www.hrw.org/news/2019/04/08/more-must-be-done-protect-academic-freedoms-under-threat-china

Pescosolido, B. A., Fettes, D. L., Martin, J. K., Monahan, J., & McLeod, J. D. (2007). Perceived dangerousness of children with mental health problems and support for coerced treatment. *Psychiatric Services, 58*(5), 619–625. https://doi.org/10.1176/appi.ps.58.5.619

Pew Research Center. (2015, December 17). Parenting in America. http://www.pewsocialtrends.org/2015/12/17/parenting-in-america/

Pew Research Center. (2018, March 1). The generation gap in American politics. http://www.people-press.org/2018/03/01/the-generation-gap-in-american-politics/

Pew Research Center. (2015, July). The complex story of American debt. http://www.pewtrusts.org/~/media/assets/2015/07/reach-of-debt-report_artfinal.pdf

Planned Parenthood. (n.d.a). PPFA consent survey results summary. https://www.plannedparenthood.org/files/1414/6117/4323/Consent_Survey.pdf

Planned Parenthood. (n.d.b). Too busy to remember birth control? https://www.plannedparenthood.org/planned-parenthood-mar-monte/patient-resources/long-acting-reversible-contraception-2

Ponsot, E. (2017, October 10). New audio reveals Harvey Weinstein propositioning a model as she desperately tries to leave. Quartz. https://qz.com/1098873/harvey-weinstein-tape-audio-reveals-weinstein-propositioning-ambra-battilana-gutierrez/

Preckel, F., Holling, H., & Vock, M. (2006). Academic underachievement: Relationship with cognitive motivation, achievement motivation, and conscientiousness. *Psychology in the Schools, 43*, 401–411. https://doi.org/10.1002/pits.20154

Pyles, L. (2014). *Progressive community organizing: Reflective practice in a globalizing world* (2nd ed). Routledge.

RAINN. (n.d.a). Victims of sexual violence: Statistics. https://www.rainn.org/statistics/victims-sexual-violence

RAINN. (n.d.b). The criminal justice system: Statistics. https://www.rainn.org/statistics/criminal-justice-system

RAINN. (n.d.c). Steps you can take to prevent sexual assault. https://rainn.org/articles/steps-you-can-take-prevent-sexual-assault

Ramirez, W. (2018, March 7). Battle for Fresno State's New Student Union building will soon come to head. *The Collegian*. http://collegian.csufresno.edu/2018/03/07/battle-for-fresno-states-new-student-union-building-will-soon-come-to-head/#.XO17gaR7lPZ

Redden, M. (2016, April 27). Oklahoma court: oral sex is not rape if victim is unconscious from drinking. *The Guardian*. https://www.theguardian.com/society/2016/apr/27/oral-sex-rape-ruling-tulsa-oklahoma-alcohol-consent

Redden, M. (2017, June 24). "No doesn't really mean no": North Carolina law means women can't revoke consent for sex. *The Guardian*. https://www.theguardian.com/us-news/2017/jun/24/north-carolina-rape-legal-loophole-consent-state-v-way

Redden, E. (2019, May 6). In Brazil, hostility to academe. *Inside Higher Ed.* https://www.insidehighered.com/news/2019/05/06/far-right-government-brazil-slashes-university-funding-threatens-cuts-philosophy-and

RichardBSpencer [Spencer, R.]. (2018, January 11). I must come to the defense of #Haiti! It's a potentially beautiful and productive country. The problem is that it's filled with shithole people. If the French dominated, they could make it great again. #MakeHaitiGreatAgain [Tweet]. https://twitter.com/richardbspencer/status/951668654969671680?lang=en

Rodriguez, D. (2017, September 5). How do you tell the difference between good and bad carbohydrates? Everyday Health. https://www.everydayhealth.com/diet-nutrition/diet/good-carbs-bad-carbs/

Rodriguez, J. (2018). Engaging race and racism for socially just intergroup relations: The impact of intergroup dialogue on college campuses in the United States. *Multicultural Education Review, 10*, 224–245. doi:10.1080/2005615X.2018.1497874

Rogers, C. R. (1959). A theory of therapy, personality, and interpersonal relationships as developed in the client-centered framework. In S. Koch (Ed.), *Psychology: A study of a science*, (Vol. 3, Formulations of the person and the social context). McGraw-Hill.

Rose, D., Thornicroft, G., Pinfold, V., & Kassam, A. (2007). 250 labels used to stigmatise people with mental illness. *BMC Health Services, 7*, 1–7. doi:10.1186/1472-6963-7-9

Ross, M., & Svajlenka, N. P. (2016, March 24). Employment and disconnection among teens and young adults: The role of place, race, and education. Brookings. https://www.brookings.edu/research/employment-and-disconnection-among-teens-and-young-adults-the-role-of-place-race-and-education/

Rudick, C. K., Golsan, K. B., & Cheesewright, K. (2018). *Teaching from the heart: Critical communication pedagogy in the communication classroom.* Cognella.

Saad, L. (2014, August 29). The "40-hour" workweek is actually longer—by seven hours. Gallup. https://news.gallup.com/poll/175286/hour-workweek-actually-longer-seven-hours.aspx

Sanburn, J. (2017, January 18). Flint's water crisis still isn't over. Here's where things stand a year later. *Time.* http://time.com/4634937/flint-water-crisis-criminal-charges-bottled-water/

Schwartz, N. D. (2013, March 3). Recovery is lifting profits, but not adding jobs. *New York Times.* http://www.nytimes.com/2013/03/04/business/economy/corporate-profits-soar-as-worker-income-limps.html

Seghal, P. (2016). Racial microaggressions: The everyday assault. American Psychiatric Association. https://www.psychiatry.org/news-room/apa-blogs/apa-blog/2016/10/racial-microaggressions-the-everyday-assault

Senn, C. Y., & Forrest, A. (2016). "And then one night when I went to class ...": The impact of sexual assault bystander intervention workshops incorporated in academic courses. *Psychology of Violence, 6*(4), 607–618. https://doi.org/10.1037/a0039660

Shierholz, H., & Mishel. L. (2013, August 21). A decade of flat wages. Economic Policy Institute. http://www.epi.org/publication/a-decade-of-flat-wages-the-key-barrier-to-shared-prosperity-and-a-rising-middle-class/

Sheffield, R. (2018, June 8). Remembering Anthony Bourdain: The man who ate the cobra heart. *Rolling Stone Magaine.* https://www.rollingstone.com/tv/tv-news/remembering-anthony-bourdain-the-man-who-ate-the-cobra-heart-629433/

Simpson, J. S. (2003). *I have been waiting: Race and U.S. higher education.* University of Toronto Press.

Singer, L. M., & Alexander, P. A. (2017). Reading on paper and digitally: What the past decades of empirical research reveal. *Review of Education Research, 87*, 1007–1041. doi:10.3102/0034654317722961

Smith, R. A. (2007). Language of the lost: An explication of stigma communication. *Communication Theory, 17*, 462–485. doi:10.1111/j.1468-2885.2007.00307.x

Smith, R. A., & Applegate, A. (2018). Mental health stigma and communication and their intersections with education. *Communication Education, 67*, 382–408. doi:10.1080/0363 4523.2018.1465988

Smucker, J. (2017). *Hegemony how-to: A roadmap for radicals*. AK Press.

Sprague, J. (1999). The goals of communication education. In A. L. Vangelisti, J. A. Daly, & G. W. Friedrich (Eds.), *Teaching communication: Theory, research, and methods* (2nd ed.; pp. 15-30). Lawrence Erlbaum.

Sue, D. W. (2010). Microaggressions: More than just race. *Psychology Today*. https://www.psychologytoday.com/us/blog/microaggressions-in-everyday-life/201011/microaggressions-more-just-race

Sussman, R. W. (2014). *The myth of race: The troubling persistence of an unscientific idea*. Harvard University Press.

Syvertsen, A. K., Wray-Lake, L., Flanagan, C. A., Osgood, D. W., & Briddell, L. (2011). Thirty-year trends in U.S. adolescents' civic engagement: A story of changing participation and educational differences. *Journal of Research on Adolescence, 21*, 586–594. doi:10.1111/j.1532-7795.2010.00706.x

Texas State University. (n.d.). Student government. http://studentgovernment.dos.txstate.edu/about-us/accomplishments.html

The BBC. (2018, November 16). Khmer Rouge leaders found guilty of Cambodia genocide. https://www.bbc.com/news/world-asia-46217896

The Institute for College Access & Success. (2011). Pell Grants not linked to higher tuition. https://ticas.org/blog/pell-grants-not-linked-higher-tuition

The Institute for College Access & Success. (2014). Quick facts about student debt. https://ticas.org/sites/default/files/pub_files/Debt_Facts_and_Sources.pdf

The Institute for College Access & Success. (2017). Student debt and the class of 2016. https://ticas.org/sites/default/files/pub_files/classof2016.pdf

The United States Holocaust Museum. (2018). Timeline of events. https://www.ushmm.org/learn/timeline-of-events/1933–1938

Ting-Toomey, S. (2005). Identity negotiation theory: Crossing cultural boundaries. In W. B. Gudykunst (Ed.), *Theorizing about intercultural communication* (pp. 211–233). SAGE.

Trostel, P. (2015). It's not just the money: The benefits of college education to individuals and society. Lumina Foundation. https://www.luminafoundation.org/files/resources/its-not-just-the-money.pdf

Tuckman, B. W. (2003). The effect of learning and motivation strategies on college students' achievement. *Journal of College Student Development, 44*, 430–437.

Twenge, J. M. (2014, October 2). Why so many people are stressed and depressed. *Psychology Today*. https://www.psychologytoday.com/us/blog/our-changing-culture/201410/why-so-many-people-are-stressed-and-depressed

U.S. Food and Drug Administration. (n.d.a). Protein. https://www.accessdata.fda.gov/scripts/InteractiveNutritionFactsLabel/factsheets/Protein.pdf

U.S. Food and Drug Administration. (n.d.b). Dietary fiber. https://www.accessdata.fda.gov/scripts/interactivenutritionfactslabel/factsheets/Dietary_Fiber.pdf

Vera, A. (2018, April 1). Howard University meets 1 of 9 student protest demands. CNN. https://www.cnn.com/2018/04/01/us/howard-university-protest/index.html

Villalpando, O. (2003). Self-segregation or self-preservation? A critical race theory and Latina/o critical theory analysis of a study of Chicana/o college students. *International Journal of Qualitative Studies in Education, 16,* 619–646. doi:10.1080/0951839032000142922

Wander, P. C., & Jaehne, D. (2000). Prospects for "a rhetoric of science." *Social Epistemology, 14,* 211–233.

The Washington Post. (n.d.). Fatal force. https://www.washingtonpost.com/graphics/national/police-shootings-2017/?noredirect=on

Webb, A. (2018, March 13). Student Government Association, student urges UGA to release statement on national walkout. *The Red & Black.* https://www.redandblack.com/uganews/student-government-association-student-urges-uga-to-release-statement-on/article_b9d0ab4e-2710-11e8-b125-67fec931d8d2.html

WebMD. (n.d.a). Anal sex safety and health concerns. https://www.webmd.com/sex/anal-sex-health-concerns#1

WebMD. (n.d.b). Things you should (or shouldn't) do after sex. https://www.webmd.com/sex-relationships/ss/slideshow-sexual-hygiene

WebMD. (n.d.c). How does emergency contraception work? https://www.webmd.com/sex/birth-control/how-emergency-contraception-works#1

Webster, M. (2008, May 6). Can you catch up on lost sleep? *Scientific American.* https://www.scientificamerican.com/article/fact-or-fiction-can-you-catch-up-on-sleep/

Wei, M., Ku, T., & Liao, Y. (2011). Minority stress and college persistence attitudes among African American, Asian American, and Latino students: Perception of university environment as a mediator. *Cultural Diversity and Ethnic Minority Psychology, 17,* 195–203. doi:10.1037/a0023359.

Whiteman, H. (2015, October 28). Caffeine: How does it affect our health? Medical News Today. https://www.medicalnewstoday.com/articles/271707.php

Williams, M. (2018, April 18). UW system students hold sit-in at regents office to protest campus cuts. Wisconsin Public Radio. https://www.wpr.org/uw-system-students-hold-sit-regents-office-protest-campus-cuts

Wohl, R. (1979). *The generation of 1914.* Harvard University Press.

Wolff, E. N. (2017). Household wealth trends in the United States, 1962 to 2016: Has middle class wealth recovered? National Bureau of Economic Research. https://www.nber.org/papers/w24085

World Healthy Organization. (2015). *Q&A on the carcinogenicity of the consumption of red meat and processed meat.* https://www.who.int/features/qa/cancer-red-meat/en/

Young, S. (n.d.). I'm not you're your inspiration, thank you very much. TEDxSydney. https://www.ted.com/talks/stella_young_i_m_not_your_inspiration_thank_you_very_much/discussion

Zaniewski, A. (2018, February 15). WSU student allegedly pulls out knife on campus. https://www.freep.com/story/news/local/michigan/detroit/2018/02/14/wayne-state-student-knife-immigrants/338807002/

Zerunyan, A. (2019, April 25). 4 suspects in the toppling of Silent Sam had their trials yesterday. What happened? *The Daily Tar Heel.* https://www.dailytarheel.com/article/2019/04/silent-sam-trial-0425

Image Credits

Chapter 1
Fig. 1.1: Source: https://unsplash.com/photos/93W0xn4961g.

Fig. 1.2: Source: https://pixabay.com/photos/laptop-office-hand-writing-3196481/.

Fig. 1.3: Source: https://unsplash.com/photos/mO9vKbG5csg.

Fig. 1.4: Source: https://unsplash.com/photos/aku7Zlj_x_o.

Fig. 1.5: Source: https://pixabay.com/photos/mentor-school-students-college-3513738/.

Fig. 1.6: Source: https://pixabay.com/photos/people-girls-women-students-2557396/.

Fig. 1.7: Source: https://unsplash.com/photos/ALGRkWz3-yc.

Fig. 1.8: Source: https://unsplash.com/photos/6RzCutNSMK4.

Chapter 2
Fig. 2.1: Source: https://pixabay.com/photos/millicent-fawcett-feminist-3990590/.

Fig. 2.2: Source: https://unsplash.com/photos/pp6HQAeT7rQ.

Fig. 2.3: Source: https://pixabay.com/photos/hand-united-together-people-unity-1917895/.

Fig. 2.4: Source: https://pixabay.com/illustrations/bisexual-intersex-transgender-683960/.

Fig. 2.5: Source: https://unsplash.com/photos/1TqTPPz3xpg.

Fig. 2.6: Source: https://unsplash.com/photos/QI3ULtlpIsQ.

Fig. 2.7: Source: https://unsplash.com/photos/ycW4YxhrWHM.

Chapter 3
Fig. 3.1: Source: https://unsplash.com/photos/TVSRWmnW8Us.

Fig. 3.2: Source: https://unsplash.com/photos/3aVlWP-7bg8.

Fig. 3.3: Source: https://unsplash.com/photos/IbLgFFIADrY.

Chapter 4
Fig. 4.1: Source: https://pixabay.com/photos/startup-whiteboard-room-indoors-3267505/.

Fig. 4.2: Source: https://pixabay.com/photos/agenda-book-calendar-daily-3991875/.

Fig. 4.3: Source: https://unsplash.com/photos/JClMcOpFHig.

Fig. 4.4: Source: https://unsplash.com/photos/Sj0iMtq_Z4w.

Chapter 5
Fig. 5.1: Copyright © 2018 Depositphotos/ AntonMatyukha.

Fig. 5.2: Copyright © 2016 Depositphotos/ skonech@aol.com.

Fig. 5.3: Copyright © 2016 Depositphotos/ HighwayStarz.

Fig. 5.4: Copyright © 2015 Depositphotos/ chiociolla.

Fig. 5.5: Source: https://www.tabc.state.tx.us/publications/brochures/BACCharts.pdf.

Fig. 5.6: Copyright © 2012 Depositphotos/ fergregory.

Index

About the Authors

C. Kyle Rudick

I grew up in Oologah, Oklahoma, a small town north of Tulsa. It was a small town, about 800 people, mostly White and rural. I went to a consolidated school, Oologah-Talala (no, I promise you, I'm not making words up!), where I found my passion in debate. I was successful in debate, and went to college on a scholarship for it. The university, Northeastern State University, in Tahlequah, had about 8,000 people, which to me was hitting big city life. I was amazed that the town had its own Walmart and two different McDonald's! I remember being so afraid my first few weeks. I didn't know how to cope with so many new people, ideas, and the culture of higher education. I felt out of place without my high school friends, and even though my parents were only 2 hours away, it felt like they were on the moon. I didn't think I would ever be successful. I was lonely, scared, and out of my element.

Slowly I began to adjust. I met people from other races, countries, ethnicities, and religions. I read books from people from all over the political spectrum. I learned how to conduct research and how to test knowledge. And, by the end, I loved college so much I decided that I would devote my life to being a part of it, and improving it. I met my advisor Dr. Amy Aldridge Sanford, who was also from a small town like mine, but who had gone on to receive her MA and PhD. Seeing her example, and with her encouragement, I started to pursue earning my graduate degrees so I could teach at the university level. After many years, and a LOT of student debt, I began working at the University of Northern Iowa in 2014.

Now, I'm an associate professor and the graduate program coordinator, and continue to find joy and hope in teaching and writing research. I am lucky in that a lot of my activism about labor, racism, and sexism has an immediate outlet in my job as a professor. My work is rooted in my deep belief that it is everyone's moral duty to dedicate their life to equity, peace, and justice. I think we could live in a world without poverty, hunger, or discrimination if we set ourselves to the task of imagining and pursuing it. That's what this book is to me—our invitation to you to join us in making the world a better place, one college campus at a time. When I am not playing video games, bass guitar, or piano, I am probably either riding my bicycle or hanging out my amazing partner Kat, and our dog Rosie, who is a very good pup.

Nicholas Alexis Zoffel

Hi, I'm Nic or more professionally known as Dr. Nicholas Zoffel. I was born in Southern California. I moved to Northern California for my undergraduate B.A. and Graduate M.A. in Communication. As I navigated higher education, I moved to the Midwest, where I earned my Ph.D. also in Communication. My thirst for education was bore out of finding human communication too often be so overwhelming that we miss opportunities for fulfillment and nuanced that we miss making connections when meeting new people.

For this reason, I majored in Communication, a discipline that provided me clarity to that process of relationship development and understanding how people share their identities. Professionally, it continues to be a space where I can collaborate with visionary people and bring ideas to diverse industries while asking "how are we ensuring that people can fulfill their potential?" This question has since ignited my passions focusing on public benefit and education, exploring academically grounded approaches, and creating spaces for collaboration with change makers. I have been fortunate enough to parlay these interests into a career as the Executive Director of a nongovernmental organization (NGO) called the Global Forum for Civic Affairs. Throughout my education and career, I have maintained the simple idea that being visionary is possible with the right relationships. In teaching, research, and professionally this means I explore how new media systems, pedagogy, community resources, and international collaborations can address the global threats posed by misinformation, misperception, & disinformation. As I seek to better understand identity, community, and attend to issues of difference, social influence, and power as part of routine relationships. I am also often a reddit upvote, tweet, FB post, LinkedIn endorsement or meme away from knowing my authentic self. As you traverse the pages of this text, you will notice a heavy connection between academic language and stories. We often call this type of embodied research ethnography. I frequently use this method to explore the dynamics of relationships that intersect various parts of higher education and within communication studies like interpersonal, intercultural, organization development, and media use. This also means that I am a heavy consumer of culture; this is a fancy way of saying that I like to travel, listen to Spotify, stream a lot of Hulu, Netflix, and professional wrestling, read a ton of social media, new media, graphic novels, and play Xbox and D&D; an endeavor I share with my wife Jennifer, our two kids, Eliana and Gabriela, and dog, Halo Shibata. This book has been a process of identity development for me and through the writing process with Kyle and Katherine (both amazing people), served as a reminder, both personally and professionally why relationships matter. As you navigate this book, please take ownership of the ideas on the pages, make it part of who you are, as I genuinely hope it engages and provides you support to find others with your visionary thinking to live your best life.

Katherine Grace Hendrix

I was born in the Central Valley in California; spe-cifically, in Fresno. This is a heavily agricultural area often called "the fruit basket of the world." I attended California State University, Fresno for my undergraduate BA in Speech Communication. I married in my senior year of college, and my husband and I both graduated from University of California, Davis. That is where I earned by MA degree in Rhetoric. After leaving the California State Scholarship Program, located in Sacramento, California, I worked at two community colleges in the Central Valley for 11 years; sometimes in the classroom, other times in management. Because

of my background in the community college system, I have a special apprecia-tion for the purpose of 2-year institutions and their value in preparing students to think critically and also be able to support themselves with a professional career or excellent trade skills. During these years I decided I wanted to conduct research on the experience of Black professors teaching in predominantly White universities (PWIs), because, at that time, I was one, although I was at a commu-nity college. So, my husband and I—now with two children—moved to Seattle, Washington, where I earned my doctoral degree. Even though I consider myself to be a West Coast baby, when I graduated most of the positions in my area of expertise were in the South, so my family settled in Memphis, Tennessee. You never know where your career will take you.

I have two major lines of research: (1) How do professors (especially those of color or of color with English as a Second Language) build their credibility in the classroom? and (2) What research gets published in the Communication discipline versus what topics are typically left out? I believe research should translate into useable information, so my activism is geared toward making universities an easier place for teachers/researchers who are not White males to succeed. Our presence, in turn, makes the college experience more welcoming for all students. When we were your age, my husband and I were constantly pushing, praying, and fighting to justify our presence in predominantly White universities. I'm excited about this book, and what my coauthors and I have researched and prepared specifically with you in mind, because we are equipping you with tools to stand up not only for yourself but for others.